Promises Not Kept

Promises Not Kept

*Poverty and the Betrayal
of Third World Development*

Sixth Edition

John Isbister

Promises Not Kept: Poverty and the Betrayal of Third World Development, Sixth Edition
Published 2003 in the United States of America by Kumarian Press, Inc.
1294 Blue Hills Avenue, Bloomfield, CT 06002 USA

Published and distributed in Europe and Africa by
PALGRAVE MACMILLAN
Houndmills, Basingstoke, Hampshire RG21 2XS UK

ISBN: 1-4039-2111-3

A catalogue record for this book is available from the
British Library.

First edition published 1991
Second edition published 1993
Third edition published 1995
Fourth edition published 1998
Fifth edition published 2001

Production and design by Rosanne Pignone, Pro Production
Copyedited by Kathleen Achor
Proofread by Beth Richards
Index by Robert Swanson, ARC Films

The text for Promises Not Kept: Poverty and the Betrayal of Third World Development, Sixth Edition is set in Sabon 10/12 Adobe Sabon.

Printed in Canada on acid-free paper by Transcontinental Printing.
Text printed with vegetable oil-based ink.

∞ The paper used in this publication meets the minimum requirements of the American National Standard for Information Sciences—Permanence of Paper for Printed Library Materials, ANSI Z39.48–1948.

Library of Congress Cataloging-in-Publication Data
Isbister, John, 1942–
Promises not kept : Poverty and the betrayal of Third World development /
    John Isbister. — 6th ed.
        p. cm.
    Includes bibliographical references and index.
    ISBN 1-56549-173-4 (pbk. : alk. paper)
1. Social change. 2. Economic development. 3. Nationalism—
Developing countries. 4. Imperialism. I. Title.
HN980.I83 2003
    303.4'09172'4—dc21
                                                    2003003743

11 10 09 08 07 06 05 04 03 02   10 9 8 7 6 5 4 3 2 1   First Printing 2003

Dedicated to my mother, Ruth,
and
to the memory of my father, Claude

Contents

Preface

For many years, I have taught in an interdisciplinary "core course" for first-year undergraduate students at Merrill College in the University of California at Santa Cruz. Initially the course was titled "Social Change in the Third World," and although both the title and the readings have changed over the years, it still focuses on the problems confronting the world's disadvantaged majority; the people living in Asia, the Middle East, Africa, and Latin America.

Those of us who founded the college in 1968 wanted to create a curriculum that would reach all our students, not just those few who were making a major commitment to third-world studies, but also the physics and the art majors, and all the others. We wanted to engage the students' intellect and challenge their minds, and we also wanted to speak to their hearts.

We designed a course that was intended to transport students quickly into the center of many third-world people's basic concerns. We insisted that the readings all be immediate and compelling. We read, for example, the diary of a poor woman living on the edge of a garbage dump in Brazil, an autobiography of a rural guerrilla, an ethnographer's account of a Pygmy tribe, a revolutionary's manifesto, a novel about Gandhi's impact on an Indian village, a village study conducted just after the Chinese revolution, a novel of a mother's burdens in Nigeria, an account of a peasant's life in the Nile valley, and many similar pieces. Some of these readings are the bases for the case studies in Chapter 2.

The course has been a success; in fact, some of our former students have come back to tell us that it remains the most vivid memory of their undergraduate years. There was always a problem with it, however. The students came to both college and the course with little background in the subject, little understanding of the basic history and problems of third-world peoples. We on the faculty were uncertain how to address this problem. We wanted to retain the immediacy and the power of the readings, and not revert to social science–type texts. At the same time, though, we saw that our students were having trouble with the context of the readings, with seeing how they fit into a broader picture.

I looked for a book that would fill the gap. It needed to be brief and attractively presented so that readers could get into it with minimum discomfort. It should deal with the great issues of third-world history, along with the present problems and the future prospects. It should present conflicting viewpoints and arguments. Most importantly, I was looking for a book that would help the students make sense of the incredibly challenging and confusing world of which they were becoming citizens.

Perhaps I did not search hard enough, but I failed to find just the right book. So I decided to write it myself, and this is the result. Over the years since the first edition, I have revised it many times—partly in response to changes in the world, and partly in response to feedback from the readers. We continue to use the book in the Merrill College core course, and it is used in other courses that deal with third-world topics in such fields as economics, politics, sociology, anthropology, and history. It is also intended for general readers who want to reflect a little more on their world.

In the years since the first edition, a great deal has changed in the world, including the collapse of the Soviet system, the end of the cold war, the new war on terrorism, the end of apartheid in South Africa, ethnic conflict and even genocide in some areas of the third world, remarkable economic progress in some regions coupled with both economic crisis and economic stagnation in other areas, and much more. The sixth edition brings the story of social change in the third world, and its betrayal, up to date. Unfortunately, the basic theme of the book has not changed. In spite of many positive developments, still, the predicament of a large portion of the world's population remains desperate; the promises made to them have not been kept.

The first three editions were dedicated to my parents; subsequent editions are dedicated to my mother and to the memory of my father. Claude M. Isbister died in 1996 at the age of eighty-two after a career of public service. His ideals were formed in the Great Depression of the 1930s, and he devoted his life to doing what he could to keep another depression from occurring. For a quarter century he worked for the government of Canada in such areas as statistical systems, international trade, fiscal policy, immigration, and energy policy. Then from 1968 to 1975, he was an executive director of the World Bank, representing Canada, Ireland, and Jamaica. He was one of the people who helped the World Bank change its focus to one of combating poverty. He consulted widely on issues of economic development; several times, for example, he conducted the replenishment campaigns for the funding of the Caribbean Development Bank and the African Development Bank. He was a doer, not a writer, and he left behind little record of his life's work. Part of his life's work, though, was that he was the most important inspiration in my life. This book is dedicated to him because, in a way, he is responsible for it.

In thinking and writing about the subject, I have accumulated many other debts. Thanks to Sir W. Arthur Lewis, now deceased, but in his lifetime the most distinguished economist to come from the third world, whose lectures and seminars at Princeton in the 1960s made the subjects of global poverty and economic development compelling to me. Philip W. Bell, the founding provost of Merrill College, invited me to join the college faculty and started this project. My colleagues Edmund Burke, a historian, and Walter Goldfrank, a sociologist, joined me in planning the first core courses in the late 1960s, and then years later helped me by reading drafts of the text. Others who gave generously of both time and insight were Dilip Basu, Paige Baty, Marla Black, Liezell Bradshaw, Roekmini Harris, Susanne Jonas, Leslie Lopez, Joseph Lubow, John Marcum, Sherri Paris, Sarah-Hope Parmeter, Daniel Scripture, Walter Smith, Patricia Sullivan, and David Sweet. Hundreds of Merrill students have helped to sharpen my arguments by engaging me in seminar discussions, and I would also like to thank the many readers who have written and e-mailed me with comments. I am particularly grateful to my wife, Roz Spafford, who helped me turn what were frequently inchoate musings into something approaching presentable prose. The remaining errors of fact and interpretation, I regret to admit, are mine alone.

As we embark upon a new century, we can hope that the next hundred years will witness the cooperation of rich countries with poor countries—and rich people with poor people—so that the scourge of poverty on a global scale will finally be eliminated. When one reflects upon the incredible social changes that marked the twentieth century, it is surely not outrageous to hope and even plan that the twenty-first will bring us this one improvement. According to the Gospel of Matthew, Jesus said, "For ye have the poor always with you." Many of Jesus' teachings should remain as moral guideposts for us, but not that one. It is time to ensure that every baby born on this planet has a fair chance at a decent, comfortable, and long life.

Chapter One

Introduction

Most people on the planet are poor. Most live in the third-world countries of Asia, Africa, and Latin America, where the typical standard of living is so far below that of the industrialized countries as to be almost unimaginable to those who have not experienced it. Many lack adequate nutrition, shelter, and clothing. They are susceptible to disease and early mortality. They are insecure, because the margin separating them from catastrophe is thin.

One of the myths prevalent about third-world people is that they are unchanging, that their societies are static. One often hears the word *traditional* used to describe the network of relationships in which they seem trapped. The opposite is true, however. The third world is undergoing rapid and sometimes chaotic social change: populations are growing and becoming more urbanized. Public health measures are lowering death rates. Within recent memory, nationalist independence movements created dozens of new sovereignties. Since then, governments have changed often, revolutions and counterrevolutions have been instigated, warfare has ensued. Modern technology has penetrated the third world and transformed production. Education at all levels is spreading.

The lives of people in the third world are changing. They are not improving, however, at least for the majority. One can find privileged groups, or even entire countries and regions, in which economic conditions have progressed and human and political rights are respected. The achievements in some parts of East Asia, for example, have been remarkable. These are the exceptions, though; most people in the third world are desperately poor. For them, the promises of social change in the third world have not been kept. The dreams of independence, a more comfortable life, security, and human rights were betrayed in the twentieth century. In this respect, the third world shared the fate of the entire world, where prospects that seemed certain were distorted and lost.

Throughout the world, twentieth-century people knew moments of intoxicating optimism. In Europe and North America, the century opened in a spirit of almost infinite expectations as the industrial revolution seemed to bring the promise of comfort and even opulence to ordinary people. In the second decade of the century, the Russian Revolution promised the overthrow of oppression and the creation of a new society in which the human personality would be free to flourish. As the midpoint of the century approached, the people of the Indian subcontinent were the first of the nonwhite world to emerge from colonialism and assume their equal place in the community of free nations. The Chinese revolution promised liberation for the most downtrodden of social groups, the peasants. In the 1960s, the American[1] President John F. Kennedy brought to the Western world a sense of limitlessness, and a new generation of young people committed themselves to the remaking of their societies. Science and technology developed exponentially, and with them the hope for prosperity for the entire world. What marked these moments was a sense of freedom, the collapse of the past's boundaries.

To recall these moments in the early years of a new century is to recall, however, how exceptional they were. Although they seemed to those in their midst to be universal, they were closely circumscribed, in both time and place. The heady enthusiasm of the first decade of the twentieth century was exploded by the guns of August 1914, as Europeans settled into the incredibly destructive First World War. A decade after that conflagration ended, the world was plunged into the economic catastrophe of the Great Depression of 1929–39. The Russian revolutionaries degenerated into tyrants and mass murderers, and their system was eventually rejected by their own people. The Second World War, beginning in 1939, was truly a worldwide conflict, in contrast to the first, which had really been just a European war. The Second World War unleashed not only unbelievable military carnage but also genocide, as the Jews of Europe were destroyed in the Holocaust. With the end of the Second World War came an era of relative peace, but it was a peace with dangerous forebodings. Nuclear technology and the cold war brought with them the prospect of global winter. As science advanced, people became aware of the limited capacity of the globe to absorb ecological change. Improvements in health conditions led to a population explosion that threatened to overrun the world. Ethnic conflicts degenerated into slaughter. Political regimes that had seemed to promise liberation delivered despotism. The twentieth century turned out to be a century of potential dangers and actual disasters, as the power of scientific technology raced wildly ahead of the wisdom of human beings in harnessing it. The subject of social change in the third world shared this prevailing theme of the twentieth century: the betrayal of the promise of progress. We will see whether the twenty-first brings the fulfillment of the hopes and dreams or further betrayals of them.

For almost all of known history, before the twentieth century, most ordinary people were poor: they were sick, insecure, poorly clothed and sheltered, and vulnerable to an early death. At times the modern world, with its extraordinary technology, has seemed to promise an end to the human condition of poverty. In fact, some countries have reduced poverty considerably: in Europe and North America, as well as Australia, New Zealand, and, more recently, Japan. Although pockets of poverty remain in those societies, and shamefully so, the great majority of the people there enjoy a comfortable life; they are reasonably secure and healthy, with enough income to cover not only the necessities but also at least some of the pleasures and even luxuries of life. The victory over poverty in these prosperous countries was one of the remarkable achievements of the twentieth century. It was one of the promises of the century to extend this material progress to all the world's people.

Yet it did not happen. The majority of the world's people, most of the people living in the third world, remained poor. Although by now most people in the third world are healthier than their forebears of a century ago and are living longer lives, the quality of life has generally not improved and has in some respects deteriorated. For hundreds of millions of people, rural poverty—which was hard but was at least embedded in a rich cultural network—has been replaced by the dislocation and alienation of urban poverty.

The plight of the third world is not only economic; it is social and political as well. The independence movements and revolutions of the middle part of the century seemed to imply a new age of freedom for third-world peoples but often produced tyranny and terror. Democracy was usually intended but often abandoned. Millions were killed in regional warfare and internal repression in Indonesia, Cambodia, El Salvador, Rwanda, China, Vietnam, Congo, and many other countries.

This book shows how many of the promises inherent in the independence of third world countries were transformed and abandoned. The story is not a simple one of good and evil. Social scientists have struggled with the issue of causality in trying to explain conditions in the third world, and they have come up with a variety of often contradictory theories, some of which are discussed in these pages.

Still, the promises that once beckoned—the promises of technology, of material comfort, of democracy, of human rights, of fairness, of basic respect and decency—have not been fulfilled in much of the world. Two major promises, in particular, have been violated. The first was the promise made by the leaders of the nationalist independence movements and the revolutions in the third world. In the three decades following the end of the Second World War, the people of the third world dismantled the European empires to which they had been subjugated. A spirit of nationalism swept their countries. A new generation of leaders proclaimed that the poverty of their countries was due to centuries of colonial exploitation; when the empires were cast off, the emerging autonomous nations would settle into the hard work of bringing prosperity and dignity to their people. They promised that the people's labor would now be used for their own progress, not for the enrichment of foreigners.

Almost every one of the new nationalist leaders made this commitment. A few months after the independence of India in 1947, Prime Minister Jawaharlal Nehru told his people in a nationwide radio address:

> We talk of freedom, but today political freedom does not take us far unless there is economic freedom. Indeed, there is no such thing as freedom for a man who is starving or for a country which is poor. The poor whether they are nations or individuals have little place in this world. Therefore, we have to produce in order to have sufficient wealth, distributed by proper economic planning so that it may go to the millions, more especially to the common man. Then not only the millions prosper, but the whole country becomes rich and prosperous and strong.[2]

Kwame Nkrumah, the charismatic president of Ghana, wrote in his autobiography in 1957:

> Once freedom is gained, a greater task comes into view. All dependent territories are backward in education, in agriculture and in industry. The economic independence that should follow and maintain political independence demands every effort from the people, a total mobilization of brain and manpower resources. What other countries have taken three hundred years or more to achieve, a once dependent territory must try to accomplish in a generation if it is to survive.[3]

The goal of an end to poverty, which was an explicit part of the independence movements, has been met only intermittently. In many cases, it has been waylaid as the new political elites have entrenched their positions of privilege.

The second promise was made by leaders of the rich countries. As they watched the nationalist movements of the third world gain momentum and win independence for their people, some of them began to see the world through new lenses. At the end of the Second World War, they had had few thoughts for the majority of the world's people living in Asia, Africa, and Latin America. By around 1960, however, with Europe now fully recovered, this blind spot began to disappear. The international institutions that the rich countries had established, especially the World Bank, began to pay serious attention to the plight of the poor countries. Foreign aid was increased. The motivations were not disinterested—the new attention paid to the third world derived mostly from the cold war competition between the Western and the Soviet blocs—but nevertheless a new spirit of cooperation between rich and poor countries developed. Promises were made that the rich would work together with the poor for economic development. No one captured and helped create this spirit better than President Kennedy. In his inaugural address on January 20, 1961, he spoke to the people of the third world:

> To those new states whom we welcome to the ranks of the free, we pledge our word that one form of colonial control shall not have passed away merely to be replaced by a far more iron tyranny. We shall not always expect to find them supporting our view. But we shall always hope to find them strongly supporting their own freedom. . . .
>
> To those peoples in the huts and villages of half the globe struggling to break the bonds of mass misery, we pledge our best efforts to help them help themselves, for whatever period is required—not because the communists may be doing it, not because we seek their votes, but because it is right. If a free society cannot help the many who are poor, it cannot save the few who are rich.
>
> To our sister republics south of our border, we offer a special pledge—to convert our good words into good deeds—in a new alliance for progress—to assist free men and free governments in casting off the chains of poverty.

One can hardly imagine such words being spoken today by an American president, or indeed by a leader of any rich country—and not because the problems of the third world have been resolved. Quite the contrary: the gap that divides the rich countries from the poor is still unconscionably large. About 15 percent of the world's population, living in the North, enjoy a standard of living that is extraordinarily more lavish than that of the world's majority. One cannot imagine an American president extending such a hand of generosity today because the American people and their government—along with most of the people of the other rich countries—have reneged on their promises to the poor.

Some people in the rich countries try to react responsibly to the terrible inequities in the world. They support nongovernmental organizations and foreign aid. They promote human rights and the settlement of refugees. They argue for constructive government policies, and they would like to proclaim that their countries are being helpful to the world's majority.

For the most part, however, the rich countries are not helpful. Outbalancing their constructive policies are the harmful ones: the geopolitical rivalries, the economic policies, and the many other ways in which the countries of the North make the struggles of the world's poor people harder, not easier. Although many individuals act in good faith, their countries largely reject their responsibilities to people outside their borders.

Notes

1. Throughout, I use the term *American* to refer to the people of the United States—with apologies to Latin Americans who believe that the term should not be appropriated by just one country in the Western Hemisphere and who prefer the term *North American*. My Canadian origins prevent me, however, from using *North American* to refer to the United States alone. Because *United Statesian* is not in use, and in the absence of another suitable adjective, I am stuck with *American*.

2. Jawaharlal Nehru, *Independence and After* (New York: John Day, 1950), 160.

3. Kwame Nkrumah, *The Autobiography of Kwame Nkrumah* (London: Thomas Nelson and Sons, 1957), x.

Chapter Two

A World of Poverty

A poverty curtain has descended right across the face of our world, dividing it materially and philosophically into two different worlds, two separate planets, two unequal humanities—one embarrassingly rich and the other desperately poor.
—Mahbub ul Haq, *The Poverty Curtain*

"And what about the people of your household?" he asked Akuebue. "They were quiet when I left them. There was no sickness only hunger."
—Chinua Achebe, *Arrow of God*

Five Lives

The story of today's third world is told best not in statistics, nor in treatises of social scientists and historians, but in the details of its people's lives. In the following pages we meet five real people whose lives have been documented either by themselves or by interviewers—five people chosen to convey something of the variety of human experience in the third world.

⤳

Mauwa Funidi is a college graduate and a college librarian in Kisangani, Congo. Her plight has been chronicled by reporter Nicholas D. Kristof.[1] When she graduated and first took her job in 1976, it paid a good salary of $300 a month; she could look forward to a middle-class life. In 1997, her salary had fallen to the equivalent of $11 a month, but even that was theoretical, because most months she was not paid at all. In any case, the library has virtually ceased to function, because the university lacks the funds to conduct classes; it has not provided money to buy books or magazines since 1982. Mauwa's principal task is to protect the dwindling collection from the wind and rain that come through the broken windows.

She cannot support herself as a librarian, so she sells charcoal on the street. "It is humiliating, it really is," she says, "but it isn't quite so debasing when all of the other university graduates are out there beside me, peddling on the street, selling cakes, palm oil, salt, sugar, soap, lemonade." Selling charcoal yields little income, so she depends, as do the other members of her family, on the earnings of her twenty-five-year-old cousin, Alphonsine, who is a prostitute at the Take-a-Peek Bar. "Everyone in the family criticizes me, but I'm the only one putting food on the table," says Alphonsine. "Mauwa always says she's afraid I'll get AIDS, but then how come she doesn't help? She just scolds, and complaining doesn't help."

"If my grandfather were alive today, he would be very sad," Mauwa says. "He would regret that his family turned out this way. . . . When he was alive, conditions were better. We had food, we had clothing, and we could afford breakfast. Now we have nothing." Mauwa's grandfather Funidi was born in 1904 in what was then the colony of the Belgian Congo. He became a chief, then moved to Kisangani and got a job as a government street cleaner in 1943. His granddaughter Mauwa was born in 1952. Funidi died in 1959, just a year before the Congo became independent. His surviving family welcomed independence with great joy and anticipation. After the first few tumultuous years of independence, Mobutu Sese Seko seized power in 1965 and later renamed the country Zaire. The country was rich in mineral resources, and the future seemed promising. Mauwa had the opportunity to attend both primary and secondary school, and she became the first member of her family to graduate from college.

As matters turned out, independence for Zaire was the beginning of a nightmare. Mobutu pillaged the country's wealth for his own purposes, just as the previous colonial regime had done. The population grew, but the economy deteriorated. The cities became enormous slums. Human and political rights were abolished, and a one-party dictatorship was established. By the 1990s, conditions in the country for most people were far worse than they had been in 1960. The jungles reclaimed the roads, and many of the people in the interior retreated into a poor, subsistence life. In 1976, Mauwa had every reason to expect that as one of the country's few college graduates, she would move to a position of leadership, but it was not to be. With the collapse of the country came the collapse of her hopes.

In 1997, a rebel alliance swept through Kisangani, on its way to take power from Mobutu and establish a new regime. Mauwa did not

expect the revolution to improve her life, and in fact warfare continued almost unabated for the next five years. When she was a young
person, Mauwa said, all the children went to school; now they are
illiterate.

↯

Shahhat is a young Egyptian *fellah,* or peasant, living in the village of
Berat on the banks of the Nile River, 450 miles south of Cairo. His
father recently died, and he lives with his mother, Ommohamed, in a
two-story house made of unbaked mud bricks with a roof of palm
branches and palm leaves. Along with about half of the villagers, his
family owns land; in his case, two acres. The other villagers work for
wages or as sharecroppers or in the local stores. The details of Shahhat's life have been recorded by Richard Critchfield, a British journalist who has written extensively about third-world peasants and who
lived with Shahhat for a year.[2]

As Critchfield explains it, an extraordinary change has come over
Berat during Shahhat's short lifetime. For millennia, the annual flood
of the Nile River determined the rhythms of agricultural life. The river
flooded each September to November, then receded, leaving a fertile
layer of silt. Crops of wheat, barley, and lentils were planted then and
harvested in April. There was just one crop a year, and summer was
a time of rest.

In the region of Berat, however, the Nile flooded for the last time
in 1966; thenceforth, the flow of the great river was controlled by the
towering Aswan Dam. The dam and its works provide continuous,
planned irrigation of fields in place of the annual flood, and continuous cultivation is now possible, with up to three crops a year.

Shahhat and most of the *fellahin* were unprepared for this
immense change in their lives. It was not simply that they now needed
to work twelve months a year, without the summer rest; the whole
technology of agriculture changed. Chemical fertilizers were required
to supplement the soil's fertility. Motorized pumps were installed.
New high-yielding varieties of grain were introduced. A government
inspector instructed the *fellahin* which crops to plant. Railway networks were expanded to gather the crops. Shahhat's people had been
peasants for generations; overnight they were expected to become
farmers, knowledgeable about the latest methods and the fluctuations
of markets.

In a sense, all this represented progress. It led to sharply increased
crop yields per acre of land, which were needed by Egypt's rapidly
growing population. More income was generated in the village. Yet the
process of technical change has not been smooth. Salinity levels in the
soil have risen and threaten the fertility of the land. The government

officials sometimes make choices that are unwise in terms of the crops' productivity or of the market for them. The railway boxcars are sometimes unavailable, and a crop has to be abandoned. In the old days, the *fellahin* were dependent, as peasants always are, on the vagaries of the weather. Now they are still dependent on the weather and on much more besides—chemical processes, international market forces, and organizational structures that are far beyond their control or even comprehension.

So Shahhat has experienced wrenching changes in his culture, and in return for enduring these changes, he has gained little if anything. He is no more prosperous, although he works more regularly than he once did. Distressed by the disruption of his life, he has left his village several times to seek his fortune in Cairo, but he has always returned. He has no savings, no protection from the uncertainties of his life. Although some of his fellow villagers have taken advantage of the new technology to amass some wealth, Critchfield demonstrates that Shahhat has not. He is confused and passive. He and his mother both trust in the providence of Allah and do not plan actively for the future. Perhaps his children, who will grow up in the new world of scientific agriculture, will be able to cope with it more creatively, but Shahhat is at a loss.

Bernard Ledea Ouedraogo is a Mossi tribesman from the Yatenga Province of Burkina Faso, formerly Upper Volta.[3] Burkina Faso is a landlocked, desert country in West Africa, one of the world's five poorest countries. It suffers from some of the worst health conditions in the world and, consequently, an average baby has a life expectancy of only about forty-four years. Ouedraogo was born in a small village, herded goats as soon as he was able, and tilled the land with his father. One day a group of French colonial administrators visited his village and, without warning, enrolled eighty-one children in a primary school. Eighty of the children stayed in school only a couple of years, not long enough to stay literate. By a mysterious combination of determination and chance, Ouedraogo persisted at school, becoming literate and much more. He moved from level to level and eventually earned a doctorate in agronomy from the Sorbonne in Paris.

He dedicated his education and good fortune to his people, the Mossi. Returning to Yatenga, he founded the modern *Naam* movement for social and economic development. The *Naam* is a traditional form of Mossi social organization, a small group formed in the village for collective work. Under Ouedraogo's leadership, *Naams* have been formed to dig wells, build dams, install mills, and in other ways improve the desperately poor economy. There are now 2,000 *Naam* associations in 1,000 villages throughout Burkina Faso, Mali, and Senegal. Ouedraogo works with international organizations such as the United Nations Children's Fund (UNICEF) to get resources for his people. Peter Adamson describes him sitting on his haunches, explaining foreign aid to the elders at a meeting: "If the load you have to carry is too heavy to lift onto your head, then it is right to be glad of the hand that helps you. But a Mossi must always use two hands of his own."[4]

The load that the Mossi have to carry is frighteningly heavy. They are still living with the legacy of the colonial administration that uprooted their society by forcing the men to travel year after year to the coffee plantations of the Ivory Coast. After the colonialists were replaced, the same migration patterns persisted, as the most able-bodied young men left to seek wages and returned only sporadically. For long periods of time, wives have lived without their husbands, children without their fathers. Meanwhile, as the population has grown, the land has had to be tilled more intensively, so the pace of soil erosion has increased. Periodic droughts have hastened the erosion. Throughout the last third of the century, the devastation in the Sahel region of Africa has been massive. As colonialism sapped the cultural strength and self-confidence of the Mossi, overcultivation and drought sapped the soil's fertility. Pictures of starving African tribespeople have become familiar sights to television viewers around the world.

Even when the rains come, sufficient grain can seldom be stored in the villages to last until the next harvest. The infant mortality rate in Burkina Faso is tragically high: 15 percent of babies die before their first birthday. The village children who survive typically decline in health once they are weaned. Many have the swollen bellies characteristic of the undernourished, and they suffer fever, pains, and rashes from parasitic infections and worms. They are underweight and have unhealed sores. They are frequently listless. The nutritional deficiencies they suffer in early childhood leave permanent disabilities that typically cannot be reversed at older ages, even if their diets improve.

Ouedraogo moves back and forth between this village world of Yatenga, the national capital of Ouagadougou, and the capitals of Europe—seeking help abroad while trying to inspire his people to work together at home. His method is to respect and build on the existing social structure of the Mossi, not to uproot it. He addresses the elders in a responsive mode:

> Did the young respect the elders in the old days? What about today? Were the taboos observed in our young days? But what about today?. . . If you are my friend is our relationship not holy? But what

about today? Would a man who was a Mossi ever tell a lie even if
tortured to death? But what about today? . . . If in the old days you
were having a siesta and a man came and knocked at your door
would you ever say to him "go away, I am sleeping?" But what
about today?[5]

When the rains come and the harvest is ample, he makes a little
progress.

Domitila Barrios de Chungara is the wife of a miner in Siglo XX, a
tin-mining camp in the central highlands of Bolivia.[6] She, her husband, and seven children live in a one-room house measuring about
twelve by twenty feet. The house is owned by the mining company,
and if her husband retires, dies, or is laid off, she will have to leave
the house within a few days. The house has no running water or sanitation facilities; these are provided centrally in facilities that quickly
become filthy. Her husband works a backbreaking and dangerous
eight-hour shift in the mines. What he earns is not enough to live on,
and Domitila sells *saltenas,* small meat and potato pies, on the street
to make ends meet.

The mine workers are members of several militant labor unions
that have periodically gone on strike for higher wages and improvements in living conditions. As Domitila describes it, the strikes have
generally been met by strong resistance from the army, with mass
arrests. On at least two occasions, there were armed confrontations,
resulting in the shooting of dozens of miners and their family members. Leaders of the union are sometimes jailed for long periods of
time or deported to Argentina or Chile.

During one strike in Siglo XX, when the union leaders were
arrested, the women in the camp went on a hunger strike to protest
the arrests and secure the freedom of the men. From this hunger strike
a permanent organization was born, the Housewives' Committee of
Siglo XX, of which Domitila is a leader. Year after year, she says, she
has worked with her comrades, both men and women, to secure a better life in the mining camp. In 1975, she was sent to the International
Women's Year Tribunal organized by the United Nations and held in
Mexico City, and it was there that she spoke and got her story out.

Her life has been unbelievably hard. During one strike, the army
invaded Siglo XX, killing workers, women, and children. Although
pregnant, Domitila was arrested, then released, arrested again, and
tortured. She was accused of being an agent for revolutionary communist guerrillas. She denied the charges and was beaten brutally. In
anger, she struck back against her torturer, biting his hand; in turn,
she was beaten into submission, and six of her teeth were broken. She
was in her eighth month of pregnancy.

It turned out that her torturer, with the bitten hand, was the son of the commanding colonel. The next day the colonel took over the proceedings. He beat her relentlessly and said, "All right, luckily you're expecting a baby. We'll take our revenge on your baby." Then he began to sharpen a knife in front of her. She shortly gave birth to a boy, alone in a filthy prison cell, and then passed out. When she awoke her baby was dead; she does not know whether he was born dead or died after birth. The colonel was summoned. Furious at being denied his revenge, he grabbed the dead baby and threw him at Domitila.

Eventually Domitila was given medical care, and she survived. She was exiled for a time to a farming area in the lowlands, but she eventually returned to Siglo XX with her husband. He begged her to give up her organizing activities so the family could have some peace. She consented for a while but eventually went back to her Housewives' Committee. The strikes and armed confrontations continued.

Domitila is a socialist; she thinks that progress can come to her coworkers only when a workers' party is in control of Bolivia. Although she has been recognized by feminists, she says that she is not a feminist:

> Our position is not like the feminists' position. We think our liberation consists primarily in our country being freed forever from the yoke of imperialism and we want a worker like us to be in power and that the laws, education, everything, be controlled by this person. Then, yes, we'll have better conditions for reaching a complete liberation, including our liberation as women.[7]

Rigoberta Menchú is a Quiche Indian woman from the village of Chimel in the mountains of northwestern Guatemala. She was extensively interviewed by anthropologist Elisabeth Burgos-Debray, and the interviews were edited into an autobiography entitled *I, Rigoberta Menchú*.[8]

Rigoberta describes how the Indians from Chimel travel back and forth several times a year between their homes and the cotton and coffee plantations on the coast, where they work as laborers. In the springtime in the village they plant maize (corn), which is their staple food. They then travel to the coast packed in lorries that are supplied by the plantations; the lorries are covered with canvas so that the villagers can see nothing of the countryside they are traversing. At the plantations, families are frequently separated. Living in huge single-room dormitories that hold as many as four hundred or five hundred people, they do the backbreaking work of tending the coffee and cotton plants. In the fall they return to the mountains, in the same lorries, to harvest the maize; then they usually return to the plantations.

They are paid very little at the plantations, and some of what they are paid is stolen from them by the labor contractors, who are Indians who have learned to speak Spanish. Rigoberta's villagers do not speak Spanish. In fact, twenty-two Indian groups in Guatemala speak different languages, so they have difficulty communicating with one another at the plantations, and they are vulnerable to being exploited by people in power whom they do not understand.

Rigoberta's life in the mountains has been a life of hardship; the maize is always in short supply, the work is devastatingly hard, and the money is scarce. But it is a life of spiritual richness. Rigoberta is connected to her family and to her fellow villagers by the rituals of birth, of maturity, of marriage, and of death. She and her compatriots reject many of the trappings of urban civilization—for example, they refuse to use mechanical grinders for their maize. The maize is not just sustenance; it is the spirit of life.

Her life has been more than hard, though; it has been calamitous. Although Indians make up 60 percent of the Guatemalan population, they were oppressed by the minority Ladino (mixed Indian and Spanish) population. She says that she worked for a while as a maid in Guatemala City, where she was fed only table scraps and saw most of her wages confiscated to buy the clothes that her mistress insisted she wear. Even the discrimination in the city might have been bearable if her mountain home had been a secure refuge—but it was not.

Chimel was often attacked by the army. Indians were killed and their belongings destroyed. Rigoberta helped build a network of traps to keep the army from Chimel, and she led the villagers into mountain camps when the army was coming. But she and her *compañeros* had no guns or modern weapons; they had only staves and machetes.

As these confrontations proceeded, year after year, Rigoberta saw her family destroyed. She says that one brother died of starvation at a plantation. Another brother, she says, was tortured and killed by the army. Her father, Vicente Menchú, was a leader in the Indian resistance movement. He was burned to death when he was part of a group that occupied the Spanish embassy in Guatemala City. Her mother was captured by the army, then raped and tortured to death.

Rigoberta is a Christian. She accepts the sacraments of the Roman Catholic Church and believes in Christ's divinity and sacrifice. The church she identifies with is the church of the poor, not the church of the clerical hierarchy. It is a church that coexists for her with the teachings of her Indian ancestors; she sees no need to reject her own traditions in order to accept Christianity.

She became a leader in the movement of the Guatemalan Indians. Her life was continuously in danger. In 1992, she was awarded the Nobel Peace Prize for standing out "as a vivid symbol of peace and reconciliation across ethnic, cultural and social dividing lines, in her own country, on the American continent and in the world."[9] The peace that came to Guatemala in 1995 was due in part to her lifetime of struggle.

The Third World

Mauwa Funidi, Shahhat, Bernard Ouedraogo, Domitila Barrios de Chungara, and Rigoberta Menchú are five among the over four billion inhabitants of the third world, the great majority of humankind, living for the most part in Asia, Africa, and Latin America.

The use of *third world* to refer to the largest portion of the globe's people dates from the 1950s in France. It is a pun, based on the terms used to describe the three social classes that had political authority in the *ancien régime* of prerevolutionary France. The first estate was the Lords Spiritual, or the clergy; the second estate the Lords Temporal, or the nobility; and the third estate the bourgeoisie or commercial class. Political power resided in the hands of the first and second estates. Consequently, in eighteenth-century France, the term *third estate,* or *tiers état,* became a revolutionary slogan. The French Revolution, beginning in 1789, was fought to a large extent by and for the third estate to establish liberty, equality, and fraternity; to transfer political power from a small oligarchy to the third estate, and thence to the people as a whole.

Alfred Sauvy and other French intellectuals, viewing the global forces that were emerging from the wreckage of the Second World War, coined the term *tiers monde,* or *third world,* corresponding to the third estate of Europe almost two centuries earlier. It connoted the majority, the dispossessed, the excluded—and it also connoted revolution. In the writings of revolutionary theorists Jean-Paul Sartre and Frantz Fanon, the term *third world* became the banner of the hungry and the oppressed.

The pun is striking. In its origins, the term *third world* carried with it a sense of opposition, tension, and struggle. The third world was a world excluded, subject to the power of alien rulers. The term itself called for change, for an extension of liberty and equality to those who did not have it. It set up an opposition between the rulers and the ruled. It drew attention to colonialism and imperialism and to their modern-day counterparts in a world of oppression and unequal power.

Over the decades, the meaning of *third world* has softened and taken on the connotation of "nonalignment." A conference of twenty-nine nonaligned nations in Bandung, Indonesia, in 1955 used *third world* to mean the newly emergent nations of Asia, Africa, and Latin America that were coming out of an era of colonialism into the status of independence. They were not to be aligned with either the first—Western, capitalist—world or the second—Eastern, communist—world. In this usage, *third world* lost much of its meaning of confrontation and opposition. It became a more neutral term, one suggesting a different way, a social path lying somewhere outside the blocs of the postwar superpowers.

Third world cannot be a completely neutral term, however, because its origins are revolutionary. It implies an opposition between the poor and the rich, and it also connotes hope. The third estate was empowered by the French Revolution and went on to become the dominant force in French society. In a similar way, the term *third world* carries with it the promise of change, the promise that those who are currently oppressed will eventually overcome their oppression and enjoy vastly better lives.

If there is a striking analogy between the world's poor of today and the third estate of prerevolutionary France, the analogy breaks down when it is extended to today's rich societies. The most privileged societies of the world today are both secular and, for the most part, democratic. Accordingly, the third world is not confronted by a first (clerical) world or a second (aristocratic) world. In one of the great ironies of modern history, it is actually confronted by the successors to the victorious third estate. The French Revolution and the European industrial revolution, also dating from the eighteenth century, released forces of creativity, technology, and expansion that completely transformed the European world and its offshoots. The medieval class system was blown away. In its place, the descendants of the third estate created a new class system: capitalism. It is the capitalist, industrial world, which was created by the third estate, that now confronts the third world.

The *third world* refers, then, to the poor of the world, those who are disenfranchised in an international system dominated by the industrialized countries: the North, the developed, the rich. For the most part, the hopes that are inherent in the term *third world* have not been fulfilled. As the twenty-first century begins, most of the people of Asia, the Middle East, Africa, and Latin America have not drawn near to the people of the rich countries in terms of either standard of living or political power.

The Extent of World Poverty

The third world today covers most of the globe. It embraces countless cultures, religions, traditions, and ways of life. Its achievements are monumental. Yet there is a single characteristic that pervades the third world, distinguishing it from the industrialized countries: widespread poverty. Not everyone in the third world is poor: there are middle-class strata as well as pockets of luxury. There are productive factories and sparkling computer centers. But the *favela* dwellers, the peasants, the underemployed, and many of the industrial workers of the third world subsist at standards of living that are low to the point of incomprehension for people living in the industrialized world.

Poverty has many dimensions. It can be thought of as an absolute condition or as relative. Absolute poverty is a standard of living so pressing that it brings with it life-threatening malnutrition and disease. The United Nations Development Programme (UNDP) has estimated the number of people in absolute poverty in the world in several ways. The most obvious criterion is simply a lack of income. Using a poverty line of a dollar a day, the UNDP estimates that about 1.2 billion people, or one-quarter of the population in the developing world, are poor, and that this figure has barely changed since 1990.[10]

Lack of income is only the beginning of an understanding of poverty, however. Other attributes include low life expectancy, adult illiteracy, underweight children, inadequate housing, child labor, food insecurity, and lack of access to safe water, to health services, and to sanitation.[11] The condition of being poor is complicated, and the dividing line between the poor and the near-poor is inexact. Clearly, however, the prevalence of poverty in the world is massive. Table 2.1 contains the UNDP estimates of income poverty in selected countries, as well as the population not expected to survive to age forty, adult illiteracy, and underweight children. More than 70 percent of the world's poor are Asians.[12] Most of the poor—more than three-quarters—live in rural areas, according to UNDP estimates. In spite of the fact that they grow crops, they endure monotonous, unbalanced diets, inadequate caloric intake, and malnutrition. They have lower health standards than urban people and have less access to clean water and sanitation facilities. They suffer the diseases of the undernourished. At each age their probability of dying is higher than that among the rest of the population.

Poverty is not restricted to this most desperate stratum of human beings, however. A great deal of the world's poverty should be thought of in relative terms—that is, poverty is a relationship. One thinks of oneself as poor only if others are rich and one's poverty is measured against that richness. The surviving Pygmies of the Congo's rain forest live at a subsistence level and suffer from diseases that have been eliminated elsewhere, but they do not think of themselves as poor. They live in a self-contained society, hunting and gathering as their ancestors did for centuries, in harmony with the forest and its spirits. But

Table 2.1 Poverty in Selected Countries, 2000

	Percentage of the Population			
Country	Less Than $1(US) per Day	Not Expected to Survive to Age 40	Adult Illiteracy (15 and Older)	Underweight (Children Younger Than 5)
Bangladesh	29	21	59	48
China	19	8	16	10
Ghana	45	27	29	25
Guatemala	10	16	31	24
India	44	17	43	47
Indonesia	8	13	13	26
Kenya	27	35	18	23
Mexico	16	8	9	8
Nepal	38	23	58	47
Nigeria	70	34	36	27
Pakistan	31	20	57	38
Peru	16	12	10	8
Senegal	26	29	63	18
Sri Lanka	7	6	8	33
Tunisia	2	8	29	4
Venezuela	23	7	7	5
Zimbabwe	36	52	11	13

Source: United Nations Development Programme, *Human Development Report 2002* (New York: Oxford University Press, 2002), Table 3.

Mauwa Funidi, the librarian of Kisangani, who actually has access to more goods and services than the Pygmies do, is desperately poor.

Poverty in this relative sense is found in every country in the world. Two of the advanced industrial countries with the highest poverty rates are Britain and the United States, with about 15 percent of the population living on less than the equivalent of $11 (U.S.) a day: desperately poor people, although their income is greater than that of the typical person in Asia or Africa.[13] The homeless living on the sidewalks in central cities or in temporary shelters, single parents in slum housing, the unemployed who have exhausted their resources, former farmers who ran into debt before losing their patrimonies to foreclosure—these are some of the faces of poverty in the rich countries. What poverty really means is the inability to make choices. A family of four in a rich country with the equivalent of $12,000 annual income is completely constrained in its choices and deeply impoverished, whereas in the world's low-income countries, where the average income per person was the equivalent of $430 in 2001,[14] a family of four with $12,000 would be privileged.

The third world and poverty are both terms of relationship. The third world is the world dominated, the world excluded from power.

The poor are the people on the bottom, the people denied the benefits of the society in which they live.

The differences in income that exist in today's world are staggering. In Switzerland in 2001, the average income per person was the equivalent of U.S.$36,970; in the United States, the figure was $34,870, and in Britain $24,230. In the poorest forty-nine countries, with almost half the world's population, the average income was $430, just more than 1 percent of the income in the richest countries.[15]

Figures like these probably overstate the gap in living standards between the rich and the poor, because they do not adequately reflect the fact that prices are lower in some third-world countries than in rich countries. A dollar, converted to rupees at the official exchange rate, will buy more rice in an outdoor market in Delhi, India, than it will in a neighborhood supermarket in Kankakee, Illinois. In an attempt to correct for this bias, the World Bank has constructed "purchasing power parity" estimates of per capita incomes; these show that living standards in the rich countries are really ten to twenty times higher than the incomes in the poorest countries of the third world.[16] It may be impossible to put an exact figure on the gap between the rich and the poor countries, but there is no doubt that it is huge.

This is the overwhelming truth about the world we inhabit: The gap between the richness of the developed countries and the poverty of the third world is so huge that it is almost beyond our understanding. How can one imagine living for a whole year on the money one now spends in just one month? It would not be a matter of "belt tightening"; it would be a totally different and devastating life. In the United States, Canada, or Britain, an ordinary family with one working parent typically lives in a house or an apartment with several bedrooms, a living room, a kitchen, at least one bathroom, running water, and a heating system. The family has a car, quite a lot of clothes, a radio, a television set, some books, and enough extra money to eat out from time to time, go to the movies, and take a vacation. The family members are generally in good health, and if they are not, they have access to modern medical technology, the expense of which is often insured. Described this way, it does not seem like a great deal. But for Mauwa, Domitila, Shahhat, Rigoberta, and the Mossi people, it is a universe apart. It is not quite as incomprehensible to them as their situation is to us, because Western popular culture—movies, magazines, and television—has swept into most corners of the world and created some impressions of middle-class life in the industrialized world. It is so distinct from their situations as to be absolutely unattainable, however.

Among the poor of the world, a family typically shares one room— and in rural areas, the room may provide shelter for farm animals as well. The family members do not have enough good food to eat. They usually (but not always) have enough to prevent starvation, but they suffer from dietary deficiencies of both calories and particular nutrients. They have few clothes, no private cars, no vacations, and no money to spend on things beyond necessities. They experience perpetual insecurity because they hardly ever have savings sufficient to tide the family over during bad times. Above all, they are threatened by bad health—high infant mortality, less than full physical development of children, susceptibility to disease, uncertain life spans.

The pattern is far from uniform—every conceivable variation exists in the third world, as in the developed world. No variation, however, can conceal the basic fact of overwhelming poverty throughout much of Asia, the Middle East, Africa, and Latin America: the almost unclothed people living in the streets of Calcutta and Bombay, the gaunt herders of central Africa whose fertile plains are slowly but inexorably eroding into desert, the peasants of northeastern Brazil driven from their homes by drought and landowners, the bark-clothed peasants of Mozambique fleeing from war zones.

One feature shared by all the world's poor is insecurity. When times are good—when the rains fall, when the market price is high—the family can be fed and a few improvements made to the dwelling. Bad luck may strike at any time, though, and wipe out the chance for survival itself. When times are bad in Africa, in India, in China, thousands starve to death. The consciousness of imminent disaster, a fear of what the future will bring, has been found by social scientists to be pervasive among the world's poor, and for good reason.

The poverty of the third world is not "traditional"; it is not an ancient way of life. The traditional cultures of the third world are rich and various, and they are closer to the surface of everyday life than traditions usually are in the industrialized world, where they have been suppressed. The old folkways of the third world have little to do with poverty. The great religions of the third world—Hinduism, Buddhism, Islam—are not apologies for poverty; they are integral worldviews that bind the generations together. The philosophies and customs that developed over the millennia led to a sense of belonging, not a sense of exclusion. Scattered throughout the world are some significant groups of people living in completely traditional ways much as their ancestors did—for example, in the rain forests of Africa, New Guinea, and some parts of the Philippines. In learning about them we can discern something about the common heritage of the human race.

The way that these traditional people live is not, however, typical of the widespread poverty that mars the face of the globe. The endless urban slums are not traditional; they are recent. The population explosion that magnifies the number of poor and threatens the very survival of the globe is a phenomenon of the last century, not of time immemorial. The poor laborers in the tobacco, cocoa, banana, cotton, rubber, and sugar fields are not obeying traditional cultural imperatives; they are producing export crops for sale in the prosperous markets, mostly in North America and Europe.

Traditional cultures generally had low standards of living in comparison with life today in the rich countries. Life in traditional societies may even have been, in the words of philosopher Thomas Hobbes, "nasty, brutish and short." People living in traditional societies were not, however, poor in comparison with the people around them with whom they had contact. In contrast, today's poor in the third world are centrally connected to a changing world—their cities, their farms, their mines, their slums all grow and change rapidly, all responding to the dynamic demands of a growing world economy. The process that transformed the world—that gave us jet airplanes, computer technology, and suburban sprawl—transformed the third world also, creating the new phenomenon of massive urban and rural poverty.

Poverty is never shared equally, even in the poorest countries. Every society has some rich, some middle income, and some poor, and the relative size of the income gap between the rich and the poor varies greatly among countries. One should not think that because India, for example, had an average income of $460 in 2001 that all Indians enjoyed that modest income. The majority of Indians had less than $460 a year, and a substantial number of Indians had very much less. Correspondingly, middle-class and wealthy Indians commanded a great deal more of the country's economic resources.

The distribution of income among different groups has been surveyed in a number of the world's poor countries, although it must be conceded that the data are suspect. The surveys have been taken in different years, using different concepts and statistical methods, and with differing degrees of accuracy. Consequently, international comparisons are perilous. Nevertheless, the latest available data appear to confirm what has sometimes been called the Kuznets curve: as countries' average incomes rise from the very poorest levels, income distribution first becomes more unequal, then more equal.[17] Put differently, it appears that when economic growth takes place in poor countries, it does not usually improve the status of the poorest; rather, it raises the rewards of upper-income groups and leaves the poor further behind. Only after a certain level of economic development has occurred can the poor share in its fruits.

Even this generalization, modest though it is, is marked by exceptions. The UNDP ranks countries according to a human development index based on health conditions, literacy, and access to goods and services.[18] It has found that a high ranking on this index is not necessarily associated with high average incomes. Some countries with strong performance in human development are Costa Rica, Korea, China, Cuba, and Argentina. Other countries, however, including some with quite strong economies, have done much less for their people, among them Angola, Pakistan, and Guatemala.

Poverty is not shared equally by the sexes. Women have access to less health care than men. They receive less schooling; consequently, their illiteracy rates are higher. They perform work that is more tedious and of lower status than men's work, and they receive less compensation. They usually work longer hours because, in addition to their work outside the home, they are almost always solely responsible for all the work inside the home. To take an example, a female lace maker in the Narsapour region of India works eight hours a day in her home (her so-called leisure time), for an average daily salary of 0.56 rupees. This is only one-third of the wage estimated to be necessary for subsistence, 1.6 rupees. It contrasts with the minimum wage in agriculture of 3.4 rupees for men. Her husband typically earns three times as much as she does. To see how little her earnings amount to, they can be compared with the cost of a sari—between 30 and 70 rupees. She works between two and four months, therefore, to earn the money to buy a dress. Her total workday lasts fifteen hours, not eight, because of the seven additional hours she spends on housework.[19]

The poor are undernourished and malnourished—with less caloric intake and less protein and vitamin intake than they need. As a consequence, many of their children do not achieve full physical and mental development. In a survey for the period 1992–98, the World Bank found that between one-quarter and one-half of children under the age of five in the poorest countries of the third world were malnourished. The proportion for China was 16 percent, but the proportion for Bangladesh was 56 percent.[20]

The poor are susceptible to disease and premature mortality at much higher rates than are the people of richer countries. Death rates have risen in recent years in much of Africa because of the AIDS epidemic. Most of the rest of the third world, however, has seen dramatic improvements in health and longevity over the last sixty years, as the benefits of public health and sanitation measures have been extended throughout the world. Yet large differences still exist between developed and developing countries. Surveys in Latin America and Africa have shown that fully 90 percent of the people studied were infested with some form of parasite. In Peru, for example, 113 out of 122 men sampled in the armed forces had parasitic infections. Ninety percent of people in an area of East Africa were found to have beef tape-worms. The prevalence of tropical diseases such as hookworm, bilharzia, filariasis, and schistosomiasis is almost universal in some areas.[21] These diseases are typically associated with pain and loss of strength, and sometimes with early mortality.

These are the bare facts about living standards in the third world—low average incomes, substantial numbers of people living in the direst and most life-threatening poverty, and an incredible gap between the poor countries and the economically developed countries. It would not be correct to call this situation a crisis, because it persists from year to year. It is a tragedy.

The Successes

Fifty years ago, Korea and Taiwan had roughly the same standards of living as Kenya and India, but today they are worlds apart. The former are two of the newly industrializing countries (NICs) of East Asia; they are joined by Hong Kong (now reunited with China), Malaysia, and Singapore. They have built their success on a strategy of producing manufactured goods, many of them embodying high technology, and exporting them to the markets of the rich countries. They have been unapologetically capitalist, although with a strong dose of government guidance. Their rapidly developing manufacturing sectors have pulled up the living standards of people throughout their countries and narrowed the gaps between the rich and the poor. As a consequence, comparatively few of their citizens now live in desperate circumstances. Each successive year they seem to have more in common with their industrialized neighbor Japan than with much of the rest of Asia.

China's average standard of living is far below that of the NICs, but its economic performance in the last two decades has been impressive. Considerable uncertainty exists about the income levels of the Chinese; it is likely that the official figures compiled by the World Bank are much too low.[22] China has experienced extraordinarily rapid economic growth since the mid-1970s, and because the rate of population growth has fallen, most of this economic growth has translated into improvements in the standard of living of the people. China has a relatively equal distribution of income, so many of the poorest have shared in the improvements. Literacy is high. Health and longevity are among the best in the third world. Much of the improvement in living standards in China can probably be attributed to a liberalization of the economy; a freeing of enterprise from the heavy, controlling hand of the Communist Party; and an opening of the country to foreign ideas, technology, and investment. The Chinese are traditionally an enterprising, innovative people, and they are now freer to pursue their goals. The achievements of China are particularly noteworthy, because it is such a large country, with more than a fifth of the world's population.

In the Western Hemisphere, Argentina, Chile, and some other countries have made progress that is more uneven than that in the East Asian NICs but impressive nonetheless. The Latin American countries were severely damaged by the international debt crisis of the 1980s, but in the 1990s, some of them rebounded, lowering but not eliminating the number of people in serious poverty.

Different Areas of the Third World Diverge

The picture of human welfare in the third world is not uniformly bleak. Some countries have succeeded in transforming themselves, and others seem to be on the right road. Within every country, at least some people have been able to provide adequately for themselves.

The successes should not blind us to the terrible poverty that remains, however, nor to the lack of economic progress among most of the world's poor. Table 2.2—showing the growth rates in output, population, and per capita incomes since 1990—indicates how unequally different regions of the world have responded to the challenges of development.

In the third world as a whole, production of goods and services grew at the rate of 3.4 percent a year between 1990 and 2001. Population growth absorbed almost half this increase, however, leaving 1.9

Table 2.2 Annual Growth Rates in Different Regions, 1990–2001

Region	Output (%)	Population (%)	Per Capita Income (%)
Lower- and middle-income countries	3.3	1.5	1.9
Europe and Central Asia	−0.9	0.2	−1.1
Sub-Saharan Africa	2.6	2.6	0
Middle East and North Africa	3.0	2.1	0.9
Latin America and the Caribbean	3.1	1.6	1.5
South Asia	5.5	1.9	3.6
East Asia and the Pacific	7.5	1.2	6.3
High income	2.5	0.7	1.8

Source: World Bank, *World Development Report 2003* (New York: Oxford University Press, 2003), Tables 1 and 3.

percent a year in growth of income per person. This rate of growth was almost the same as the rich countries experienced. Because the rich countries started from a higher base, however, their people enjoyed a much greater absolute increase in income.

Moreover, it is likely that little of the new income in the low-income countries accrued to the poor. Although the available data are not sufficient to prove the point, the earlier discussion of the Kuznets curve leads one to think that most of the minimal economic improvement went into the pockets of the relatively well-off, not the poor.

Table 2.2 also indicates the marked variation among the different regions. The experience of the countries that made up the former Soviet Union—in Europe and Central Asia—was catastrophic. Their economies contracted at a rate of more than 1 percent in the 1990s, with a faster decline earlier in the period and some recovery later. Sub-Saharan Africa saw stagnation and worse. With the world's highest fertility levels, population growth in Africa absorbed all the economic growth; in many areas of the continent, average living standards fell, in some cases below the meager levels that existed at the time of independence in the 1960s. In the Middle East and North Africa, and also in Latin America, output growth exceeded population growth, leading to a certain improvement in living standards.

The table shows a completely different picture for Asia: steady improvement in the south, and spectacular improvement in the East. The differences within Asia are still striking, however. For example, absolute poverty is endemic in India and much less common in China, as Table 2.1 showed. The East Asian NICs have transformed themselves so thoroughly and have become so industrial that they are almost at a European level, but many other Asian countries are still desperately poor. Throughout the vast Asian continent, however, economic growth and social transformations are occurring broadly, changing the lives of many if not most people.

The developing world today is marked, therefore, by tremendous divergences and inequalities, both within and between countries. Within many countries, the gap between the rich and the poor is large, often larger than that found in the industrialized countries. Although the gap is narrowing in some countries, it is widening in most, as the fruits of economic growth flow disproportionately to those who are already richer and more powerful. Turning to international comparisons, certain countries seem to have found the key to steady growth and improvement in living standards, but some are stagnating and still others regressing.

Perhaps we are nearing the end of the period when the term *third world* is a meaningful description of the societies of Asia, Africa, the

Middle East, and Latin America. If current trends continue, the differences within that group will be as great as any differences between the third world as a whole and the industrialized, developed world. The success stories of South Korea and some other Asian countries, well publicized as they are, should not lead us to forget the overwhelming reality of poverty in the world. Although it is easing in some regions, it is growing and intensifying in others. Many of the world's people are subject to stagnant or falling incomes and increasingly precarious health. The prospect of an end, or even an overall reduction, in world poverty is not in sight.

The Betrayal of Responsibility

The people in the rich countries bear some responsibility for the poverty of the third world. There are two dimensions to this responsibility. First is a difficult set of questions related to causality: How did the economic progress of the rich countries help or hurt the prospects of the poor? How did the empires of the rich affect the lives of the poor? How are the policies of the rich today affecting the standards of living of the third world? These complex questions are addressed in subsequent chapters.

There is a much simpler dimension to the responsibility of the rich, however, a dimension completely independent of one's answers to the questions in the previous paragraph. Living in a world of obscene inequality, the privileged have a moral responsibility to do what they can to improve the lot of the less privileged. This responsibility arises from the common humanity of all people; we are a single species. It is a responsibility recognized by most ethical and religious systems.[23] It is a responsibility urged upon the rich by spokespeople of the world's poor in countless conferences and forums. It is a responsibility willingly embraced by many people and institutions in the rich countries. Taken as a whole, however, and with those honorable exceptions, the rich countries have rejected and betrayed their responsibility to the third world.

The evidence that the rich do not recognize their responsibility to the world's poor is hard to avoid. Only a few of the smaller European countries have met the United Nations' goal of contributing 0.7 percent of their annual income in the form of aid to poor countries. The most recent figure for Britain is 0.32 percent and for the United States a remarkably low 0.10 percent.[24] When the agenda before the governments of the rich countries is to cut their budgetary deficits, the most vulnerable items include foreign aid, because it has only weak domestic constituencies.

Perhaps the rich avoid grappling with the inequity on the planet and their responsibility for it because a full understanding would seriously threaten the sense they have of themselves. Most people in North America and western Europe do not think of themselves as rich beyond imagination, and certainly not as oppressors. On the contrary, they see themselves as comfortable, perhaps, but still struggling to make ends meet; as financially insecure, but hoping to do a bit better in the future. Most see themselves in the position of the little guy, fighting for some advantage against forces that are more powerful.

In their own societies and daily lives, that kind of an attitude makes sense, but from a global perspective, it is nonsense. Most people in the North live lives of incredible luxury compared with almost everyone in the South. There are exceptions—the poor in the North, the rich in the South—but not many. If Americans and Europeans were to think of themselves in this sort of global context, as constituting the world's privileged, they might then face painful questions relating to their responsibilities. They might have to ask themselves: Where does our responsibility lie? Does our material comfort require others to be poor? Are we making world poverty worse, or are we part of the solution? Should we try to be part of the solution? What solutions might there be? Will an attack on world poverty require sacrifices from us? What kind of sacrifices?

These are questions that most people in the developed world would prefer to avoid. It is stretching an analogy only a bit to recall the "good Germans" of the 1930s and 1940s who knew nothing about the Holocaust being perpetrated by the regime to which they gave loyalty because they did not want to know. If people in the rich countries today know nothing about the hunger and disease of India, Congo, Cambodia, and Honduras (to say nothing of the slums in their own cities), it is in large measure because they would prefer not to, because the knowledge would powerfully threaten their rather complacent sense of themselves. If they turn their backs on the majority of the world's population and address only their own problems, it is because it would be shocking and dangerous to do otherwise.

The privileged are turning their backs. Most people in the developed countries, having achieved a comfortable standard of living, are largely oblivious to the fate of the world's majority and to their own responsibility for that fate.

One should not overstate the argument. People in the rich countries cannot solve the problems of the poor countries by themselves. The destiny of the third world is in the hands of its people, to make of it what they will. It is they who will determine their future, not North Americans or Europeans. To think otherwise is to perpetuate a peculiarly

modern form of cultural imperialism, to conceive of the rich as puppet masters, manipulating the strings that make the rest of the world
dance. They do not.

There is plenty of responsibility to go around for the predicament
of the world's poor, and third-world leaders can claim a lot of it. Military regimes have attacked their own people, protected the exploiters
of their own poor, and squandered billions on armaments. Nationalist leaders have wasted resources on flashy, self-serving projects.
Voices of the needy have been squelched. The principal drama of the
third world rests in the third world, among its own people.

Still the prosperous countries and their institutions—their governments, armed forces, corporations, voluntary associations—powerfully
affect the constraints within which the third world must determine its
future. Having played a central role in the creation of the world's
inequities, they could allow themselves to be used constructively. They
will not help by being missionaries, by trying to bring the ideology of
free markets or even democratic institutions to the third world. The
people of the poor countries will do that well or badly by themselves,
and there is not much that the rich can do about it. Their responsibility is to reform their own institutions, to lend a hand that is open
and not clenched, to be helpful and not harmful to the world's poor.
This is a task that is achievable and is also respectful of the third
world, not manipulative.

Notes

1. Nicholas D. Kristof, "In Congo, a New Era with Old Burdens," *New York Times*, May 20, 1997, A1.

2. Richard Critchfield, *Shahhat, an Egyptian* (Syracuse, N.Y.: Syracuse University Press, 1978).

3. Ouedraogo's story is told in Peter Adamson, "The Rains," in *The State of the World's Children, 1982–83,* ed. James P. Grant (New York: Oxford University Press, 1982), 45–128. Further details appear in Frances Moore Lappé, Rachel Schurman, and Kevin Danaher, *Betraying the National Interest* (New York: Grove Press, 1987).

4. Adamson, "The Rains," 116.

5. Adamson, "The Rains," 117–18.

6. Her book, edited from tapes by Brazilian journalist Moema Viezzer, is Domitila Barrios de Chungara, *Let Me Speak: Testimony of Domitila, a Woman of the Bolivian Mines* (New York: Monthly Review Press, 1978).

7. Barrios de Chungara, *Let Me Speak,* 41.

8. Rigoberta Menchú, I, *Rigoberta Menchú,* ed. Elisabeth Burgos-Debray (London: Verso Books, 1984). The veracity of some of Menchú's assertions has been challenged in David Stoll, *Rigoberta Menchú and the Story of All Poor Guatemalans* (Boulder, Colo.: Westview Press, 1999).

9. The *New York Times*, October 17, 1992.

10. United Nations Development Programme, *Human Development Report 2002* (New York: Oxford University Press, 2002), 18.

11. For estimates of some of these attributes, see *Human Development Report 2002*, Table 3.

12. UNDP, *Human Development Report 1997*, 27.

13. UNDP, *Human Development Report 2002*, Table 4.

14. World Bank, *World Development Report 2003* (New York: Oxford University Press, 2003), Table 1.

15. World Bank, *World Development Report 2003*, Table 1.

16. Ibid.

17. World Bank, *World Development Report 2000/2001* (New York: Oxford University Press, 2001), Table 5.

18. UNDP, *Human Development Report 2002*, Table 1.

19. For extensive information on the status of women in poor countries, see UNDP, *Human Development Report 2002*, Tables 22 through 27. The Narsapour example is described in Jeanne Bisilliat and Michele Fieloux, *Women of the Third World: Work and Daily Life*, trans. Enne Amann and Peter Amann (Cranbury, N.J.: Associated University Presses, 1987).

20. World Bank, *World Development Report 2000/2001*, Table 2.

21. See Andrew M. Kamarck, *The Tropics and Economic Development: A Provocative Inquiry into the Poverty of Nations* (Baltimore: Johns Hopkins University Press, 1973), chap. 7.

22. Ross Garnaut and Guonan Ma, "How Rich Is China? Evidence from the Food Economy," *Australian Journal of Chinese Affairs* 30 (July 1993): 121–46.

23. For a fuller discussion of the responsibility of the rich to the poor, see John Isbister, *Capitalism and Justice: Envisioning Social and Economic Fairness* (Bloomfield, Conn.: Kumarian Press, 2001).

24. UNDP, *Human Development Report 2002*, Table 15.

Suggestions for Further Reading

See Bibliography for full details.

Domitila Barrios de Chungara. *Let Me Speak: Testimony of Domitila, A Woman of the Bolivian Mines.*

A. S. Bhalla and Frederic Lapeyre. *Poverty and Exclusion in a Global World.*

Richard Critchfield. *Shahhat, An Egyptian.*

Carolina Maria de Jesus. *Child of the Dark.*

Buchi Emecheta. *The Joys of Motherhood.*

A. M. Khusro. *The Poverty of Nations.*

David Landes. *The Wealth and Poverty of Nations: Why Some Are So Rich and Some So Poor.*

Frances Moore Lappé, Joseph Collins, and Peter Rosset, with Luis Esparza. *World Hunger: Twelve Myths.*

Oscar Lewis. *The Children of Sanchez: Autobiography of a Mexican Family.*

Rigoberta Menchú. *I, Rigoberta Menchú.*

Deepa Narayan and Patti Petesh, eds. *Voices of the Poor, from Many Lands.*

Stuart A. Schlegel. *Wisdom from a Rainforest, The Spiritual Journey of an Anthropologist.*

Chapter Three

Explanations of Underdevelopment

By dependence we mean a situation in which the economy of certain countries is conditioned by the development and expansion of another economy to which the former is subjected.
—Theotonio Dos Santos

The tragedy of the dependency perspective lies in its assumption that the world-system must be transformed before meaningful internal changes can occur. If one begins with such a pessimistic assumption, the task becomes so daunting that politically innovative strategies are dismissed in favor of symbolic tilting at transnational windmills.
—Paul M. Lubeck

There could be no greater slur inflicted on our capabilities: we are nincompoops, we are unable to ensure a local supply of exploiters, the process of exploitation has to be initiated elsewhere. . . . This itself is neocolonialism of a sort.
—*Economic and Political Weekly,* India

How are we to understand the tragedy described in Chapter 2—the massive and swelling poverty that plagues the third world—side by side with the unprecedented prosperity of the industrial countries? Why has social change in the third world come so often to a dead end? Social scientists have advanced some answers to these questions, but their answers are not simple—and in some respects, they are contradictory. Many of the answers can be grouped into three different schools: modernization, dependency, and Marxism. This chapter explores these three schools, searching for clues to explain why the promise of a better life has been empty for so many people.

Modernization theory is the dominant philosophy of social scientists in the developed countries; it is the worldview that most of them adopt in their attempt to understand the origins of poverty and underdevelopment, and it includes few hints that the rich are responsible for the plight of the poor. Modernization theorists focus on deficiencies in the poor countries—the absence of democratic institutions, of capital, of technology, of initiative—and then speculate about ways to repair these deficiencies.

Dependency theory asserts that economic growth in the advanced capitalist countries created third-world poverty in its wake. The argument is not simply that the third world is poor in comparison with the industrialized world; rather, it is that the development of the industrial system in Europe and North America fundamentally changed and impoverished most of the societies of Asia, Africa, and Latin America. Theorists of this persuasion argue, therefore, that poverty in the third world cannot be understood without reference to the entire international system.

This argument has been developed in detail by social scientists in the third world as well as in the developed countries. Different writers in the dependency school have different approaches, and some of the debates are quite significant,[1] but the school is united in seeing the structure of modern third world societies, and the problems that beset them, as responses to the capitalist growth of Europe and North America. The dependency school stands in opposition to the argument of modernization theorists and Marxists that the origins of poverty are to be found internally, within the social structures of the third-world countries themselves.

The Marxists focus their attention on the class structure in poor countries and the mechanisms that exist for exploitation, that is, for the appropriation of surplus production by the dominant class. If the dominant class is capitalist, the exploitation and the appropriation of surplus may be accompanied by economic growth. If, however, the class structure of the country is feudal or some other noncapitalist type, the surplus is likely to be wasted and the country mired in stagnation.

The term *Marxist* may be a bit confusing, because many dependency theorists consider themselves to be Marxist, and in truth, one would have to acknowledge that some of the most creative Marxist thinking in recent decades has come from within the dependency school. Sociologist Aidan Foster-Carter resolves the problem by referring to the dependency school as neo-Marxist.

These three schools do not exhaust the ways that have been used to understand world poverty. Furthermore, the disagreements within the schools have often been as great as the gaps between them. Nevertheless, the three basic approaches are distinct. An acquaintance with them is the best way to begin to grasp the causes of inequality and poverty in the world.

Modernization Theory

Modernization theory is the mainstream school of scholarship about poverty and economic, social, and political development in the countries of the third world. A great deal of useful, even brilliant, work has been carried out within this framework. The adherents of this approach do not actually see themselves as a cohesive school; they are more inclined to emphasize the disputes among them and to dismiss the dependency school and the Marxists as irrelevant or excessively doctrinal or political. There are a number of common elements to the modernizationists' analyses, however, and they can be usefully drawn together.

An important idea in this school is the concept of the traditional society. The modernizationists think of today's third-world societies as being largely traditional; they also think of western Europe as having been traditional in the long period before the era of modern economic growth and cultural change.

According to this view, the essence of a traditional society is that it is stagnant and unchanging. Its values are spiritual values, not the values of individual self-betterment. Its rhythms of life are circular, not linear and progressive; one always returns to the same place. The traditional world is emotionally comfortable, a world in which each person has a place that is secure, a place in the family among the pantheon of ancestors. The traditional person identifies with his or her ancestors and emulates them. Daily work is carried out just as it always has been, not to secure a profit but to perform one's duty, to maintain one's place in the society. Nothing is innovative, and there is no attempt to "better" one's lot. No distinction exists between daily life and spiritual life—it is all one. Almost any religious system can serve as the basis for a traditional society. Referring to French Canada of the nineteenth century, historian A. R. M. Lower wrote:

> The life of the peasant is a series of ritual occasions, planting and harvesting, being born, coming of age, begetting, dying. . . . All are one family, interrelated if not in this generation, in the last or the next. All give unquestioned obedience to the great mother goddess, the earth-mother, who can easily be made to wear a Christian dress. . . . His religion is among the simplest and oldest of all creeds, Catholic almost by accident.[2]

The picture of traditional life painted by the modernizationists is not a negative one. It is an integrated life in which the spirit, the family, the larger group, and the work tasks all combine to form a seamless whole, a life in which there is no estrangement, no alienation. From an economic point of view, however, it is a poor, subsistence life, a life that has no hope of accumulation, income, or wealth. No sense of progress inheres in it. When time is circular, when the most honorable task is to imitate one's ancestors, there can be no breakthroughs, no fundamental changes, no development.

Historians in the modernization school argue that about five hundred years ago, most people in the world were poor, living in traditional social arrangements. Scholars disagree as to whether average standards of living in western Europe were the same as or higher than average standards of living in Asia at the time.[3] Whatever the answer, there is no question that most people, everywhere in the world, lived at a very low standard compared with the norms in today's wealthier countries.

Sparks of scientific discovery occurred in widely scattered parts of the world—in the Middle East, in China, in Africa, and in South America. For a variety of historical reasons, however, scientific inquiry led to consistent technological innovation mainly in western Europe. Science and the entrepreneurial spirit combined there to produce little pockets of productivity: higher yields per acre of crops, more seaworthy ships, advancements in weaponry, more efficient techniques for artisans. These pockets of productivity grew—they widened and deepened—gradually transforming the societies of Europe and later of Europe's offshoots in North America and elsewhere. The engine of this economic growth was capitalism.

To understand the modernizationists' view, one must know what they mean by capitalism. The term *capital* is used in diverse ways by different groups of people. In common parlance, *capital* is often synonymous with money, as when a broker says, "I have some capital to invest in the stock market." But this is not how the word is used by modern social scientists.

For mainstream economists (often called neoclassical economists), capital is a means of production, that is, something that is used in the production of other things. To distinguish it from other means of production, such as land and labor, the term *capital* is reserved for those means of production that have themselves been previously produced. Included in capital are factories, machines, and tools that have been produced at some prior time and are currently used for making goods or providing services. Capital can include highways, trucks, harbors, airplanes, and even inventories. Natural resources, such as deposits of iron ore, are not considered capital, because they have not been produced.

For mainstream economists, capitalism is the social system under which this capital is privately owned. At the center of this view of capitalism is the market, the institution in which sellers and buyers come together on a voluntary basis to exchange goods and services in return for money, at a price. Privately owned capital is used to produce goods and services, which in turn are sold in markets, at prices that are determined through the interplay of supply and demand.

Included in this view of capitalism is an important role for the government. Earlier generations in Europe and North America, influenced by the laissez-faire ideas of Adam Smith and his followers, may have argued that government was a threat to capitalism, but in the modern world, it is clear that governments are central partners in most capitalist systems. In Britain and the United States, for example, about one-third of the goods and services produced are paid for by governments at all levels. Governments in capitalist countries build the infrastructure—the roads, airports, waterways, educational systems—that is needed to maintain the system; they provide for the military; they regulate the private sector through a series of rules, subsidies, price controls, and oversight agencies; and they patch up the loose ends of the system with welfare programs. In the Great Depression of the 1930s, there was a danger that the capitalist societies of North America and Europe would collapse because of their own rigidity; they were saved first by the Second World War and then by government economic policies and the development of public welfare programs. Governments in the capitalist countries learned to spend, tax, regulate, legislate, and produce in ways that supported the capitalist system and that compensated for its unevenness and shortcomings. Capitalism today in no way implies the absence of government activity; what it implies is that governments support the system of private ownership of the nation's productive capacity.

Economic historians in the modernization school argue that innovation and technological growth became self-sustaining in Europe because they were embedded in the capitalist system. Individual capitalist entrepreneurs were in competition with one another. They knew that if they did not struggle aggressively, their competitors would overtake them, capture their market, and ruin them. So each capitalist had to be at the forefront, working as hard as possible to develop better products and expand output. Each tried to enlarge profits by keeping costs low and increasing revenues. The capitalists used some of those profits for their own consumption, but a much greater share was used to invest in more capital equipment in order to produce more goods. Growth became the only constant; the fundamental tenet of European societies during the industrial revolution was that each generation would outperform its parents in terms of production, wealth, and, eventually, standard of living. According to the people who view the growth process through these lenses, each feature of the capitalist system conspired to promote growth. Workers who were mobile and unencumbered by artificial restrictions sought employment where they could be most productive and earn the best wages. Financial institutions searching for the highest rate of return on their funds invested in the most promising new activities. Firms that were in competition with one another cut costs and thereby promoted efficiency. Particularly important was the role of entrepreneurship: the lure of profits drew adventurous people into uncertain, risky projects, thereby creating wealth and eventually raising standards of living.

Initially, the workers were excluded from the benefits of the industrialization process, working long hours for minimal wages in health-threatening environments. Conditions in the early European factories and the towns that surrounded them were frightening. Contemporary economists in the nineteenth-century British "classical" school actually predicted that the poor would remain poor and grow in number, surviving at little more than a subsistence level. Modern scholars in the modernization school stress the fact that these predictions proved false. As history unfolded in twentieth-century Europe and North America, wealth was increasingly distributed among the population—not equally, of course, or even equitably. Wealth was distributed widely, however, as workers were drawn into the productive sphere to enjoy the benefits of the quickly advancing technology. Poverty remained, but it was scattered. To a large extent, poverty occurred not among the working people but among those who for one reason or another were unable to work. The undeniable poverty that still exists within capitalist societies should not, say the modernizationists, obscure the fact that the capitalist system created for most people much higher overall levels of production, income, and wealth than were ever known before.

Many social scientists emphasize the political modernization that accompanied the economic modernization. Feudal autocratic monarchies were challenged by representatives of the people and eventually displaced—in some cases gradually, over centuries, as in Britain; in other cases through revolution, as in France. Individual freedoms were ensured—of association, of speech, of religion. Representative forms of government were established, and the principle that governments are to be democratic, that they are responsible to the people, was won. Political parties were formed and free elections regularized. The rule of law was made supreme and the independence of the judiciary guaranteed. The exact form of government differed in each country of the modernized world, but the common element became democracy. Political modernization and economic modernization went hand in hand, inseparable, exalting the position of ordinary people to a status not known in previous regimes that were both poorer and more despotic.

According to at least some of the modernizationists, capitalism was as responsible for political freedom as it was for the wealth of the developed countries. Capitalism, they argue, is a system of decentralized power, with many different people controlling the wealth of the country. In a socialist or autocratic system, economic power is centralized; as a consequence, only one political voice is tolerated. But the dispersion of wealth among many capitalists, and eventually among the workers as well, allows for a variety of political power bases. Politicians and competing political parties can turn to any number of sources for financial support, so diversity and debate are kept alive. The two phenomena, capitalist economic development on the one hand and political freedom and diversity on the other, are so closely connected as to be inseparable. Capitalism needs political freedom, say the modernizationists, in order to preserve the openness required for the flourishing of entrepreneurial innovation, and a liberal political order needs the diversity of power centers that only capitalism can provide.

The modernizationists argue that the poverty and backwardness of the third world can be understood simply as the failure of those societies to kindle the same sparks of creativity. The third world was left behind at the starting block; it neglected to transform itself. Without a commitment to science, to free inquiry, to technology, to the spirit of enterprise and competition, to democracy and the rule of law, it stagnated as it had for centuries, while the societies of the Northern Hemisphere grew both economically and morally.

According to this way of looking at the world, then, there are two poles: modern and traditional. The modern world is what economists sometimes call rational. It is inhabited by people who are constantly trying to do the best they can for themselves, to optimize, to maximize. The modern world is based on research and development and on the goal of efficiency. It is driven by the search for profit and wealth, as people take risks to do things in new and better ways, in the hope of improving their lot. It is based on competition and on the laws of the marketplace that reward success. The modern world is forward-looking, committed to growth and improvement. The modernizationists argue that the task before the underdeveloped countries is to transform themselves from tradition to modernity, that is, to follow in the footsteps of the now developed countries. The title of the influential book by Nobel Prize–winning economist Theodore W. Schultz is revealing: *Transforming Traditional Agriculture*. Schultz paints a picture of traditional agriculture as being in a state of equilibrium in which little changes and in which there is little possibility of change, because the ancient folkways are perfectly adapted to providing as much security as possible in an inherently dangerous world. To transform this traditional world, he maintains, new opportunities must be provided to peasants—new incentives, new rewards, new technologies, new knowledge. With these new stimuli, the traditional, unchanging subsistence peasant can be converted into a productive, surplus-creating, modern farmer.

Fortunately, argues the modernization school, there is every chance that the world's poor countries can succeed in this transformation from the traditional to the modern, because they have an advantage that the Europeans lacked. They can follow in the footsteps of those who have come before. In fact, because the path to modernization is now charted, the poor countries can avoid some of the false starts that delayed the progress of the pioneers. Furthermore, the rich countries can lend a helping hand to the poor, offering them technology, markets, capital, and encouragement.

People who base their worldview on the modernization theory often think in terms of stages through which all countries must pass on their journey to a high standard of living. Some of these stages are fairly simple and obvious—for example, agriculture to industry to services, or rural to urban to suburban. One of the more powerful, although more complex, stage theories of modernization was presented in Walt Rostow's 1960 book *The Stages of Economic Growth*. Rostow identifies five stages, using the metaphor of the takeoff of an airplane:

1. *The traditional society.* The airplane is at rest. The society's culture is prescientific, with the great majority of the population living in a traditional way at a bare subsistence level.

2. *The preconditions for takeoff.* In this stage, the equilibrium of the traditional society is challenged—perhaps by science or by foreign commerce or by invasions. The traditional organization of the society is upset, and the opportunity is presented for fundamental social change. At this stage it is only an opportunity, however; the forces of tradition may yet reassert themselves and prevent further modernization.

3. *The takeoff.* "We come now," wrote Rostow, "to the great watershed in the life of modern societies. . . . The take-off is the interval when the old blocks and resistances to steady growth are finally overcome."[4] The takeoff occurs when political power accrues to a group that regards economic growth as its main business; when the country's savings rate, as a proportion of national income, doubles;

and when modern technology is applied to a few leading sectors, both agricultural and industrial.

4. *The drive to maturity.* This stage corresponds to the increase in altitude of the airplane. It lasts perhaps two generations, and it is the period in which economic growth spreads from the initial few leading sectors to a wide range of activities. The country becomes an active participant in international markets, exporting new goods and producing for domestic use goods that were formerly imported. As the country reaches maturity, it is able to use modern technology to produce if not every good in the world then at least every good it chooses to.

5. *The age of high mass consumption.* This stage corresponds to the high-altitude, high-speed, long-distance flight of the airplane. In this fifth stage, the fruits of growth are finally transferred to the mass of the population. No longer are the people called on to sacrifice for future growth. Now their broad standards of living rise steadily and predictably. The country has sufficient wealth to turn its attention to social welfare, that is, to extending the fruits of growth in at least a minimal way to those people who were not able to participate directly in the growth.

Since Rostow's book first appeared, the modernization school has produced an enormous amount of creative scholarship. What remains constant throughout this literature is the idea of two poles, tradition and modernity, with the transition between them seen as the task of our age. For some writers, the issue is primarily one of individual psychology. In the traditional society, they believe, people are rooted in ancient ways of relating to one another and of conceiving problems. They venerate their ancestors and think of time in a circular, repetitive way. The transformation to modernity requires a breaking of these ways of thought—the creation, for example, of a "need for achievement," to use psychologist David McClelland's phrase—a celebration of individual success as opposed to group affiliation.

Other writers view the tradition-modernity dichotomy from a more social and political point of view. A traditional society may be one in which the ruling group uses its power to confiscate the wealth of the country so that it can support itself, for example, in ostentatious consumption. What is needed is a class of entrepreneurs who will mobilize the country's wealth for productive investment, to create the technology and the capital needed for growth. Economist Everett Hagen suggests that these entrepreneurs may come from a minority group whose progress toward positions of power in the traditional society has been blocked.

Still others, like Theodore Schultz, see the problem as one of economic incentives. It is rational for people in traditional societies to avoid change and progress, because change entails risk, and risk, in turn, leads to the possibility of disaster—a possibility all too imminent for people living at a subsistence level. The transformation out of tradition therefore requires that low-risk opportunities and incentives be provided to people, so that they can opt for higher productivity and incomes.

Opinions differ as to whether the impetus for modernization comes from within the society or from without. From within, it may come from a class of "new people" who were not formerly part of the power structure. Or it may come from a formerly elite group in the traditional society that has been displaced. Proponents of external sources of change point to the technology that is available from the more advanced countries, to the colonialism and imperialism that disrupted traditional societies, to international corporations that seem to jump national boundaries without noticing them, to foreign media, to travel, and to trade. Any of these groups or forces can upset the equilibrium of traditional societies, setting them on the road to change and modernization.

Modernization theorists have a variety of approaches for understanding social change, but the central idea is that the world's task is the transformation of traditional societies. It follows that the main unit of analysis in modernization theory is the nation. Rostow wrote, "the whole transition we are examining took place historically within a system of nation states and of national sovereignty,"[5] and this perspective has not changed. In the modernization school, each country can be looked at separately. The first airplane to take off from tradition was Britain in the late eighteenth century, and it was followed over the next century by France, Germany, and other European countries and by the United States, Canada, and Australia. The twentieth century saw the takeoff of Russia and Japan and several smaller Asian countries. The rest of the world's fleet is still at the airport, their airplanes grounded. Their countries are still stagnant, still traditional, as they have been for centuries.

The challenge to modernize is one that faces each country separately, as it tries to get its airplane into the sky. What Britain, the United States, and Japan did, Zimbabwe, Colombia, and China can do. Their methods may differ somewhat, depending on national factors, but in each case they must find a way to break away from tradition, to free the innovative spirit and direct their human, physical, and financial resources toward productivity and growth. Their task is to follow the example of those airplanes that have already taken off, perhaps not in every detail, but in broad measure.

As the countries of the third world struggle to get their planes into the air, the rich countries can show them the way and offer tangible assistance. According to this way of looking at the issue, the industrial world can be of the greatest help to the third world by growing quickly and creating and diffusing the technology needed by the third world. The corporations of the rich countries can utilize that technology in their branch plants in the poor countries. The financial institutions of the rich countries can provide funds for the economic development of the poor. And the affluent consumers of Europe and North America can provide expanding markets for the exports of Asia, the Middle East, Africa, and Latin America.

It is a benign picture. With just a bit of imaginative license, one can see long ropes attached to the tails of the rich countries' speeding supersonic jets, ropes with hooks trailing at their ends. The hooks are dangling free, but they are out there, waiting to be snared by any of the grounded planes that choose to move into position. Once snared, the planes of the third world will be pulled into flight.

What could go wrong? Two things. First, the planes on the ground may choose not to snag the offered hooks. In Rostow's terms, they may not develop the preconditions for takeoff—the education, the legal systems, the political systems, and the mobility needed for growth. They may allow their populations to grow so fast that they lack the stamina for takeoff. Second, the planes that are already flying may slow down and lose the power to lift the grounded planes into flight. This is an important proposition of modernization theory: the already developed countries must continue to grow if they are to assist the poor. Without growth in the developed world, there will be no new capital for investment in the third world and no expanding markets to stimulate third-world exports and economic development.

No conflict need mar the relationship between the rich and the poor, according to the modernizationists. They profess no ethic, for example, that the existence of great wealth in a sea of poverty might be unstable or immoral. They do not fear that the world's benefits might be limited and that the accumulation of wealth in some hands might destroy the promise of advancement for others. Quite the opposite. As modernization theorists describe it, part of the world has raised itself from poverty to affluence; now the rest of the world has every opportunity to do so and can even turn to the developed countries for assistance.

The modernizationist view of the world is not without its moral imperatives for the rich. If the poor countries are to modernize, it is important that the rich countries not turn their backs on them. Foreign aid, foreign investment, planning assistance, expanding markets, technology transfer, even the Peace Corps—all these are productive connections between the rich and the poor that the rich should nurture. In other words, proponents of modernization stress government policy. In fact, many of them are most comfortable in the role of advisers—to their own governments, to third-world governments, and to international agencies.

This aspect of the modernization school can hardly be overstressed. As scholars, its practitioners are interested in identifying root causes of growth, historical patterns, and sound predictors. The analysis usually comes around, however, to government policy—and for many in the school, it is fair to say that the scholarship serves primarily as a backdrop and justification for policy recommendations. An important part of their agenda is to participate in the councils of state, to influence development policy. It was no accident that Rostow himself became one of the closest advisers to President Lyndon B. Johnson.

Many of the modernizationists' insights into government policy have been fruitful. Economists in the school have advanced important propositions about trade and tariff policy; planning techniques; agricultural pricing policies; the use of monetary, fiscal, and financial policy in poor countries; appropriate technology; employment policy; and much more. Demographers and public health professionals have helped establish family-planning programs. Consultants with expertise in such fields as political systems, legal systems, medicine, labor unions, cooperatives, and media have lent their advice, some of which has been useful and well taken.

It is somewhat dangerous to put a political label on the modernizationists, but for most of them, "liberal" fits pretty well. Most are not conservative; they do not regard the current state of the world as optimal. Neither are they radical (or Marxist, or socialist); they see no need for fundamental political and social change in the rich countries, nor for revolution in any country. They are reformers. They are on the side of the world's poor, and they think that more can be done to help them. What is needed, they think, is better policies, more technology, more aid, freer markets, sounder planning. Most importantly, they see no necessary conflict between the world's rich and poor, between the capitalist markets of the industrial world and the traditional societies of the third world. The ideal is partnership, the serving of mutual interests.

Dependency Theory

Dependency theorists critique the modernization school. They believe that the growth of today's rich countries has impoverished the third world and that the forces of international capitalism still block its progress.

Dependency theory is an outgrowth of Marxism; many of the central ideas of dependency find their original expression in a 1957 book by Paul Baran, the leading American Marxist economist of his generation, titled *The Political Economy of Growth*. It was at the hands of Latin American social scientists, however, that *dependencia,* as they called it, became a major intellectual movement. The most important precursor of the dependency school was Raúl Prebisch, an Argentinean economist who was secretary of the United Nations Economic Commission for Latin America in the 1950s and of its Conference on Trade and Development (UNCTAD) in the 1960s. The ideas of dependency were later developed by Celso Furtado, Theotonio Dos Santos, Osvaldo Sunkel, F. H. Cardoso, and other Latin American social scientists. Outside Latin America, the most important writers have been Samir Amin of Senegal, André Gunder Frank of Germany, and Immanuel Wallerstein of the United States. To a major extent, therefore, dependency theory has been a product of the third world itself; this is one important way in which it differs from the modernization perspective, which has been developed almost exclusively in the major universities of the developed countries.

To the modernization theorists, underdevelopment is a state or a condition; for most of them, it is synonymous with tradition. To those in the dependency school, however, underdevelopment is a process. Underdevelopment is not just the failure to develop; it is an active process of impoverishment. Aidan Foster-Carter put it nicely when he described André Gunder Frank's use of *underdevelop* as a transitive verb, as in "I underdevelop you."

It is simply not true, argue the dependency theorists, that third-world societies are in a primitive, unchanged state. To the contrary, they have been formed, even created, by their interaction with the world's rich (and, not incidentally, capitalist) countries.

Dependency theorists acknowledge that before the sixteenth century—that is, before the era of modern economic growth—the world's major regions were essentially unconnected to one another. In that premodern period, it may make sense to think of the societies of today's third world as having been traditional. Before the sixteenth century, the empires of the world were not global in scope. In the sixteenth century, however, argues Immanuel Wallerstein, the most influential social historian of the dependency school, capitalism started to develop as a world system. Capitalists from Europe began to seek profits from around the globe. The search for profits, through the production of agricultural goods for sale in faraway markets and through long-distance commerce, became the dominant world force. Europeans seeking profits gradually came to control the rest of the world—sometimes formally and administratively through colonial empires, but also informally and commercially, without legal administrative control but with the economic power to strike unequal bargains.

From the sixteenth century on, capitalist markets dominated the world, and these capitalist markets fundamentally changed the social structures of the third world. The process continued for more than four centuries and still continues today. Dependency theorists argue that although the era of formal colonial empires is almost past, neo-colonial capitalist domination still remains, and third-world social structures continue to be dependent on the industrial world. The workers of the poor countries produce raw material exports for the rich countries. They work for foreign companies, and they are caught up in the geopolitical power struggles of the economically advanced countries. They are required to speak the languages of the colonial powers and to use their currencies.

It is not the case, then, that the poor countries are in some sort of primitive, unchanged state. For better or for worse, they have been changed by centuries of contact with the world's rich countries. For the most part, say the dependency theorists, they have been changed for the worse. The poverty of the third world is not traditional, and it is not accidental. It is the necessary companion to the richness of the developed countries. As a condition for its own development, the industrial world required cheap raw materials from the third world. The expansion of the industrial world therefore shaped the structure of the emergent third world, deforming it, impoverishing it, and rendering it incapable of balanced development.

An example shows how the dependency school sees the process as having worked. More than a generation ago, Eric Williams, a young West Indian who would later become prime minister of the newly independent country of Trinidad and Tobago, argued that the slave trade between Africa and the Caribbean islands was responsible for the emergence of a commercial middle class in Britain.[6] British ships brought slaves, captured in the interior of Africa and traded at its shores, to the Caribbean; there, the ships exchanged their cargoes for the sugar grown by the slaves on plantations. The sugar and molasses were then either exported back to England or traded in the North American colonies for farm products, which in turn were sent to England. The trade provided rich profits that were invested in British enterprises, as well as cheap food that was needed for a growing

British industrial workforce. Both the profits and the cheap food were the basis for the British industrial revolution and, consequently, for the growth of a bourgeois middle class in the imperialist country.

This example shows the essence of the dependency approach—the actual creation of underdevelopment. The requirements of British capitalism led to the corruption and despoliation of the African population. Dependency theorists would say that it is wrong to characterize West African societies of the twentieth century as essentially traditional, because they were fundamentally uprooted and changed by centuries of the slave trade. In the Caribbean region, British capitalism led to the dominance of a plantation system that met no local need and that actually depended on the continuing poverty of its labor force for its commercial success. The sugar plantations of the Caribbean are not traditional; they were instituted to meet a need in the economically advanced countries, and they persist to this day for the same purpose. The profits of the triangular trade accrued in Britain, where they were reinvested and eventually raised the average standard of living in the metropolitan center. The third world was left with skewed, impoverished economies and devastated populations—while the core of the world system gained comfort and prosperity.

In other regions of the third world, although the details of the history are different, the broad outlines are the same, claim the dependency theorists. Workers were organized into labor gangs on plantations to produce rubber, cotton, cocoa, jute, sugar, tobacco, and many other products for use as either raw materials or consumer goods in the rich countries. Peasants were lured or forced out of their subsistence cultures and into the production of agricultural goods for export; they thereby became vulnerable to the fluctuations of world markets. Mines in the third world produced bauxite, tin, and many other minerals for the industries of Europe and North America. In all these cases, the success of the capitalist system depended on labor earnings in the third world staying low so that imports into the core countries could remain cheap and profits correspondingly high.

Dependency theorists argue that the particular legal structure of colonialism was not of primary importance. In some cases, the third-world area was ruled as a possession of a European power. In other cases, the Europeans exerted indirect economic control over nominally independent countries. The end result was much the same, whether in the British Raj of colonial India or in the independent countries of nineteenth-century Latin America. The world was integrated into a single trading system, with the advancement of the rich countries at the capitalist core being contingent on the impoverishment of the third world.

Dependency theorists see the same sorts of exploitative processes occurring in today's international economy. They are critical of the role that multinational firms have played in recent decades in the third world. A typical multinational, with its head office in the United States, Europe, or Japan, may control operations in dozens of separate countries. Its size and power are such that it can dominate a weak third-world host country—bargaining from a position of strength for concessions, distorting the structure of the domestic economy, creating vast income gaps, and imposing its own priorities—to such an extent that the country is rendered incapable of genuine development. Dependency theorists also criticize the tariff policies in the rich countries that dictate the sorts of industrial patterns the poor countries can choose. They see the great banks of the rich countries sucking resources out of the third world. They see international investors destabilizing currencies and whole societies as they shift billions of dollars around the globe with lightning speed. They fault international economic agencies such as the World Bank, the International Monetary Fund, and the World Trade Organization for imposing policies in the third world that are favorable to the rich countries. Taken together, they believe, all these features make up the phenomenon of globalization that, although not new, has recently become much more intense.

The dependency school does not focus solely on the export industries of poor countries. Initially, the third world was underdeveloped as its workers were forced into low-wage occupations to produce goods for export to the rich core countries. In the last several decades, however, many poor countries have turned to industrial development. The dependency theorists see even this industrialization as being weak, as being subservient to the rich countries and incapable of leading to real improvement for the masses of poor people. The industries are often controlled by foreign owners. They produce goods only for the rich minority of local people, and they use modern, labor-saving technology so as to employ few people. Many workers are attracted to the cities in the hopes of getting relatively good jobs in one of these new factories, but few jobs are available. The consequence of the industrial expansion is therefore often massive unemployment, an increase in urban poverty, and an even greater gap between the rich and the poor.

The dependency school recognizes a growing bourgeoisie, or capitalist class, in most third-world countries, but it does not believe that this class has the independence and strength to lead its countries to sustained growth, as the capitalist class did in the core countries. The third-world capitalists are themselves a dependent class, responding primarily to foreign signals and incapable of undertaking the risks and responsibilities needed to transform their countries in any fundamental way. André Gunder Frank offered the model of a descending series of power centers. At the core in Europe and North America lie the real powers; in the third world, capital cities are groups of people who are dependent on the foreigners but who dominate leaders in the provinces; in turn, the provincial leaders are dependent on the capital city groups but dominate local groups, and so on.

Much of the analysis in the dependency school has to do with what its adherents call unequal exchange. In international trading markets, third-world countries are seen as giving up much more than they get. Raúl Prebisch and many of the writers who followed him have focused, for example, on what they see as the declining "terms of trade" for the third world. They see the relative prices of third-world exports falling over time and the prices of their imports from the industrialized countries rising. The consequence is that it takes more and more pounds of coffee, for instance, to buy a tractor. Brazil can be successful at increasing yields and producing more coffee, but in return for the sale of that coffee it will get fewer, not more, tractors. Because of its commitment to trading relationships with the rich countries, Brazil makes itself poorer.

The dependency theorists argue that a circular trap causes the terms of trade to fall. Export prices are low because wages in the third world are low, and prices of industrial goods are rising because wages in the rich countries are high and rising. In turn, wages in the third world are low because the terms of trade are moving against the third world, and wages in the industrial world are high because the rich countries have been able to exploit the poor. Exploitation creates poverty, which permits more exploitation, and the circle goes around.

André Gunder Frank and some others in the dependency school have concentrated not so much on the allegedly declining terms of trade as on the removal of the economic surplus from the third world. Profits and savings that might have been used productively in the poor countries are siphoned off to the rich countries in a reverse Robin Hood maneuver, stealing from the poor to give to the rich. Frank argues that the plunder of the third world began with the discovery of gold and silver in Latin America in the sixteenth century and continues today. Multinational corporations, he says, bring little new money into a third-world country when they invest in a new factory; instead, they borrow the money from local savers. When their enterprises make profits, however, they repatriate those funds back to their home countries. The consequence of international investment is that the third world loses resources.

Another strand within the dependency school does not focus on unequal exchange and is even willing to admit that the international economic system may lead to the creation of some new wealth in the third world rather than simply to its expropriation. These theorists believe that the heart of underdevelopment today lies in the creation of a rigid, unproductive social structure in the third world, a social structure dominated by the puppets of the rich countries. This relatively small group of local people controls the agricultural and industrial development of the third world. The puppets benefit—indeed, grow rich—as a result of their relationship with foreign companies and foreign investors, but they keep their gains to themselves. Connected as they are to the foreigners, they are unable to expand the development effort in ways that would improve the living conditions of the people as a whole.

Most members of the dependency school claim that economic subservience often leads to political subservience. Groups in power in the third world serve essentially at the convenience of the political and business power centers in the core of the international capitalist system. The core states support clients in the periphery who can be counted on to serve their interests, in broad outline if not in every particular. The U.S. government, for example, heaps military and economic aid on regimes in countries that favor private enterprise and that welcome American business investors. If and when these clients are displaced by groups that have the welfare of the local people closer to heart, they are attacked by the core in all sorts of ways, including militarily, as occurred in Chile in the early 1970s and Nicaragua in the 1980s.

It is therefore pure ideology, say the dependency theorists, to regard third-world societies as traditional, primitive, or unchanged. They have been formed by capitalist development just as surely as have the rich countries—only in their case, they have been underdeveloped, impoverished, and made less capable of meeting the needs of their people.

Modernization theory sees capitalism as a creative force that was responsible for the growth of the developed countries and is capable of impelling the third world to higher standards of living. The only problem, say the modernizationists, is that it has not really been tried in the third world. Dependency theory comes to the opposite conclusion. It sees international capitalism as the ruin of the third world. Far from being a stranger to capitalist ways, the third world has been intimately involved in the capitalist system for centuries. The economic growth of the world's rich countries is seen as having been dependent on the accumulation of capital, and to a large extent, this accumulation came either directly or indirectly from the third world. The profitability of firms depended on the wedge between the selling price of their goods and the costs of inputs. It was critical that costs be kept low, and this became the function of the third world: to provide the raw materials for industrialization at cheap prices.

The modernization school sees the rich countries as being at least potentially the salvation of the poor. The dependency school sees them as being the main obstacle to the well-being of the poor. It will come as no surprise, then, to learn that the political allegiances of the two schools are different. Modernization theorists are by and large liberal and procapitalist, whereas dependency theorists are socialist and frequently revolutionary.

Although dependency theorists share a fair consensus about the diagnosis—about the origins of poverty in the third world—they have a number of prescriptions for the best form of response. Not all the responses are anticapitalist. One view held by some in the dependency school is that the best course of action is for the third world to fight fire with fire, to transform capitalism from the enemy of the third world into its savior. Whatever damage international capitalism may have caused in the past, the third world should use today's forms of capitalism to break out of its dependent state. They can point to success stories in this mold. Japan emerged from the devastation of the Second World War with an aggressive capitalist economy that incorporated some of the communitarian forms of its previous feudal structure. Over the course of several short decades of remarkable growth, Japan has overtaken the living standards of the original core capitalist countries. Coming along a little later, Singapore, Hong Kong, Taiwan, South Korea, and Malaysia all embarked on the same path, unleashing the creative spirits of capitalist entrepreneurs to develop manufacturing sectors that are challenging those of the Northern societies.

This strategy is regarded with suspicion by most in the dependency school, however. Although capitalism may be having some success in scattered parts of the third world, it is also reproducing the tensions and inequities that are found in the economically advanced countries. Because capitalism is based on competition, it will lead inevitably to greater chasms between the haves and the have-nots within each country. Capitalism is not, they argue, a strategy that can work for the great majority of the world's poor.

A liberal wing of the dependency school argues that capitalist free enterprise should remain but that it should be subject to strong guidance and even control by the central governments of poor countries. This would ensure that capitalism is directed to serving the real needs of the people and not the external demands of foreign markets. Proponents of this view argue for tariff barriers against foreign imports, effective government economic plans, public financial institutions that favor some sectors over others, and so on.

Most of the dependency school adherents regard these measures as halfhearted and naive. They call for full socialist revolutions in the third world and the expropriation of private enterprises, both foreign owned and domestic, so that the people as a whole, acting together through their governments, can combat the destructive forces of capitalism. For still others, the focus of the socialist revolution is not on the third world at all but on the rich countries, where the source of the problem is. And for another group, the problem can never be resolved on a national level, because it is global in scope: the long-run goal is a socialist world government that will completely change the dynamic of international relations and permit the creative development of third-world societies.

Marxism

The legacies of Karl Marx are almost infinite. Some of the most vitriolic debates in the history of scholarship have been between contending schools of Marxists, each claiming to be the true interpreter of the teachings of the nineteenth-century master. The conflicts have carried over into the study of the development of the third world. Many of the dependency theorists consider themselves to be Marxist, writing in the tradition of Marxist scholarship and using well-known Marxist categories. Dependency theory has been attacked since the 1970s, however, by more orthodox Marxists who argue that it has abandoned the central tenets of Marxism. Dependency theory, they argue, deals only with surface phenomena, not with the true underlying causes of development and social change.

The resurgence of Marxist thinking about the third world has been so strong that one can now say that it represents a separate school, a school that is antagonistic to both the modernizationists and the dependency theorists. The basis of this Marxist school is the analysis of the class structures of third-world societies rather than the growth of resources and technology (as in modernization theory) or foreign domination (as in dependency theory).

In classic Marxism, social change is the result of conflict between classes, between groups of people who have different relationships to the productive structure of the society. Workers struggle against capitalists, for example, or peasants against landowners. Out of these confrontations may come impoverishment, dynamic growth, revolution, socialism, or any number of other changes. The struggle between classes may itself change the class structure. Most Marxists are not dogmatic about how a third-world society will change; they insist, however, that the source of the change is the unending battle between different classes.

Three principal conclusions distinguish the Marxists from the dependency theorists. First, Marxists argue that the fundamental forces for social change are internal to third-world societies, not external to them. Second, they argue that capitalism is quite capable of producing growth in the economies of the third world. Third, they argue that imperialism, both in its historical form and in its current neocolonial form, is often an agent of progress, that it may operate in such a way as to propel third world societies on the path to capitalist growth. In all these conclusions, the Marxists lie closer to the modernizationists than to the dependency theorists, but it must be added that the Marxists look at the third world very differently from the way the modernizationists do.

At the basis of Marxist thinking lies the idea of the mode of production,[7] that is, the class structure that exists in a society and that leads both to production and to exploitation of the working population. Marx identified different modes of production, each with its characteristic class structure. For example, a slave society was one mode of production, with two basic classes: slave owners and slaves. The slave owners owned all the means of production, both human and nonhuman. In spite of the fact that the slaves produced everything, they were given only enough subsistence to reproduce themselves; the remaining product was expropriated from them and used for the consumption of the slave owners and for the reproduction of the nonhuman means of production.

Feudalism was the mode of production characteristic of medieval Europe, after the slave systems of the ancient world and before capitalism. In feudalism, the two basic classes were the nobility and the serfs. The serfs performed the work on land that was held in common by them, and they were exploited by being forced to transfer some portion of their produce, their labor time, or both to their lords.

Capitalism, as Marx described it, was the mode of production that grew out of European feudalism. The feudal classes were transformed into capitalist classes by the process of the "alienation" of labor. In feudalism, serfs had customary rights to the use of the land and the tools needed to produce agricultural output. Feudal lords eventually discovered that they could make monetary profits by using the common lands for the grazing of sheep and the selling of wool to textile merchants. They "enclosed" the commons—that is, they fenced off the land and drove the serfs from it. This was the alienation, or separation, of labor from the means of production. In feudalism, workers had assured access to land and to tools; it was their birthright.

Capitalism arose when the workers lost this access and were left with nothing but their own hands.

Thus arose the two fundamental capitalist classes: the working class, which did not own or have access to any of the means of production and therefore had to enter into a wage contract with the capitalists, and the capitalist class, which owned the means of production and hired the workers for wages. Capitalist exploitation occurred through the wage, which represented much less than the full value of what the workers produced. The capitalists expropriated this surplus value, the value produced by the workers over and above the wage. They used the surplus value primarily to produce more capital—adding to the means of production, hiring more workers, expropriating more surplus value, and increasing profits.

It followed from Marx's analysis that capitalism was a tremendously powerful engine of growth. The capitalists, in competition with one another, vied to increase their surplus expropriation and outproduce one another. In so doing, they greatly increased the productive capabilities of their countries. It was not a pretty process. The creation of a capitalist labor force in the first place, by enclosure or related means, always entailed the destruction of a precapitalist (or traditional, to use the modernizationists' term) way of life and often entailed massive amounts of bloodshed as well. The human devastation that followed the birth of capitalism, chronicled in the first volume of Marx's *Capital,* is a powerful antidote to the smooth, benign, mathematical growth models of modern neoclassical economists. Once capitalism was established, its progress was always uneven—between countries as well as within countries. Some countries, areas, industries, and people jumped ahead; some were left behind or even destroyed. Workers were exploited to unbelievable lengths in the first factory and mill towns; there were dismal generations of long hours, low pay, child labor, malnutrition, and disease.

Eventually, in the most advanced capitalist countries, the benefits of increased production were extended to many of the workers. This was not, however, a development that Marx himself foresaw, writing in the middle of the nineteenth century. He predicted instead that the contradiction between ever richer capitalists and ever poorer workers would eventually lead to the collapse of the capitalist system and its replacement with socialism, by which he meant essentially the end of class warfare and exploitation and their replacement by a system in which the benefits of production were shared equitably.

The modern Marxist school returns to many of Marx's views about nineteenth-century European capitalist development. It argues that capitalism can develop in the third world and is, in fact, developing in many areas of it. Third-world countries can have their own autonomous capitalist classes that are capable of producing, reproducing, and growing, just as the capitalist classes did in the currently advanced countries. Modern Marxists do not see capitalism in the same way that the dependency theorists do—as a global system with all the power and the benefits accruing to the core countries and only poverty, underdevelopment, and weakness in the third world. They fully understand that third world countries are intimately involved in international networks of trade, investment, and finance, but they argue nevertheless that they have internal autonomy, that the local capitalist classes can have their own power and not simply be subservient to the international system.

The Marxists recognize other possibilities. The capitalist class may be dependent on foreigners and incapable of leading its country to economic growth, but if so, this is a consequence of its own internal weakness vis-à-vis contending classes at home.

The Marxists do not, of course, see capitalism as the only mode of production that can increase productivity in the third world. Countries may opt for socialism; the socialist regime may be capable of mobilizing the peasantry and working classes for development, or it may be too weak to be successful. The point is that the source of the strength or weakness of the dominant class must be sought internally, in its relationships with other classes, not externally. To quote Agustin Cueva:

> Dependency theory holds that the nature of our social formations is dependent on how they are integrated with the world capitalist system. But, is it not more correct to state the inverse? Is it not the nature of our societies that determines their links with the capitalist world? Thus, for example, if Bolivia after the 1952 revolution had followed a similar course to that of the Cuban Revolution, it would not today be a dependent country.[8]

The argument between the more orthodox Marxists and the dependency school over the role of wage labor in capitalism is particularly interesting. A classic Marxist definition of capitalism is that it is a system of wage labor. Because the working class is free and because it does not own the means of production itself, workers must offer their labor power to the capitalists in return for a wage. In most Marxist writing, the wage contract is the occasion for class conflict between workers and capitalists. The workers produce all the value, but the wage they are paid represents only a fraction of that value— hence the stage is set for protracted struggle as the workers try to increase their share and the capitalists resist.

The dependency theorists have either explicitly or implicitly rejected the identity of capitalism with a wage labor system. Immanuel

Wallerstein, the intellectual leader of a variant of the dependency approach known as world systems analysis, has made the case most clearly. From the sixteenth century on, he argues, it is important to see capitalism as a world system, not just as the national system of several countries of Europe. The core of the capitalist world system was in western Europe, where a regime of wage labor grew up. This core gradually exerted its dominance over the rest of the world, beginning with eastern and southern Europe and eventually extending its influence throughout Asia, the Middle East, Africa, and Latin America. In time, most of what is now the third world became integrated into the capitalist world system, providing food, raw materials, markets, and profits for the core countries. The third world was a component of world capitalism, but for the most part, it did not have a wage labor system. The third world had all sorts of other arrangements for securing a supply of labor, including slavery, peonage, indentured servitude, sharecropping, and independent peasant production. The fact that the third world had different, nonwage ways of dealing with labor did not mean that it was any less a part of the capitalist system. So, according to the dependency school, what is unique about capitalism is not wage labor but the private ownership of the means of production by a class of profit-seeking capitalists and the buying and selling of the goods they produce through worldwide markets. Like the mainstream, neo-classical modernizationists, the dependency school sees capitalism as essentially a system of market relationships, not a class struggle mediated by the wage contract.

The Marxists are not persuaded by this argument that capitalism is consistent with any and all forms of labor organization. They maintain that such a position is equivalent to saying that the defining characteristic of capitalism is the market. Nonsense, they say; markets exist in almost every social system. Ancient Athens, which was a slave society, had a thriving market. The defining characteristic of capitalism is the class struggle between workers and bosses. This class struggle occurs when workers are alienated from the means of production and are therefore compelled to work for the capitalists for wages. And the class struggle is essentially an internal, national phenomenon.

One subject on which the Marxists and the modernizationists differ in interesting ways is the role of government in the third world. Western economists and other social scientists in the modernization school spend a good deal of their time identifying "obstacles" to development and then recommending government policies that can overcome those obstacles. The implied assumption is that the government stands separate from the society, that by making the right choices it can steer the country around the obstacles to development.

A typical obstacle might be that the country's manufacturing sector is hampered by insufficient markets, so that it cannot produce on a scale large enough to become efficient. Government policy can address this problem, perhaps by erecting tariff barriers to keep out foreign manufactured goods that take away markets, or perhaps by negotiating with rich countries to reduce their tariffs so that the third world manufacturers can enjoy expanding markets abroad. For the modernizationists, the government is not a part of the problem; the government can be the solution to the problem if it adopts the right policy.

The Marxists see the government not as a neutral and beneficent outsider but as an integral part of the social structure of the country. The government is controlled by the ruling classes, and government policies are an expression of the interests of those classes. The dominant classes may or may not be capable of progressive development. If they are, government policies will help move the country forward; if they are not, government policies will be harmful to development. It would be a mistake to see the government as standing in opposition to the dominant societal groups or as being able to use its policies to direct development in a way not wanted by those groups. Unlike the modernizationists, therefore, the Marxists do not see government policies as fundamental.

Although the dependency model dominated thinking about development in Latin America in the 1960s and early 1970s, it did not prove to be all that attractive to social scientists in Africa and Asia.[9] Even in Latin America, it has met increasing resistance from the left in recent years. Correspondingly, the Marxists' investigations of social change in the third world have become increasingly lively.

In Kenya, for example, an interesting debate has arisen about the mode of production. Some writers believe that in the era before Western imperialism, Kenya had a sort of capitalist society, with wage labor. Others have identified different modes of production. Sociologist Goran Hyden claims that Kenya had what he calls a "peasant mode of production," with small household units of production.[10] Marxist students of Kenya view British imperialism ambivalently. Although imperialism exploited the Africans, it may have broken down a stagnant mode of production and opened the way for capitalism. When Africans regained control over their country after the independence movement, they were able to build a capitalist system on the remnants of imperialism. Paul Lubeck writes:

> The brutal intrusion of white settler agriculture undermined many precapitalist institutions and practices that otherwise would have resisted the penetration of capitalist relations of production. Therefore, after

the successful anti-imperialist Mau Mau insurrection, an indigenous bourgeoisie inherited a productive base in capitalist agriculture with large units of production and a disciplined state bureaucracy.[11]

The dependency theorists see third-world plantations and mines as subservient institutions, subject to the whims of consumers and importers in faraway lands and consequently lacking the strength to transform their own societies. The Marxists, in contrast, see them as capitalist firms, with a labor force working for wages and a class of owners expropriating profits. These capitalist firms may well be capable of growth, and the capitalist class may embark on other ventures that will fundamentally change the local society. It is possible, of course, that the capitalist class will fail in its historical mission of reproducing capital and leading its society to higher productive standards, but if it does, the fault will lie within itself and not with its foreign puppet masters.

The Marxists have an easier time dealing with the capitalist success stories of the third world than do the dependency theorists. In the 1960s and 1970s, the giants of Latin America—Brazil and Mexico— were particularly successful. From the early 1970s through the early 1980s, the oil exporters of the third world enjoyed striking growth. In the 1980s and 1990s, attention turned to the successes of the Asian newly industrialized countries (NICs): Taiwan, Singapore, South Korea, and Hong Kong. The oil exporters may be a special case, but in the other countries, growth has been led by private firms in partnership with supportive governments; the countries have borrowed technology from abroad and aggressively sought new markets both inside and outside their borders. Dependency theorists sometimes claim that this growth is doomed to failure in the long run because it is dependent on foreigners, or they concentrate on the new forms of exploitation caused by the growth—the new urban slums and impoverished peasants, for example. The world systems variant of the dependency school explains the growth of these countries by thinking of them as a "semiperiphery," which embodies some features of the core and some features of the periphery and consequently is able to enjoy some economic growth and some improvements in standards of living.

The Marxists, in contrast, see the economic success of these countries as validating their view that the capitalist class in third-world countries is sometimes capable of becoming the engine of growth. They acknowledge the human devastation that capitalism often leaves in its wake, the destroyed peasant cultures, the urban slums, and the overworked wage laborers. Capitalism is always uneven and unfair, they argue; certainly it was a massively destructive force, as well as a creative force, in Europe, and it will show both faces in the third world as well. The capitalist system is, after all, class warfare.

Marx himself believed that capitalism was a necessary stage in social evolution, for although it was exploitative, it was the only mode capable of developing the productive resources of a country. Although he dealt almost exclusively with Europe, he also wrote a series of articles about India in which he welcomed imperialism as breaking down the structure of feudalism and thereby opening the way for capitalism. Socialism, he believed, would follow the self-destruction of the mature capitalist system. As matters actually turned out in the twentieth century, however, none of the mature capitalist societies collapsed—although there were several close calls during the Great Depression of the 1930s—and the socialist revolutions all occurred in poor countries. One of the pressing questions, therefore, has been whether socialism offers a better path for economic and social development than capitalism does.

The great majority of the writers in the dependency school believe that socialism is a more hopeful path. In contrast, the modernizationists look to capitalism and free markets (guided, to be sure, by government planning). The Marxists have a rather ambiguous position. Ultimately, they see capitalism as the enemy, because it exploits the workers. For the present, however, capitalism may be the best choice for many third-world countries, provided that it is a system with strong internal coherence that can develop a country's productive capabilities. For Marxists, socialism is the ultimate goal, but that goal may have to wait until the capitalist engine of growth has done its work. The Marxists, of course, are divided on this question; many in Latin America look to socialist Cuba as a model, for example.

The rebirth of this classically Marxist perspective coincides, ironically, with the decline of communism in much of the world, beginning in the late 1980s. In the Soviet bloc countries, communist regimes collapsed. In China and Vietnam, the regimes continued, but the economies turned increasingly to market capitalism. How could such a period be a fruitful one for the resurgence of Marxist thinking?

The answer is that Marx was a student of capitalism, not of communism. He had little to say about the structure of a communist society. Leaders of communist movements in the twentieth century found no blueprints in his writings and had to turn instead to Lenin. Marx had a great deal to say about the historical development of capitalism, however, and about the class conflicts inherent in capitalism. Consequently, as capitalism grew stronger in the late twentieth century, so did the opportunities for Marxist social analysis.

Limitations of These Approaches

The three principal perspectives on the third world—modernization, dependency, and Marxism—are all valuable. Although they differ and in many respects are contradictory, they all have insights that can help one begin to understand the causes of poverty in the world.

It is useful to consider a variety of different theories at the same time rather than just a single view. The truth is that social reality is infinitely complicated, confused, and puzzling. It consists of more than six billion human beings, each one of whom is a thinking, creative person. Society can be thought of as a ball of tangled string: there is no consistent pattern to it, no way of adequately describing its twists and meanderings. Nevertheless, one tries. One way of trying is to cut a cross section through the ball with a sharp knife and then attempt to describe the surface that has been created. It is still difficult to find a pattern in that surface and to describe it in words, but it is easier than the impossible task of analyzing the whole ball of string. Even if one could adequately describe the flat, cut surface, however, the problem remains that different people will choose to cut the ball at any number of different angles. They will discover different patterns and will come up with different explanations. All the explanations are "true," but they are also partial and therefore in a way untrue, because they do not comprehend the full complexity of the ball of string.

This is the basic problem in trying to make sense out of the many variations of development theory, the many explanations of why there is so much poverty in a world of riches. All the variations have useful, accurate insights—but they are all partial. The same could be said of theories that are Freudian, Keynesian, Christian, or deconstructionist. The human mind has not reached the elevated point at which there is a single superior school of social science that dominates all others. That being the case, it behooves one to be open to different approaches.

Take, for example, the debate between modernization and dependency theorists about whether the present-day cultures of the third world are best thought of as traditional or dependent. In reality, the cultures of the world are marvelously varied; they are both traditional and dependent. At the heart of even the "modern" societies of Europe and North America is much that is traditional, with roots extending far back before the capitalist epoch. The religious forms of the rich countries—the many variations of Christianity and Judaism—have ancient origins and yet are still vital presences for many. They are not disappearing; some forms, such as charismatic and fundamentalist

Christianity, are growing stronger as people turn to them to make sense out of constant change and dislocation. Likewise, and to a much greater extent, in the third world, religions, philosophies, family structures, and attitudes toward fertility and death often have roots that go back centuries and even millennia and certainly deserve to be called traditional. These traditional values are not by themselves responsible for poverty, though. The dependency theorists are often correct in seeing poverty as imposed on the third world from outside.

Nigerian novelist Buchi Emecheta's wonderful book *The Joys of Motherhood* describes the anguish of a traditional village woman who tries to adapt to the modern world by providing educational opportunities for her eldest son.[12] Modernizationists could read the novel as a case study of their philosophy, seeing the mother drawn out of the traditional world toward the world of modern education, which promises to transform if not her life then the lives of her children. That is not quite how the narrative proceeds, however. The son attains ever higher levels of Western education, finally disappearing into the clouds of an American graduate school, never to be heard from again in his mother's lifetime. She has sacrificed everything for her son's education and is left impoverished by her struggle. The foreign world has taken her principal resource, her son, and given her nothing in return. So the novel can also be read as a case study in dependency.

Shahhat's world is a mélange of the dependent and the traditional. He grows wheat and lentils for export to the markets of Cairo and beyond, and he copes unsuccessfully with the modern agricultural technology of irrigation systems, chemical fertilizers, and hybrid strains, all imported from abroad. At the same time, his unquestioned faith remains with Allah, the age-old deity.

What is an almost gentle mixture in Shahhat's life is a devastating conflict in Rigoberta Menchú's. She is exploited in the coastal export plantations, scorned in the capital city, and attacked in her village by an army supported by the United States. At the same time, she clings to a traditional culture whose roots go back long before the arrival of white people in Mesoamerica, a culture that gives her the strength to resist the assaults of the dominant world. In the richness of these few lives, one sees the limits of any single social theory.

Why Does Poverty Persist?

There is no end in sight to world poverty. As Chapter 2 showed, poverty is retreating in some areas of the world but advancing in others. This is so in spite of the extraordinary explosion of science and technology in the last two centuries and in spite of the nationalist and revolutionary movements that appeared to bring autonomy to third-world people in the twentieth century. The technological and political changes seemed to promise a better life for the majority of the world's people, but that promise has somehow been betrayed. It is difficult to know why. The three theories have three different approaches to an answer, all of which have some validity.

In comparing the three approaches, one notices first that the modernizationists tend to deny the very phenomenon under discussion. That is, the modernizationist view is almost by its nature optimistic. It shows that well-designed policies can lead to progress, and it sees progress at every turn. Most social scientists of the mainstream Western variety acknowledge that there is terrible poverty in the third world, but they see the poverty slowly disappearing over time. The dependency school takes the opposite view. Underdevelopment is inherent in the world order, as long as the world is dominated by rich capitalist countries. The Marxists are eclectic: poverty may or may not disappear, depending on the class structure and the strength of each country.

Although the modernizationists are generally optimistic, their scholarship contains a number of clues about why poverty continues and worsens. The issue for the modernizationists frequently comes down to policy—policy of governments in both the poor and the rich countries. Rural Indians are still desperate, a modernizationist would argue, because the Indian government has neglected agriculture and stressed industry, because it has failed to develop extension programs that reach the villages, because it has not packaged the new agricultural technology to make it accessible to farmers with smallholdings, and so forth. Poverty is growing in the Philippines because the government made the wrong choices about development strategy, because it protected markets for local industries that turned out to be inefficient and neglected to encourage its export industries. The U.S. government is culpable because it cut back its foreign aid and failed to direct what aid remained to the countries and projects where it would do the most good. These are the sorts of answers that some modernizationists turn to when trying to understand the failure of development.

A growing group of right-wing modernizationists blame government policy in a different way. Their argument is that there is too much policy, that governments of both the rich and the poor countries try to regulate and govern in far too much detail. What governments should do, they believe, is step back and let the free market take over the task of development. Taken to an extreme, as it often is, this sort of critique departs from the modernization school altogether, becoming a kind of free-market conservatism that completely loses interest in the problems of the less fortunate. Still, many people who are genuinely liberal modernizationists also believe that government control has been excessive. Socialist countries such as Cuba have stagnated, they say, because the state tried to direct the economy through a central planning office. In contrast, free-market, capitalist South Korea has thrived because the government kept its hands off and allowed entrepreneurs to seek profits.

In any case, the modernizationists usually see governments as autonomous bodies, capable of making whatever choices they please. The fact that they make harmful choices about policy is therefore the principal cause of stagnation and poverty where those phenomena persist.

For both the dependency and the Marxist schools, government policy is far from the central cause of poverty. Writers in both schools are critical—even scornful—of many government policies, but they do not see governments of either the rich or the poor countries as autonomous bodies. All governments are seen as acting in the class interests of the dominant groups. If governments do not have much autonomy, it is beside the point to criticize them for their policies. One must go a step further and explain why governments act the way they do.

For the dependency theorists, of course, the betrayal of the promise of social change in the third world lies exactly at the heart of their analysis. The capitalist world system never for a minute held out the hope of real progress to the third world. It despoiled and impoverished the third world. The cause of continuing poverty is therefore the failure of the third world to break its ties with the rich capitalist countries. For most dependency theorists, only full-scale socialist revolutions will suffice. Without revolutions, in which the mass of the people take control of their societies, the exploitative ties with the capitalist world will remain, and third-world people will continue to be sucked into a life of dependency and poverty.

For the Marxists, the explanation of continued poverty is most often the failure of a dynamic capitalist class to emerge from the social systems of the past. In a Latin American country, for example, the dominant class may be the owners of the great landed estates, people who are content to exploit their tenants and live in luxury off the rents but who have no commitment to entrepreneurship and to industrial, commercial development. If the landed class controls the government and the military, then the country's policies will result in poverty, not in social change and progress.

Assessment

The dependency school has an insight into the underdevelopment of the third world that is centrally important, one that is simply missing from the modernization and the Marxist perspectives. The past several centuries have seen massive changes in the economic structure of almost every area of the third world, and in almost every case, these changes have come in response to the dynamic of global capitalist economic growth. Most of the population of Latin America—whites, mestizos, and blacks—are, after all, the descendants of immigrants from the colonial era. Many areas of the third world depend on one or two staple export goods that are grown on plantations or produced in mines: bauxite in Jamaica, coffee in Brazil, cocoa in Ghana, copper in Zambia, sugar in Cuba, rubber in Malaysia—the list goes on. Where plantations do not dominate, peasants on small plots produce for the market. The markets for many of these goods are in the rich countries, and the fortunes of the poor rise and fall as the prices of primary products fluctuate in world markets. Capital and technology invade third world countries from the capitalist core, as do manufactured and sometimes even agricultural goods. Even the population explosion, which threatens to overwhelm some parts of the third world, was caused for the most part by imported technology—public health, sanitation, and medical care—that lowered death rates while leaving birth rates high.

Although many remnants of traditional mores are still alive in the third world—cultural, philosophical, and economic—the dependency school is correct to see the third world not as a stagnant, unchanged place but as fundamentally transformed. It does not follow from this, however, that third-world countries are bereft of autonomy. Many dependency theorists argue that only if third-world countries cut themselves off from their ties to the capitalist world will they regain the internal strength to achieve progressive social change. This is not true, however. Taiwan and South Korea successfully intensified their connections to the international market system.

What is most valuable about the dependency school, then, is that it focuses attention on the international context of the third world. Its writers are correct to insist that economic growth is a global phenomenon, the benefits of which have been concentrated unevenly in the fortunate countries. The dependency school can be seriously misleading, however. It denies the strength of the capitalist third world, and most of its adherents hold that socialism is the only road to progress in the third world.

Dependency theory can all too easily turn into a kind of cultural imperialism of the left. In the eyes of dependency theory, the main actors on the world stage come from the advanced capitalist countries, with the third world appearing in only a passive and manipulated role. This does an injustice—even when the task at hand is to locate the source of exploitation (as the quotation from the Indian journal at the beginning of this chapter states). People in the periphery are as capable of inhumanity as are people in the core: It is the third world that is to be held accountable for genocide in Rwanda and Cambodia, for human rights abuses in Argentina and Uganda, for repressive religious fundamentalism in Iran, for military adventurism in Iraq. Those evils have taken place in the context of world affairs, but it is perverse and ultimately demeaning to argue that the third world has not generated its own villains.

The third world also has its successes. The world's largest democracy, for all its enormous problems, is India. The world's most creative, state-directed approaches to social and economic change have been in China. The economic success stories of Hong Kong, Taiwan, and South Korea are the result of the commitment of the people of those societies, not the manipulations of outsiders. The courageous turn to democracy in Latin America in the 1980s was a testament to the strength of the Latin peoples.

The insight to be gained from dependency theory is not, therefore, that the people of the third world are puppets, not that the source of all initiative for social change lies at the core of the capitalist system. It is not true that third-world countries can progress only if they cut themselves off from the capitalist system through socialist revolutions.

If it were the case that dependency analysis led inevitably to a prescription for socialist revolution, then recent world events would signal the bankruptcy of dependency analysis. As eastern Europe jettisoned socialism, as the Soviet Union collapsed as both a socialist economy and a political entity, and as it became clear that most of the remaining socialist countries in the third world could retain their political structure only by totalitarian control over their people, the once proud claims of socialism lay in tatters.

The usefulness of dependency theory does not lie, however, in its connection to socialism or in the conclusion that third-world societies lack autonomy. The most important insight of dependency theory is that the social and economic structures of much of the third world have been created in response to the imperatives of the developing capitalist North. We are not a world of separate nation-states, independent of one another; we are one world, completely entangled with one another.

It follows that the development of the third world is both an international and a national phenomenon. The context within which the third world exists is an international one; world capitalism and the political relationships between the great powers set the parameters within which the poor of the world must function. But the responses of third-world countries to these outside forces are just as important in determining their fate. It is from this perspective that the modernization and the Marxist schools have more insight, notwithstanding their major differences.

The Theories as Worldviews

The three theories—modernization, dependency, and Marxism—have been developed for the most part as explanations of social change on a broad, global scale. Marx's principal subject was the growth of industrial capitalism in western Europe, whereas both the modernization and the dependency theorists have tried to explain the growing gap between rich and poor countries. The theories have additional applicability, however. They are really worldviews, general philosophies, ways of seeing and understanding reality at almost any level. They can be used in the most surprising ways. Marxism, for example, is the basis for a great deal of inventive thinking in modern literary studies.

Modernization and dependency can be helpful in understanding the difficulties that different racial groups have communicating with one another in the industrialized countries.[13] Whites often view racial problems with bewilderment. "What is the problem?" a typical white person seems to be asking nonwhites. "I took care of business, got an education, worked hard, earned a decent income, and provided for my family. It wasn't easy, but I did it. Why don't you do the same? Go to school, get a job, save your money, and enter the middle class."

To which people of color frequently reply, at least to themselves, "Are you kidding? How can I take care of business when you are standing on my neck?"

"Surely you can't be talking about me," the white replies. "I'm not standing on anyone's neck. I'm not a racist; I think everyone deserves the same opportunity. I took advantage of mine; now you get to work on yours."

And the reply comes back, at least implied, "You know the problem we face is not only white racism, which is deeply embedded in all the social institutions we encounter, but also the fact that you won't admit to your racism, and therefore refuse to deal with it."

These sorts of attitudes are at the base of much of the conflict over race. Whites seem to believe that everyone plays on a level field, whereas minorities believe that the field is sloped disastrously against them. Facts that are obvious to one group are invisible to the other, so the argument is seldom joined constructively. Statements seem to go floating into the air, misconstrued or ignored by those to whom they are addressed. One way to understand this is to see that the whites view the world as modernizationists, the nonwhites as dependency theorists. No wonder we cannot hear each other.

Notes

1. For an excellent discussion of disputes within the dependency school, see Magnus Blomstrom and Björn Hettne, *Development Theory in Transition: The Dependency Debate and Beyond: Third World Responses* (London: Zed Books, 1984).

2. A. R. M. Lower, "Two Ways of Life: The Primary Antithesis of Canadian History," *Canadian Historical Association Report* (1943): 8.

3. See Paul Bairoch, "International Industrialization Levels from 1750 to 1980," *Journal of European Economic History* 11 (fall 1982): 269–333; Angus Maddison, "A Comparison of Levels of GDP per Capita in Developed and Developing Countries, 1700–1980," *Journal of Economic History* 43 (March 1983): 27–41.

4. Walt W. Rostow, *The Stages of Economic Growth: A Non-Communist Manifesto,* 2d ed. (Cambridge: Cambridge University Press, 1971), 7.

5. Rostow, *Stages of Economic Growth,* 107.

6. Eric Eustache Williams, *Capitalism and Slavery* (New York: Russell and Russell, 1961).

7. Not to be confused with the means of production, discussed in the section on modernization. A means of production is a physical thing, such as a factory or a worker. A mode of production, as used by Marxists, is a social structure or a set of relationships between classes.

8. Agustin Cueva, "Problems and Perspectives of Dependency Theory," *Latin American Perspectives* 3 (fall 1976): 15.

9. See Blomstrom and Hettne, *Development Theory in Transition,* for a good presentation of this.

10. Goran Hyden, *Beyond Ujamaa in Tanzania: Underdevelopment and Uncaptured Peasantry* (London: Heinemann, 1980).

11. Paul M. Lubeck, ed., *The African Bourgeoisie: Capitalist Development in Nigeria, Kenya and the Ivory Coast* (Boulder, Colo.: Lynne Rienner, 1987), 19.

12. Buchi Emecheta, *The Joys of Motherhood* (New York: George Braziller, 1979).

13. I am grateful to a former student, Roekmini Harris, for the insights in this section.

Suggestions for Further Reading

See Bibliography for full details.
Samir Amin. *Unequal Development: An Essay in the Social Formations of Peripheral Capitalism.*

Schlomo Avineri, ed. *Karl Marx on Colonialism and Modernization.*

George L. Beckford. *Persistent Poverty: Underdevelopment in Plantation Economies of the Third World.*

Magnus Blomstrom and Björn Hettne. *Development Theory in Transition: The Dependency Debate and Beyond: Third World Responses.*

André Gunder Frank. *Capitalism and Underdevelopment in Latin America.*

Walt W. Rostow. *The Stages of Economic Growth: A Non-Communist Manifesto.*

Immanuel Wallerstein. *The Capitalist World-Economy.*

Eric Williams. *Capitalism and Slavery.*

Chapter Four

Imperialism

Our wounds are still too fresh and painful to be driven from our memory. We have known tiring labor exacted in exchange for slavery. . . . We have known ironies, insults, blows which we had to endure morning, noon and night because we were "Negroes."
—Patrice Lumumba

By the old Moulmein Pagoda
Lookin' eastward at the sea
There's a Burma girl a settin'
and I know she thinks o' me
For the wind is in the palm trees
And the temple bells they say
"Come you back you British soldier
Come you back to Mandalay."
—Rudyard Kipling, "Mandalay"

Whatever happens we have got
The Maxim gun and they have not.
—Hilaire Belloc, *The Modern Traveller*

Imperialism shaped today's third world. Europeans, and later Americans, spread out over the entire globe, annexing vast areas, conquering foreign lands, and administering millions of nonwhite people. In many areas, imperialism took the form of colonization by white settler families who displaced the local people, often violently.

Modernizationists seldom pay much attention to imperialism; implied in their conviction that third-world societies are "traditional" is the view that imperialism had few lasting effects and certainly did not transform the third world in any fundamental way. For Marxists and dependency theorists, however, the history of imperialism is critical to

66

an understanding of the third world and its poverty today. Marxists see imperialism as having shattered old class structures; they see the classes and class conflicts of third-world countries today as having arisen in response to the dislocation of imperialist domination. The dependency theorists go further; as explained in Chapter 3, they see imperialism and modern-day neocolonialism as having created under-development and poverty in the third world. Whatever the differences between the latter two approaches, they are surely correct in under-standing imperialism as one of the most important forces of our age.

Imperialism let loose the social forces that generated the poverty that is the current common denominator of the third world. It created the national boundaries of most third-world countries. It provided their national languages. It was the source of the ideologies that drive many of the political movements of the third world. It laid out the trade patterns and transportation networks that frame third-world economies. It called forth the plantations, the mines, and the primary products that the third world sells abroad. Imperialism destroyed local crafts and manufactures. It pulled millions into urban slums and posed opportunities for new elites to accumulate wealth and power. The imperialists brought with them public health measures that low-ered mortality and caused the unprecedented population explosion in the third world.

The Creation of the European Empires

Any precise dating of European imperialism would be arbitrary; as good a date as any for its onset is 1492, the year that Columbus set out on his first voyage of discovery. Not coincidentally, this is also the year that the Spanish finally expelled the Moors, who had lived for centuries in Spain; before 1492, a unified Spanish state capable of supporting transatlantic exploration did not exist. The end of formal imperialism came almost five centuries later, in the early 1960s, with the explosion of "new nations" around the globe as the former colonies took their seats in world councils. The end of the European empires coincided, again not by chance, with the exhaustion of Euro-pean strength following two devastating world wars.

For almost five hundred years, the powers of Europe expanded outward over the globe. The imperialist urge took many forms and rhythms. At times it was marked by the dominance of a single Euro-pean country, at times by competition among several. It featured mas-sive overseas settlement in some cases, administrative and military control in others, and informal economic domination in still others.

Its high point came at the beginning of the twentieth century, when almost every area of what we now think of as the third world was under the direct authority of an imperial power or was subject to indirect control.

The history of European imperialism falls fairly neatly into three periods: 1492–1776, global expansion; 1776–1870, British dominance and the withdrawal of other imperialists; and 1870–1914, the "new imperialism."

1492–1776: Global Expansion

In the first period, imperialism followed the voyages of discovery. In the late Middle Ages, Europe had had some overland contacts with Asia, but most of its communities were isolated. With the discovery of better shipbuilding techniques, the isolation was broken. The late fifteenth through seventeenth centuries were the age of seafaring exploration: of Columbus's journeys across the Atlantic, Vasco da Gama's trip around Africa to India, Magellan's around-the-world voyage, and the Dutch expeditions to the Cape of Good Hope and eastward into Asia. The history of the first phase of European imperialism can be traced in the succession of world maps the cartographers drew: largely imaginary at the beginning, but gradually gaining precision over the centuries.

The first great European empire consisted of the Spanish dominions in America, followed quickly by Portuguese colonies. After Columbus came other explorers, and then bands of soldiers who took possession of the mainland. Before the might of European weaponry, ancient empires crumbled and were destroyed: the Aztecs by Cortez in Mexico, the Incas by Pizzaro in Peru. The soldiers were followed soon after by the friars, whose sacred mission it was to salvage souls and who succeeded at the expense of wiping out whole cultures. It would be hard to say whether the soldiers or the priests were more destructive. Together, in their search for wealth, hegemony, and spiritual conversion, they dominated a continent, destroying millions of lives and subjecting the survivors to servitude.

The Spanish forced the native Americans into bondage both in agriculture and in the mines. They established the system of agricultural *encomienda,* under which the natives worked on the Spanish estates for four days a week, leaving them three days to tend to their own subsistence plots. In theory, the natives were granted rights analogous to those of semifree serfs in feudal Spanish manors, but in most cases, their rights were abridged and their lives were often taken. When the native Americans proved unable to withstand the rigors of their new situation, their labor was supplemented by African slaves.

The discovery of silver in Peru in 1545 sealed the fate of the Spanish colonies. The amount of silver ore was staggering; for decade after decade, it was extracted at a fearful human cost and sent back to Spain, where it transformed the metropolitan society. Purchases increased, prices rose, and commerce prospered, first in the Iberian Peninsula and later throughout western Europe, as the riches of the Americas spread. In what was to become a common imperialist experience, however, the native and black miners shared none of the prosperity; their lot was slavery, disease, and death.

For the most part, the Spanish did not settle in the Americas; soldiers, administrators, and priests were sent out from the homeland, but few women joined them. The unions of Spanish men with local women spawned a new population—mestizo, or mixed blood. Looked down upon by the pure-blood Spanish, they nevertheless assumed a position of privilege vis-à-vis the native Americans that still exists today. Rigoberta Menchú's oppressors in Guatemala were Spanish-speaking mestizos.

The Spaniards' record of destruction of the local people and their societies in South America was exceeded by that of the British Empire in North America. Whereas the Spanish merely administered South America, British families actually settled in North America. By the seventeenth century, they constituted a population of more than a million along the eastern coast of the continent. Farther north, in the valley of the St. Lawrence River, the French settled in smaller numbers. The British settlers were eventually hemmed in by the French empire along the St. Lawrence, Great Lakes, and Mississippi systems and by the Spanish to the south. In a series of wars, the British overcame their competitors and took possession of the continent. In so doing, they almost completely exterminated the native populations, something neither the Spanish nor the French had succeeded in doing. The destruction of the North American Indian was a necessity for the British because of the large number of settlers who flowed in, carving farms out of what was once the hunting ground of the natives. The destruction was so complete that today most of the remnants of Native American society that persist are in the barren desert of the U.S. Southwest, which the white man did not covet for agriculture.

The culture and living standards of the United States are founded, therefore, on the most genocidal imperialism the world has known. It is a fact that most Americans would prefer to forget. Americans pride themselves on a certain anti-imperialism, a moral superiority to the British, French, and Dutch, who held so much of the world in domination. They flatter themselves with revolutionary nostalgia. But the truth is that Americans—at least white Americans—are the beneficiaries of an unparalleled destruction that almost totally eliminated an entire race.

Into the Americas, both North and South, the imperialists brought a new population group—black slaves from Africa. Millions of people were captured in the African interior, traded at the coastal ports, and transported in packed, inhuman conditions to the New World. They were set to work on the plantations and in the mines that produced much of the new wealth, and they bred successive generations of slaves. Although Africa had been a source of slaves for centuries, the magnitude of the slave trade exploded after 1700 as the plantations of the New World expanded, producing sugar and cotton for Europe. The islands of the Caribbean—the West Indies—became fabulously productive in the eighteenth century, importing hundreds of thousands of slaves and exporting sugar and molasses to the prosperous new consumers of England and France. The plantation system spread throughout both South and North America, generating huge profits for the colonial traders.

In the first phase of European imperialism, through the eighteenth century, Africa and Asia were incorporated into the world trading network but were not as thoroughly settled or as tightly ruled as were the Americas. Slave-trading bases were set up at West African ports, but the European traders seldom ventured inland. The only white settlement in Africa occurred at the southern tip of the continent, where Dutch settlers, eventually adopting the name Boers, established farmsteads in the plains spreading out behind the Cape of Good Hope. Christian self-righteousness was the ideology of the Boers, as it had been of the Spanish and the French imperialists in America. Whereas the French and Spanish had set out with a Catholic mission to convert and rescue native souls, however, the Boers were equipped with an intolerant Calvinist faith that identified themselves as the saved and the natives they encountered as the damned—the distinction made crystal clear by God's choice of skin color. The Boers would prove to be the most tenacious of the colonialists: only in the 1990s were their descendants, the Afrikaners of South Africa, forced to concede political control to their former subjects.

The Portuguese explorer Vasco da Gama opened the sea route from Europe to India, around the Cape of Good Hope, in 1498. A lively and profitable oceangoing trade followed. The Portuguese sometimes terrorized the Indians, killing and mutilating them and destroying their ships and their cities, but they did not rule them or settle on their territory. Their motive was commercial profit. India, the East Indies, and other areas of Asia offered a wealth of merchandise for Europe, including both agricultural products and crafts. Indian cottons became prized possessions in European households, as did pottery and rugs. The most valued agricultural products from the East were spices and tea. Asia did not offer much of a market for European products, however. Because the Asians sold but did not buy very much, their treasuries gradually amassed much of the gold and silver that had found its way to Europe from the Americas. A global economy was beginning to form.

The Portuguese were succeeded in Asia by the other imperial powers—the Dutch, Swedes, British, French, and Danes. Seventeenth- and eighteenth-century trade with Asia was usually carried out by chartered trading companies, not directly by the European rulers. These were not companies as we know them today, but institutions that had been given the authority by their crowns at home to establish order and to rule, if necessary, in order to create profitable commercial relations. Eventually the authority of the great crown companies was replaced by direct military and administrative rule by home governments. While they lasted, however, their existence made it clear that the motive of imperialism was commercial.

By the middle of the eighteenth century, a worldwide imperial system of commerce had come into existence. Cotton, spices, silk, and tea from Asia mingled in European markets with ivory, gold, and palm oil from Africa; furs, fish, and timber from North America; and cotton, sugar, and tobacco from both North and South America. The lucrative trade in enslaved human beings provided cheap labor where it was lacking. The profits accrued in Europe, increasingly in France and Britain as the Portuguese, Spanish, and then Dutch declined in relative power. It was a global network, made possible by the advancing technology of the colonialists.

1776–1870: British Dominance and the Withdrawal of Other Imperialists

Scholarly debate rages unchecked over the question of whether to view the century between 1776 and 1870 as a period of imperialist decline or imperialist expansion. The conventional view, held by students across the ideological spectrum, has been that it was a period of decline, the consequence being that the resurgence of imperialism after 1870 requires particular new explanations. The American Revolution of 1776 divided the richest jewel of the British Empire from its homeland and led many in Britain to question the cost of maintaining an empire. As the eighteenth century ended and the nineteenth ensued,[1] it seemed to many in Britain that the country's trading companies were strong enough to prosper without any help from the government. The proponents of "free trade," who adopted the teachings of political economists Adam Smith and David Ricardo, argued that the

British would be better off if the government withdrew its controls over trade and commerce. The British gradually dismantled their system of protective tariffs and loosened their control over the colonies. The remaining settlements in British North America were defended against the United States in the War of 1812, but they were then increasingly granted self-government and left on their own, eventually to become the Dominion of Canada. Prime Minister Benjamin Disraeli called the colonies, in a famous phrase, "millstones around our necks." The British withdrew from some of the territory they had administered—for example, the Orange Free State and Transvaal in South Africa—and intended to abandon more.

The contrary view is that the British imperialist thrust did not cease at all in the nineteenth century. If there was perhaps a loosening of administrative rigidity in some areas, it was only because economic dominance and commercial profit could proceed without it. Gallagher and Robinson, writing in 1953, coined the expressive term "the imperialism of free trade." The concept is particularly apt in Latin America. As the Spanish and Portuguese power receded and the South American countries became independent around 1820, they traded their formal legal imperial control for an informal, but no less dominating, rule by the British. From Mexico south to Argentina, the Latin American economies were structured increasingly to produce primary product exports for the British market—beef, sugar, coffee, gold, silver. The British ruled by the power of the purse, not by military force, but the power of the purse was even stronger, purchasing the allegiance of merchant middle classes.

Even in the middle of the nineteenth century, the boundaries of the formal British Empire were expanded in places: there were annexations in Africa, the Indian subcontinent, Australia, New Zealand, and British Columbia. Gallagher and Robinson pointed to conditions in the empire, not in the metropolitan center, as determining whether the formal boundaries of imperial rule were to grow. If political conditions in an area of the empire were sufficiently stable to permit the unimpeded flow of trade, then annexation was an unnecessary expense. "Once entry had been forced into Latin America, China and the Balkans," they wrote, "the task was to encourage stable governments as good investment risks." But if rebellion, anarchy, or the challenge of another imperial power occurred, the Crown needed to take over. The clue to understanding mid-Victorian imperialism was "trade with informal control if possible; trade with rule when necessary."[2]

The Gallagher and Robinson thesis, that imperialism continued vigorously although informally during the nineteenth century, is doubtless correct when applied solely to Britain. The British never withdrew from imperial rule; their spectacular economic growth in the nineteenth century gave them the ability to intensify control over their colonies. The clue to understanding mid-nineteenth-century imperialism, however, is that it was almost exclusively British; the other countries of Europe, unable to compete with the British, withdrew from much of their imperial territory. With the final defeat of Napoleon in 1815, the French retired as a world power. The Spanish and Portuguese had been declining, and the 1820s saw the revolt of their Latin American colonies. At the Congress of Verona in 1822, the British, whose ships by then had uncontested rule over the Atlantic Ocean, made it clear that they would not tolerate any further presence of the Spanish and Portuguese in the newly independent South American states. The American Monroe Doctrine of 1823 further excluded European colonies in the Americas. The British were the only world power left, and in the half century from 1820 to 1870, they dominated the international economy with little threat to their position. They appeared to be indifferent to imperial rule precisely because they were so strong. Beneath the surface, their imperial authority was growing, administratively in India and informally but strongly in Latin America.

1870–1914: The "New Imperialism"

If the withdrawal of the British from imperialism in the middle of the nineteenth century was illusory, the withdrawal of the other European powers was quite real. The resurgence of European imperialism in the last quarter of the century was therefore a startling new phenomenon. Dubbed the "new imperialism," it was quick, explosive, and competitive. Besides the British, it involved the French, Belgians, Germans, Italians, and Portuguese, as well as the Americans and Japanese. Between 1878 and 1914 (when the onset of the First World War turned the Europeans' aggressive tendencies against one another), the imperial powers annexed 17 percent of the world's territory at an average rate of 240,000 square miles a year.[3] The pace of acquisition was extraordinary.

Most dramatic was the scramble for Africa. The French carved out a massive empire stretching from North Africa bordering the Mediterranean Sea, through most of the western bulge of that continent, into central equatorial Africa and the Congo. The British established control over the Gold Coast, Nigeria, and other smaller areas of West Africa, as well as Kenya and Uganda in East Africa. They expanded through Egypt south into the Sudan and also occupied part of Somalia. From their colonies in southern Africa, the British also expanded north into the Rhodesias and Nyasaland. The Portuguese established control over Angola on the west side and Mozambique on the east side of southern Africa. King Leopold II of Belgium formed a private company in 1878, the International Congo Association, that was completely separate from the Belgian government; the association established control over the huge interior area of the Congo. The Germans carved out colonies in South-West Africa, Cameroons, and Tanganyika. The Italians took control of Libya in North Africa and Eritrea and part of Somalia in the east.

The ruler of the newly formed German nation, Count Otto von Bismarck, called a conference of the imperialist powers in Berlin in 1885 to establish some order among the wolves in their dismemberment of Africa south of the Sahara Desert. Certain rules of conquest were agreed to, and the pace of imperial acquisitions accelerated. Before 1870, Africa had been the unknown continent; within a few short years, it was completely divided into spheres of European influence. The boundaries of the colonies were entirely arbitrary, reflecting only the accidents of military and exploratory expeditions; they bore no relationship to tribal ethnicities, natural geographic boundaries, or economic realities.

The parceling out of sub-Saharan Africa was the most dramatic event of the new imperialism, but it was not the only one. Closer to the borders of Europe, an imperialist struggle unfolded over the remnants of the great Ottoman, or Turkish, Empire. The multiethnic and religiously tolerant Ottoman Empire stretched from the Balkans through Turkey to the Russian steppes, and thence through Persia, Palestine, and Egypt across the southern shore of the Mediterranean to Algeria and Morocco. In the nineteenth century, its internal communications weakened, its administration became more rigid, and it fell behind the Europeans technologically. As its power ebbed, some of its outlying areas were snatched up by the European imperialists. The Russo-Turkish War of 1877 led to the separation of much of the Balkan Peninsula north of Greece from the Ottoman Empire. The Suez Canal was completed in 1869, and in order to protect it, the British occupied Egypt in 1882. The occupation was thought to be temporary at the time, but it lasted until 1956. The French expanded into North Africa, with colonies in Algeria and Morocco and a protectorate over Tunisia. The weakness of Turkey and its inability to modernize itself fast enough to keep abreast of its European neighbors led to continuous struggles for its territories and eventually to the outbreak of the First World War in 1914. The Ottomans joined the losing side of that war and suffered the complete dismemberment of their empire in the postwar peace settlement. Turkey was established as a small republic confined to Asia Minor, and the remaining territories of the empire became mandates under the supervision of the League of Nations: Syria and Lebanon controlled by France, Palestine and Iraq by Britain.

In the Indian subcontinent, the late nineteenth century saw an intensification of British control. The British government had taken over rule from the East India Company in 1858 following the Indian Mutiny; thereafter, British administration stretched with the railway throughout the breadth of India. In 1885, to counter a threat from the French, the British annexed Burma, across the Bay of Bengal from India, and they also set up a protectorate in the Malay states. Farther east, the French established control over a major portion of Southeast Asia, including Cochin China (later Vietnam) and Laos. The Dutch, long the dominant power in the East Indies, consolidated their control over the vast archipelago that became known as Indonesia.

The interior of China was not occupied during the nineteenth century, but the imperial powers dominated it. In the so-called Opium Wars of 1839–42, the British broke down the Chinese refusal to trade with the imperial powers and forced the Chinese to import opium. Tariffs on other goods fell, and foreigners were given permanent rights in a number of treaty ports. The ruling Manchu dynasty declined in strength throughout the nineteenth century and was militarily defeated by the Japanese in 1894–95. The British, French, Germans, and Russians, determined to retain their rights to Chinese trade, were unwilling, however, to permit Japanese hegemony in the area. The United States, which by the late 1890s was an important Pacific military power, announced its Chinese open-door policy in 1898, under which annexation would be disallowed and all the imperial countries would have trading rights and other legal privileges. The Chinese were permitted to keep their own governmental and administrative structure, but that structure was controlled by outside countries in a particularly demeaning way. Not only were all Europeans removed from the jurisdiction of Chinese courts of law, but so were all Chinese who had disputes with Europeans.

In the Americas, the late nineteenth century saw a continuation of British hegemony, and it also saw the growth of U.S. imperialism. With the Monroe Doctrine of 1823, the United States had announced its interest in Latin America and its unwillingness to allow the resumption of European imperialism in the Western Hemisphere. In the Mexican War of 1845, the United States annexed half of Mexico, the territory stretching from Texas to California. In 1898, the United States went to war with Spain, easily winning and thereby ending Spain's four centuries of American empire. As a consequence of the war, Cuba became independent but was under the protection of the United States. Puerto Rico and the Philippines were annexed directly by the United States. In a separate action, the United States annexed Hawaii in 1898.

The Pacific islands were partitioned among the imperialists in the 1880s and 1890s. The British established rights over parts of New Guinea and over numerous smaller island groups, including the Gilbert and Ellice Islands and the Cook Islands. The Germans also had holdings in New Guinea as well as in the Solomons, the Carolines, the Marshalls, Samoa, and others. The French possessions included Tahiti and a shared dominion with the British over New Hebrides.

By the early twentieth century, almost all the world was under control; the empires were complete. The United States had effected a transition from colony to imperial power, and Japan was beginning to exercise control over adjacent areas on the Asian mainland. The British domains were divided into two parts: areas of white settlement that were achieving independence from the mother country, and areas with predominantly nonwhite populations that were being administered more tightly. Latin America was, for the most part, nominally independent but under the effective control of British commerce and investment. Sub-Saharan Africa and North Africa were carved into European colonies, as was most of Asia and the Pacific. China, although not completely colonized, was humbled and controlled by the Europeans. It was the high point of European power, the culmination of four centuries of expansion. It seemed destined to continue; there was hardly a hint that it would not. Any prediction at the time that the European empires would crumble in a few short decades would have seemed bizarre.

The Causes of Imperialism

A great deal of ink has been spilled on the question of why the nations of Europe created empires around the world—and in particular, why there was such an orgy of imperialist gluttony at the end of the nineteenth century. In 1902, British economist J. A. Hobson ascribed the new imperialism to underconsumption, to the failure of the European masses to buy the goods produced by European industry. As a consequence, the European industrialists had to export their capital abroad in search of new markets—and to secure those capital investments and markets, they needed to acquire imperial control. A socialist reformer, Hobson argued that imperialism would end if income at home was redistributed from the rich to the poor, so that ordinary people had the resources to buy the capitalists' output.

V. I. Lenin's 1917 tract, *Imperialism, the Highest Stage of Capitalism,* used some of Hobson's analysis, but with a more ominous twist. Lenin believed that mature capitalism necessarily led to rich monopolists on the one hand and to impoverished workers on the other. As Marx had predicted, the capitalist system was about to collapse because the workers could not buy the industrial products. Lenin argued that the export of capital to foreign lands, or imperialism, represented the last futile attempt of the capitalist system to avoid its demise. Lenin, of course, was not a reformer like Hobson but a revolutionary, and he did not believe that the capitalist-imperialist system was capable of rescuing itself.

The Hobson-Lenin thesis ultimately fails as an explanation of late-nineteenth-century imperialism because, although the Europeans invested heavily abroad, very little of their investments went to the newly acquired colonies; a great deal more of it went to the Americas and to India. In particular, almost none of the European foreign investment went to Africa, where the greatest acquisitions of territory occurred.

A more promising economic explanation of late-nineteenth-century imperialism is the voracious demand of the industrializing countries for raw materials and for food imports from the world's tropical areas. Some have argued that it was their fear of being cut off from their sources of supply that led the imperialist countries to acquire territories. Other writers have explored military strategy as a cause of imperialism, most importantly, the need of each European power to establish a worldwide system of naval bases and of military supplies. Gallagher and Robinson, as noted earlier, pointed to conditions in the colonies themselves: the main motive of imperial expansion was to quell disorder among the natives. Economist Joseph Schumpeter advanced the most antieconomic thesis of all. Imperialism made no sense economically, he argued; as any classical economist could demonstrate, free trade, unfettered by any government controls, was the most profitable. Imperialism therefore represented an atavistic throwback to an earlier, irrational era.

These attempts to explain late-nineteenth-century imperialism are all useful, if partial. Behind them, however, lies the unexpressed assumption that imperialism is an anomaly, that it is unusual for a powerful country to exert political, military, economic, and cultural dominance over weaker peoples. If it is unusual, it must be explained by some unique coincidence of forces.

Imperialism is not exceptional at all, however. To a large extent, the history of civilizations is the history of empires. Greeks, Romans, Mongols, the Ming dynasty, Ottoman Turks, Tartars, Aztecs, Incas, and countless other peoples established dominance over strangers. Sometimes they conquered nearby lands, eventually incorporating them into their own country. In other cases, their empires were far-flung and never fully integrated. The former Soviet Union was, in effect, the Russian empire. The United States was created as an empire, expanding across a large portion of an entire continent, displacing Native Americans and Mexicans and annexing territories in the Atlantic and Pacific Oceans.

Empires are the normal way in which political power is exercised, not the exception. A system of independent, autonomous, sovereign nation-states—the system of world organization that most of us consider the norm—is actually exceptional. It has never really existed before the present. Greek and Roman times knew city-states and empires, but not nation-states. European nation-states were created in the breakup of medieval feudalism over several centuries. The process of European nation building was not really completed until just more than a century ago, with the unification of Germany and Italy in 1870–71. One should think of Europe as being organized into nation-states only for a period of generations, not for time immemorial. In the third world, it would be an anachronism to think of the areas ruled by the imperialists as having been divided into countries before their conquest. India was ruled by shifting coalitions of princely hegemonies; Africa was organized predominantly along ethnic and tribal lines, without clear geographical boundaries; China was itself an empire. The current nation-states of the third world were created as a consequence of the disintegration of the European empires; they did not predate the empires.

Living in the early twenty-first century, one thinks of the nation-state as almost a sacred entity, worthy of one's patriotism, with legitimate power to command lives and allegiances. From this perspective, empires—the dominance of one people over another people—seem illegitimate, illegal, and in every respect reprehensible. Empires may be reprehensible because they institutionalize oppression and dominance, but they are not exceptional. It is not just the third world that has been formed by imperialism: it is the whole world. European culture resulted from the Hellenistic empire, from the Roman Empire and, in the Middle Ages, from the Holy Roman Empire. Canada, the United States, Australia, and New Zealand are creatures of the British Empire. Empires have been the dominant force of social change in history and have formed the world's civilizations. Imperialism is the means by which the world was integrated, technology was transferred and adapted, and the social organizations within which we live were established.

The fundamental cause of imperialism, then, lies not in the particular structure of late-nineteenth-century capitalism, or in a particular strategic competition, but in the existence of unequal power. Throughout human history, strong powers have dominated the weak. Unequal power can generally be traced to the uneven development of technology. Almost without exception, the imperial centers have been those that have developed the most advanced military technology and productive methods. The Assyrians, the Greeks, the Romans, and in modern times the Europeans all had access to technology that was superior to that of other peoples. They used this technology to dominate and exploit their neighbors for their own benefit. Their imperialism was masked with idealism—they persuaded themselves that they had the sacred mission of expanding civilization, salvation, economic development, or peace—but what lay at the base of each instance of imperialism was simply the dominance of the weak by the powerful.

The age of European imperialism, the imperialism that created the modern third world, should be seen, therefore, as one phase in the unending stream of imperialism that constitutes world history. It was unique principally because it was the first imperialism to cover the entire globe. The British Empire was the first to be able to claim that the sun never set on it. It stretched from Ireland to North America, through the Caribbean Sea and Latin America, over much of Africa, the Middle East, the Indian subcontinent, parts of China, and islands of the Pacific Ocean both great and small. The Spanish, the Portuguese, the Dutch, the French, the Germans, the Italians and, more lately, the Americans all established geographically dispersed empires as well. What allowed them to dominate the whole globe, as the earlier empires had not, was the tremendous development of science and technology that spurred the growth of capitalism. It was technology that allowed small groups of adventurers, soldiers, and settlers to dominate vast millions. Cortez conquered Mexico with only a few hundred men because of the superior weaponry and horsemanship he commanded. Small numbers of British were able to rule the millions of Indians because their garrisons had modern arms.

Before the period of European hegemony, the growth of technology had never been so rapid and so constant. Although previous empires had enjoyed technological advantages, those advantages had been mostly static, unchanging. Now change became the only constant, as the method of scientific experimentation was applied to all sectors of human endeavor, including agriculture, crafts, manufacturing, weaponry, shipbuilding, and power sources. An explosion of technology transformed the European world by raising standards of living to undreamed of heights and transformed the third world by allowing imperial control of it. Imperialism, in turn, fed the growth of the European economies, providing them at various times with plundered gold and silver, with commercial profits for investment in domestic enterprises, with a cheap source of primary products and raw materials, and with an outlet for profitable investment. From the very moment that Europe began to cast off the constraints of the stagnant Middle Ages and develop its economic and technical resources, it also began to dominate the world. This domination created the conditions that exist now in the third world.

From this perspective, what seems to be the strange history of nineteenth-century imperialism can be understood simply. After Napoleon's defeat in 1815 and the independence of the Spanish and Portuguese colonies in the Americas around 1820, all the European countries except Britain withdrew from their imperialist adventures. Why did the British continue to expand while their competitors withdrew? The answer is that the industrial revolution began in Britain in the late eighteenth century; by the early and mid-nineteenth century, the system of manufacturing in factories, using water and steam power, gave the British an enormous advantage in economic and military strength. No other country dared to challenge the British. Britain's strength was so dominant that it could appear in some respects to withdraw from imperial rule while retaining control over an entire world system of trade.

The new imperialism of the late nineteenth century, which involved competition among many countries, followed from the fact that the other countries caught up with Britain technologically. The French, Germans, Russians, Americans, and Japanese all learned from the British, copying their industrial methods and improving on them, achieving their own industrial revolutions fifty to a hundred years later. By the late nineteenth century, they were on a par with the British. Not until the twentieth century would Britain actually fall behind its competitors, but by 1880, the competitors had reached such strength that Britain could no longer dominate world commerce. As soon as the other European countries became industrialized, and as soon as their strength approached Britain's, they too sought empires. The British, of course, were not about to surrender their preeminence, so they were forced to become more aggressive.

The new imperialism resulted, therefore, not from some particular feature of mature capitalism, as Hobson and Lenin surmised, but from the emergence onto the world scene of a multitude of industrial powers that were jealous of one another and vying for advantage.

These countries competed at first overseas in their empires and later in the catastrophic First World War.

The Culture of Imperialism

The legacy of the European imperialist age is pervasive, extending to every area of culture and economy. No part of that legacy is more permanent or personal than the transformation of language. In most regions of the third world, the common and official language is not a native language at all but the European language of the imperialist. This is not the case universally, with the most notable exceptions being China and the Arab Middle East. China retained its linguistic uniqueness because it was not completely occupied by the imperialists, and also because its own two principal languages, Mandarin and Cantonese, are spoken by such a large number of people. In the Middle East, Arabic was spoken over such a wide area and had such status that it could not be displaced. Most other peoples of the third world were invaded thoroughly by European languages, however. The common languages of Latin America are Spanish and Portuguese. Although numerous native American languages persist in Latin America, they are spoken in isolated pockets and lack the power to facilitate communication among large numbers of people. Rigoberta Menchú cannot communicate with most of the other people of the Guatemalan highlands, because they speak twenty-two different ethnic languages. In the Caribbean islands, English and French are spoken along with Spanish. Most Africans speak a European language in addition to an ethnic language, and the European languages—be they French, English, or Portuguese—are the official languages of the independent countries. The common language of the Indian subcontinent—made up today of India, Pakistan, and Bangladesh—is English. Hindi is recognized as an official language of India, but it lacks the universality to unite the country, as English does. Some countries have rejected their colonial languages; the Indonesians no longer use Dutch, and the Vietnamese no longer use French. But the Philippines, incorporated into the fledgling American empire less than a century ago, uses English as a common tongue.

Many of the indigenous languages, although not all, still persist— they are the languages of the local marketplace and of the home—but they do not often function in national communications or in government or official discourse. The European language is often promoted by the central government as a way of overcoming tribal and ethnic divisiveness, of encouraging national unity.

The displacement of native languages by foreign ones was a consequence of the unequal power of the imperialist confrontation. With few exceptions, the imperialists refused to learn the local languages and essentially forced the native people to learn theirs.

The imperialist languages do bring the people of the third world into communication with the ideas and information of the broader world. They allow the novelists, poets, songwriters, scholars, journalists, and statesmen of the third world to address a worldwide audience. There is a terrible price to be paid for the abandonment of one's own language, however.

Languages run as deep as the soul, and they are not, in their most basic functions, translatable. A European or an American who has tried to translate Shakespeare into French or Molière into English knows that the subtle nuances are lost, transformed into something else. How much greater the shock in moving from Xhosa (a southern African language) into English. Xhosa is the language of the spirits, of the ancestors, of the forests and the plains, and of the gods of the rivers. No translation into English can save these concepts as anything but museum pieces.

Some ideas that are fundamental in third-world cultures cannot be thought in the imperialist's language. Among the Managalase, for example, an ethnic group of 6,000 people in New Guinea, marriage negotiations are extraordinarily delicate; they are conducted entirely in the rhetoric of allegory and metaphor. Skillful use of the language is required to avoid open embarrassment of any of the parties and to advance ideas into the public discourse without appearing to have made them directly. If anything goes wrong with the linguistic interactions, the marriage can collapse, and with it political alignments within the community. Without the Managalase language, marriage negotiations would be impossible.[4]

When the imperialists imposed their languages, therefore, they stole ways of thinking from third-world people and replaced them with their own. By refusing to learn the local languages and to accept them on an equal basis, they planted a sense of psychological and cultural inferiority among their subjects. It was the ultimate imperialism: mind control. The damage continues in the postimperialist age, as the European languages grow stronger and the ethnic languages weaker.

Along with language came the traditions and cultures of the conquerors. The conflict between the imported culture and the native one was long and protracted, and it is not over yet. The imported culture is on the advance, however, the local one in retreat. Laura Nader, a social anthropologist at the University of California, tells the seemingly benign story of how the Kaiser Aluminum Company set up a plant in the interior of Ghana and provided medical benefits for its employees and their dependents. The workers welcomed the medical benefits and assumed that they would be available to all the members of their extended families, which included dozens, in some cases even hundreds, of people. Sorry, said the company, its generosity did not extend quite that far, just to the *nuclear* family—the husband, the wife, and their children. The nuclear family, however, was not a relevant concept to the people of this ethnic group. In order to be eligible for medical care, the workers had to make artificial divisions in their families, creating distinctions and privileges where none had existed before. The company was not consciously evil; quite the contrary, in its own eyes it was beneficent and proud of it. It was the more powerful of the two cultures, though, and its effect on the local family structure was catastrophic. Many examples exist, of course, in which the imperial power was not so beneficent.

One of the most powerful tools of cultural disruption that the imperialists brought with them was their Christian religion. Christianity, whether of the Catholic or the Protestant variant, provided the imperialists with an aura of superiority and a sense of mission. The aura of superiority is not surprising; every religion gives its adherents the conviction that they have the truth. But the sense of mission was particularly harmful. Christianity was not willing to coexist with other faiths; it demanded conversions. The conversion was a highly charged symbolic moment in which the new adherent rejected his or her sinful, error-filled past and adopted the new dogma. We know that many of the converts to the imperialists' religion went through the ceremony with proverbially crossed fingers, that Christianity in fact coexisted in many souls with a wide variety of other beliefs. Nevertheless, the basic Christian intolerance of other worldviews meant that converts frequently experienced a massive shift in belief systems.

The traditional religions that the imperialists encountered varied a great deal from culture to culture, but a common thread was that most of them grew organically out of the daily lives of the people. They provided an explanation of the rhythms of ordinary life; there was frequently no real distinction between the spiritual life and the daily life of work and family. Christianity cut this unity asunder because it was a foreign belief system with foreign symbols and artifacts; its god was the god of the conquerors, not the god of the local soil and the nearby river. Christianity supported in subtle and not so subtle ways the authority of the imperialists; it cloaked their actions in a veil of respectability.

Shortly before his murder by the police, Steven Biko, the leader of South Africa's black consciousness movement, discussed the influence of Christianity on his people. His description could apply to many other areas of the third world:

> We as blacks cannot forget the fact that Christianity in Africa is tied up with the entire colonial process. This meant that Christians came here with a form of culture which they called Christian but which in effect was Western, and which expressed itself as an imperial culture as far as Africa was concerned. Here the missionaries did not make the proper distinctions. This important matter can easily be illustrated by relatively small things. Take the question of dress, for example. When an African became Christian, as a rule he or she was expected to drop traditional garb and dress like a Westerner. The same with many customs dear to blacks, which they were expected to drop for supposed "Christian" reasons while in effect they were only in conflict with certain Western mores. . . . Black theology does not challenge Christianity itself but its Western package, in order to discover what the Christian faith means for our continent.[5]

Even when the Christian missionaries failed to convert the heathens, they often succeeded in disrupting their societies by sowing seeds of mistrust in their own belief systems and by introducing alien ideas. In *Arrow of God,* Nigerian novelist Chinua Achebe weaves a rich tale of how a Christian missionary confounded the villagers' beliefs in their local gods. Ezeulu, the priest of the paramount god Ulu, has the responsibility each year of calling the harvest festival, the Feast of the New Yam. He knows when to call it because at each new moon during the year, he eats one of thirteen sacred yams that have been stored from the previous festival. When all the yams are eaten, it is time for the new festival and the harvest. This year, however, Ezeulu has been imprisoned by the British colonial authorities for more than a month and has consequently missed eating a sacred yam at two new moons. He refuses to call the festival until the yams are eaten. This refusal, which he regards as an act of obedience to Ulu, threatens to throw the village into chaos, because the yams that have been planted will rot in the ground if they are not harvested on time. The missionary, Goodcountry, provides a "solution" to the village's problem by having the Christian church sponsor a harvest festival. Goodcountry assures the villagers that if they take part in the Christian festival and harvest their crops, his god will protect them against the wrath of Ulu. He thereby succeeds in separating the village from its traditional priest and its traditional god. Achebe closes his novel with these sentences:

> The Christian harvest . . . saw more people than even Goodcountry could have dreamed. In his extremity many an Umuaro man had sent his son with a yam or two to offer to the new religion and to bring

back the promised immunity. Thereafter any yam that was harvested in the man's fields was harvested in the name of the son.[6]

Christianity provided a moral cloak that could mask the destruction wrought by the imperialists. Massacres were justified in Latin America on the grounds that they led to the advancement of the Christian faith. In the California missions, Spanish padres held natives in virtual slavery, while apparently persuading themselves that they were saving their souls. In China in the nineteenth century, Christian missionaries encouraged the addiction of millions of people to the opium that was imported by the British.

Not all the effects of Christianity in the third world were negative; the balance of gains and losses is complex. Note that Steven Biko's statement quoted above does not condemn Christianity per se but rather the association between Christianity and Western imperialism. The Christian churches with their messages of redemption have provided a tool to many third-world groups in their struggles for self-determination. In South Africa, where almost all African organizations were banned until recently by the white government, the Protestant churches and their leaders stood out as centers of black resistance. In Latin America, the local Catholic clergy with their "liberation theology" inspire hope and resistance among the poor. But the losses and the costs have been staggering.

The Europeans brought with them not only their religions but also their secular ideologies. The early Spanish, Portuguese, Dutch, and French colonizers carried with them a belief in autocracy, monarchy, even the divine right of kings. It was an ideology that oppressed the common people at home and oppressed the colonial natives even more heavily. By the nineteenth and early twentieth centuries, however, the reigning European ideologies had liberalized. It is one of the marvelous ironies of imperialism that it brought to the third world the very ideas that would eventually liberate the third world—the ideas of freedom, equality, democracy, socialism, and revolution. Social movements in the third world took these European ideas, adapted and melded them—sometimes with indigenous belief systems—and used them in the struggle against imperialist control.

The story of Indian independence illustrates the use of British ideology, combined with Indian beliefs, to defeat the British. The great Indian nationalist and spiritual leader Mohandas Gandhi was trained in London as a lawyer and became thoroughly committed to the doctrines of English common law that bestow unchallengeable rights of legal equality on all subjects of the Crown. After leaving England, he discovered that British imperial practice deviated from the common law when he experienced severe racial discrimination against Indians in the Union of South Africa. In response to racism and in order to secure the British right of equality, he developed the attitudes and techniques of nonviolent resistance. He later used this system to lead the movement for the independence of India. The rights he was asserting were part of British doctrine, not Indian. Indian society, with its rigid caste system rooted in Hindu scripture, did not recognize the equality of all people. The Gandhian nonviolent resistance movement had a base in Indian culture, but Gandhi was also deeply influenced by the writings of American philosopher Henry David Thoreau. Gandhi combined these initially foreign ideas with his own religion, Hinduism, and that of his brothers and sisters in India, Islam, to fashion a compelling social movement that eventually drove the British from India and captured the imagination and allegiance of people throughout the world. The story of Gandhi is a particularly apt one for illustrating the interconnectedness of the world, for in leading the revolution in race relations in the United States, the Reverend Martin Luther King Jr. turned to the example of Gandhi, using Indian ideas that had their antecedents in London and in Massachusetts. Imperialism opened the third world to the liberating ideas that would eventually bring about its defeat.

Liberalism was not the only ideological export of the imperialists. Socialism and Marxism found their way to the colonies in short order too. Ho Chi Minh, the future leader of the Vietnamese communist revolution, developed his ideas in the working-class cafés of Paris's Left Bank and from the insurrectionary French journals published in the years after the First World War. He traveled to Moscow in the early years of the Russian Revolution, soaking up the ideas of Marx and Lenin. The movement that he led for decades in Southeast Asia was a mixture of classic Marxism and traditional Vietnamese patriotism.

China's revolutionary leader Mao Tse-tung did not travel to an imperialist center, but he steeped himself in the communist ideology emanating from Europe. The successful communist revolution he led was based on Marxist principles, although he adapted them broadly to the Chinese reality. Most importantly, what was a doctrine of urban, working-class revolution in Russia became the practice of rural, peasant revolution in China. If Chinese communism had its own tints, however, it was, first of all, communism, the doctrine of German scholar Karl Marx.

Almost all the social movements of the third world have had this character, adapting ideas from the center of Europe to the local conditions. In recent years, the most significant exception to this rule has been the Iranian revolution of the Ayatollah Khomeini, based solidly on fundamentalist Islamic doctrine and rejecting any hint of European ideology. The genocidal extremism of the Khmer Rouge movement in Cambodia also represented a radical turning away from foreign doctrines. Still, the exceptionalism of these cases shows all the more clearly how, in most instances, the third world has adapted the ideas of its oppressors.

The Foundations of Third-World Poverty

In the economic sphere, the legacy of imperialism is central. The dependency theorists are correct in insisting that imperialism formed the economic structures of the third world, which even today leave the vast majority of the human race in desperately poor conditions.

An earlier section argued that the existence of European imperialism can be explained primarily by unequal power: by the military, technological, and economic strength of the Europeans in contrast to the relative weakness of what became the third world. The fact that the late-nineteenth-century European economies had a particular capitalist structure is much less important than Hobson, Lenin, and their followers claimed. As long as European technology was dominant, imperialism would have occurred anyway, even if the European societies had had a different sort of noncapitalist structure.

When we turn to the other side of the story, however, to the effects of imperialism on the economies and societies of Asia, the Middle East, Africa, and Latin America, the fact that the imperialists were capitalist is centrally important. The essence of capitalism is alienation. The factors of production—land, labor, and capital—are treated in a capitalist system as commodities to be bought or sold. They are not part of a person's birthright. In many peasant societies, in contrast, the factors of production are inherently connected as part of an integrated system. A person is born to a village society and automatically cultivates the land bequeathed to him by his people, using the product to sustain his family. The peasants, although usually exploited by a landowning or ruling class, are nonetheless secure in knowing their place in the world. The advent of imperialism broke this world apart, creating labor forces that worked for wages on other people's projects and land that could be bought and sold. Imperialism converted the peasants of the third world into separate components of the capitalist system, components whose survival depended on the vagaries of global markets over which they had no control.

Before the arrival of the imperialists, the majority of the people of the third world were involved in producing food for their own use—as hunters and gatherers in some regions, but for the most part as culti-vators of the soil. They typically produced only what they needed to survive. Any surplus food was used to support a ruling group, but this was usually a small portion of production. Imperialism changed this picture. It did not totally displace subsistence production, of course, because people still had to eat. On top of subsistence production, however, the imperialists imposed the production of primary export commodities—agricultural goods and minerals from the colonies that were intended for use in the metropolitan centers. The colonies were turned into a vast production system for sugar, cacao, tobacco, wheat, cotton, meat, fish, jute, coffee, coconuts, rubber, wool, palm oil, rice, bananas, ground nuts, indigo, tin, gold, silver, bauxite, copper, and many more products.

As Europe developed its manufacturing industries in the nine-teenth century, and as its own peasants were drawn off the land and into its unspeakable cities, it required new sources of primary agri-cultural commodities—both to feed the urban labor force and to pro-vide raw materials for the factories. It was no coincidence, then, that colonial export production intensified at the same time that capitalist industrial production was growing in Europe; the colonial exports were required for the growth of industry at the imperial centers.

Imperialism produced a world of economic specialization: manu-facturing in the core of Europe, and agricultural and mining produc-tion in the periphery of the third world. The doctrines of free trade and comparative advantage provided an intellectual justification for this specialization. Free trade and economic specialization were to the advantage of every country, taught classical economist David Ricardo, even if some countries were more efficient in the production of every good and some countries were less efficient. What mattered was rela-tive efficiency, or comparative advantage. A poor colonial economy might be less efficient than Britain in the production of crops, but as long as its disadvantage in crops was less serious than its disadvantage in manufacturing, both it and Britain would be better off if it special-ized in agricultural production, shipping its surplus crops off as exports to Britain and importing British manufactures. It was a lovely theory, promising benefits from international trade to all participants.

One of the lasting puzzles of economic history is to assess whether this Ricardian theory of comparative advantage really works. One fact is clear: as Ricardo and his followers posed the theory, it is far too narrow. It is easy, and even trivial, to grant the Ricardians' main conclusion that at any given time a country will do better by special-izing in those goods for which it has a comparative advantage. The more difficult question is whether that specialization will be to the benefit of a poor country in the long run. The economic case to be made against imperialism is that the colonies' specialization in primary production impoverished them in the long run by making their economies incapable of sustained economic development.

The case against comparative advantage, and against the world division of production brought about by the imperialists, is not entirely easy to make, because there are obvious counterexamples, the best of which is Canada. From the sixteenth century to the twentieth, Canada fit precisely into the imperialist economic mode: it produced primary products for export to Europe and imported European manufactured goods. On the basis of those primary exports, it was successful; it developed into one of the richest countries in the world, with a standard of living higher than that of most European countries. Canada developed its economy to a high level by exploiting a series of primary exports, or "staples." In the sixteenth century, the French discovered the rich fisheries off the coast of Newfoundland. Their successors ventured inland, eventually across the entire continent, in search of beaver furs, which were processed into felt hats for European consumers. The fur trade was succeeded by timber and then by the greatest staple export of all: wheat. In the twentieth century, wheat was supplemented by minerals. Immigrants flocked to the new land to develop each staple export as it came along. The income they generated was used both to raise their standard of living and to reinvest in productive activities designed for local use. In Canada, primary exports became the engine of sustained economic growth. A national manufacturing sector grew up behind the staples to meet the needs of the local settlers, and in this way, Canada developed a technologically advanced, productive modern economy.

To cite the Canadian example is to show, however, how exceptional it was, for the export industries established in most of the rest of the colonial world did not lead automatically to self-sustaining economic growth for the local population. Far more often they led to poverty, to destitution on the land, and to urbanization without hope. Even in Argentina, which for many decades resembled Canada and as late as the 1920s had a higher standard of living based on its beef export industry, stagnation eventually set in.

The best answer to the question of why the concentration on colonial agricultural export production led to stagnation in the third world instead of to prosperity (as in Canada) lies in the fact that the exports transformed the social structures of the third world (but not of Canada) in such a way as to render genuine economic development less likely. The heart of social transformation in the third world was the fact that the local labor force or the land, or both, had to be wrested, often forcibly, from their existing uses. The problem of forcibly changing the use of local labor and land did not arise in Canada, because there the native population was either exterminated or shunted off to reservations, leaving behind lands that for the most part had never been tilled. In the third world, in contrast, the local populations generally stayed and were in possession of the land.

The colonialists in the third world often confronted intensive labor shortages. Frequently the local people did not constitute the sort of labor force that capitalist enterprises required; they were not willing to give up their subsistence pursuits and work for wages—at least not for the low wages normally offered. In some cases, forced labor of the local people resulted in many deaths—for example, in the mines and plantations of the Spanish empire in Latin America. The slave trade was the first answer to this problem—millions of Africans were shipped to the Western Hemisphere—until it was effectively shut down toward the beginning of the nineteenth century. As the nineteenth century progressed, however, the need for colonial labor only increased, so other expedients were developed. Indentured service, or the labor contract, became common; it was a system by which people committed themselves to work in a foreign land for a period of years in return for a guaranteed wage and a return passage home. Indentured Indians, Chinese, and other Asians were shipped long distances to work in semifree conditions in the imperialist plantations. Many did not return to their homelands; their descendants today create ethnic heterogeneity in many areas of the third world.

In addition to importing labor, the Europeans devised ways of forcing the local people to work for them. In Indonesia, the Dutch established the "culture system," a kind of throwback to European medieval feudalism, under which native people were required to devote a certain portion of their land and labor to the production of export products; this system took the place of taxes. A common technique in Africa and elsewhere was to impose a hut tax or a head tax. These taxes had to be paid in the imperialist's currency by each person. Because the peasants did not earn or use this currency in their villages, they had to earn the currency by working as laborers for the white man. The head tax led to the pernicious colonial theory of the "backward-bending supply curve of labor": the lower the wage rate, the longer the natives would work, because their goal was to earn a certain fixed amount in order to be able to pay the hut tax. It was a system of forced labor, pure and simple. Frequently, taxes did not induce sufficient work, however, and they were supplemented by more direct means: the compulsion of labor by military force. The use of armed force by King Leopold of Belgium in the Congo to create a labor force was particularly notorious.

The formation of a capitalist labor force, an army of laborers working for wages, has never been an easy process. European historians from Marx onward have documented the terror, bloodshed, and misery imposed as European feudal peasants were forced off the land to which they had common-law rights and into the filthy cities and deadly early factories. In the colonies, the goal was somewhat different—to move the peasants from subsistence village life into commercial agriculture—but the process was often equally devastating. At least in Europe the descendants of the displaced peasants eventually came to enjoy rising incomes; for most people in the third world, there has been no payoff to speak of so far.

If the accumulation of a labor force was a problem, the amassing of land to be used by capitalist enterprises for export crops was even more difficult. Most of the land was already occupied. The Europeans were faced with the need either to expel the local people from the most fertile land or to persuade them to grow export crops in their villages. Expulsion was often the order of the day. In some parts of southern and East Africa, settlers carved out farms reminiscent of European commercial farms. The Boers at the Cape and later in the Orange Free State and Transvaal, and the English settlers in the highlands of Kenya, worked cattle ranches and wheat farms, hiring African labor in limited numbers to help them. The land distribution in southern and East Africa became unbelievably skewed, with the Europeans—a small proportion of the population—owning the great majority of the land and the Africans crowded into small areas with inferior soil.

Far more common were large plantations in Africa and Asia that were owned and overseen by Europeans and worked exclusively by natives. In the nominally independent countries of nineteenth-century Latin America, the plantation owners (or *hacendados*) were generally local people of pure Spanish or Portuguese descent; the peons were of native or mixed races. Plantations were created for rubber in Malaya, rice in Vietnam, tea in India, coffee in the Belgian Congo, bananas in Honduras, sugar in Cuba, cocoa in the Gold Coast, and many other crops throughout the colonies. Landholding patterns became incredibly unequal; it was common in many areas of the third world for a scant 1 or 2 percent of the landowners to control at least half of the arable land. The land available for peasant use was reduced proportionately. Many of the peasants, having lost their land, had to work as wage laborers, usually for very low wages, on the great plantations.

Export crops were often grown by village peasants along with their subsistence crops. It was the essence of the Dutch culture system in Java, for example, to require this kind of dual agriculture by the peasants. The system was not confined to Indonesia. Cotton and rice were grown in Egypt, wheat in India, palm oil in the Congo, ground nuts in French West Africa. It was common for the same crop to be grown by both plantations and independent peasants in the same area. Malayan rubber, for example, was grown both on large-scale plantations and in small scattered plots.

The imperialist world economy, and the insatiable demand of European industrialization for food and raw materials, transformed the agricultural sectors of the third world, where the great majority of the populations were located. Imperialism forced millions of people to migrate, it separated masses of people from the land and recreated them as wage laborers, and it brought village-based peasant agriculture into world markets.

In assessing this tremendous impact, it is helpful to return to the comparison of the third world with Canada, because Canada parlayed a succession of primary exports into steady economic growth and one of the world's highest standards of living. Why did the concentration on primary exports not pay similar dividends in the third world? It is a puzzle. Some of the answers that have been given over the years are not very satisfying. Raúl Prebisch and some other Latin American economists argued that the problem was declining terms of trade— essentially that the prices of primary products were falling in world markets to such an extent that even though third-world countries were selling more and more, they were earning less and less and could afford fewer imports of manufactured goods. The argument is valid for some primary exports and for some countries during some periods, but recent scholarship has shown conclusively that as a general explanation for the continuing poverty of the third world, it collapses. Certainly it cannot be a general explanation for the poverty of primary exporters, for if it were, Canada would be poverty-stricken as well.

Another line of argument has been that the imperialists and their successors sent the profits they earned back to their homelands rather than reinvesting in local enterprises. Modern imperialism and neo-colonialism are seen through these lenses as a way of looting the third world, just as surely as the sixteenth-century Spaniards looted the gold and silver of the Americas. This argument has some substance, because there certainly were enormous transfers of funds from the colonial areas back to Britain and the other core powers. It is not really satisfactory, however, as an explanation of continuing poverty, because profits were repatriated from Canada too, and even after subtracting the repatriated profits, considerable new wealth stayed in the colonies as a consequence of the export activities.

A more promising explanation is that of F. S. Weaver, who argues that the export industries created new wealth and that the wealth reinforced whatever social structure already existed in the colony.[7] In Canada, the British settlers who populated most of the country outside the province of Quebec were entrepreneurial capitalists to begin with. There was no question of transforming them from feudal or subsistence peasants—they were capitalists from the day they entered the country, in the sense that they were committed to the market, to buying and selling, to producing for export and not for their own use. The income they earned was reinvested in the expansion of their small-scale enterprises, including family farms.

In the colonies of what is now the third world, conditions were different. The relationship that the imperialists had to the natives, and that the *hacendados* had to the peons, was one of oppression. So when the ruling classes in the third world accumulated wealth through the export of primary products, they used that wealth and the power that went along with it to intensify the oppression of the local people, thereby reinforcing their own status. Imperialism reinforced the conditions that were already there. Profits were used to expand plantations, but for the local people, this simply meant being part of a larger labor force, separate from their ancestral homes and working for minimal wages. In theory, peasant-based export agriculture might have been more beneficial to the local people, but in practice, there were severe limits to the expansion of peasant agriculture, because the people stuck to their subsistence farming techniques; consequently, sufficient wealth seldom flowed to the villages to allow them to escape from their poverty.

One could imagine conditions under which agricultural and mineral exports could have led to the prosperity of the third world—if the local people had not been oppressed, if they had been able to benefit from their own work, if they had been allowed the freedom to be creative and inventive. These were not, however, the conditions of the European empires.

An enormous system of worldwide trade in primary commodities grew up; it was a system that depended on impoverished labor forces that were, in many cases, pulled unceremoniously away from their villages and cultures. Income was earned in the colonies from these export industries, but it was not earned by the working people who might have been able to use it creatively to improve their lives. It was earned by upper and middle classes, who used it to increase their consumption and to secure their control over the poor.

By contrast, the primary export producers in Canada—the fur traders, the lumberjacks, the small farmers, and the miners—slowly accumulated wealth and increased their demands for manufactured goods that could be produced locally. Over time, an integrated economy was developed, with primary exports and manufacturing both growing and supporting each other. In the third world, because most of the new income was kept from the workers, people could not afford manufactured products. The Latin American "structuralist" school has been particularly successful in showing how the local income generated by imperialist trade went into the hands of an increasingly well-off minority of the population, who turned to European imports to satisfy their demands for sophisticated consumer goods. No mass market for simple manufactured goods ever arose, so local manufacturing could not get a start.

As the colonialists concentrated on single export crops, they often impaired the local people's ability to grow their own food and even destroyed the ecosystems that permitted the growth of food. Political scientist Sehdev Kumar demonstrates how French taxation policies in West Africa forced peasants to devote ever-increasing areas to the cultivation of ground nuts. This forced food production out into areas that had previously been used for grazing; the nomads of the area were therefore compelled to graze their animals on smaller areas of land. The overgrazing eventually resulted in desertification and with it the cycles of starvation that came to the Sahel region in the twentieth century.[8] Similar stories can be told in many areas of the third world. In the short run, it may have been advantageous for West Africa to concentrate on ground nut exports, as the Ricardian theory of comparative advantage would prescribe. The income went into the hands of the elite, however, not to the laboring people, and in the long run, the very ecosystem that permits people to survive was damaged.

If imperialism harmed the self-sufficiency of third-world agriculture, it absolutely devastated its manufacturing. Before the age of imperialism, the third world had not enjoyed industrial production such as currently exists in the developed countries. Factory production is a result of the European industrial revolution. Most third-world areas did, however, have thriving craft sectors, producing textiles, pottery, household utensils, and the like. These were systematically destroyed by the imperialists, not at the muzzle of a gun but as a consequence of marketplace competition. The European industrial revolution spewed out manufactured goods that were much cheaper, and often of higher quality, than the colonies' crafts. The imperialists had no motive to protect the local crafts; on the contrary, they had every incentive to open up local markets to European exports. Imperialism therefore led to the collapse of manufacturing and craft production in the third world.

Swiss economic historian Paul Bairoch has constructed some remarkable statistical tables showing how the European industrial revolution and imperialism went hand in hand with the destruction of the craft sector in much of the third world. Table 4.1 contains index numbers of industrial output per person in different countries in different years. The average level of industrial output per person in Britain in 1900 is set at 100, and all the other numbers are shown relative to that level. As an example, in 1860, the United States' level of industrial output per person was 21 percent of the United Kingdom's level in 1900.

Table 4.1 shows that among the developed countries, Britain established a lead in industrialization in the nineteenth century but was overtaken by the United States by the eve of the First World War. Most dramatically, it shows the near disappearance of industrial, or craft, output in the third world over the same period. Note that in 1750, just before the beginning of the British industrial revolution, third-world industrial output per person was almost as high as Britain's and substantially higher than in the American colonies. During the nineteenth century, though, third-world industrialization declined, so that by 1900 it was just 2 percent of the British level.

Bairoch has compiled a wealth of additional data making the same point in different ways. He shows, for example, that between 1830 and 1900, total industrial output of the third world fell almost by half. In 1750, the third world produced 73 percent of the world's manufactured goods; in 1913, only 7 percent.

It is clear that the effect of imperialism on third-world manufacturing and crafts was catastrophic. This is another example of the limited relevance of the theory of comparative advantage. In the nineteenth century, the Europeans were at a comparative advantage, and the third

Table 4.1 Index Numbers of Industrial Output Per Person

Region	1750	1800	1830	1860	1880	1900	1913
Developed countries	8	8	11	16	24	35	55
U.K.	10	16	25	64	87	100	115
France	9	9	12	20	28	39	59
Germany	8	8	9	15	25	52	85
U.S.	4	9	14	21	38	69	126
Canada	—	5	6	7	10	24	46
Third world	7	6	6	4	3	2	2
China	8	6	6	4	3	2	2
India	7	6	6	3	2	1	2

Note: Numbers are relative to the industrial output per person in Britain in 1900—set at 100.

Source: Paul Bairoch, "International Industrialization Levels from 1750 to 1980," *Journal of European Economic History* 11 (fall 1982): 294.

world at a comparative disadvantage, in the production of manufactured goods. The Ricardians would argue that the result—the concentration of manufacturing in Europe and its disappearance in the third world—was for the best. Manufacturing production all but disappeared from the third world, but that is no reason to worry, teaches the theory, because consumers in the third world were able to buy cheaper and better goods from the Europeans.

This was true enough, in the short run. The long-run effects were hardly advantageous to the third world, though, because an entire class of independent craftspeople disappeared. They were, for the most part, people with highly developed skills who were used to making business decisions on their own, and many of them were to some extent entrepreneurial. They might very well have been able to adapt the new European technologies to their own needs and, as a consequence, could have led the way to the economic development of their societies. They were wiped out. Almost the entire Indian textile industry was eliminated because of the import of cheap cotton goods from Britain.

The economic effects of European imperialism were therefore massive. Millions of people were pulled away from their accustomed pursuits to work in capitalist and export enterprises. Almost all were kept at low, subsistence incomes, without an opportunity to share the benefits obtained from export production. Land that had been tilled for centuries for subsistence food crops was expropriated for the growth of export crops. In the countryside, single-crop agriculture brought with it ecological deterioration. Manufacturing and crafts disappeared, and, as a consequence, the economies of many third-world areas became much more specialized and concentrated.

The Population Explosion

One of the most pervasive and transforming effects of imperialism was the population explosion in the third world, which began at the end of the imperialist era, between the two world wars of the twentieth century. Population growth is determined almost exclusively by the gap between birth rates and death rates. For example, a country like Mexico, which has an annual crude birth rate of twenty-five per thousand people and a crude death rate of five per thousand, has a population growth rate of twenty per thousand, or two percent a year. This may not seem like a high rate, but a population growing at two percent a year will double in just thirty-five years, quadruple in seventy years, and so forth.[9] Congo, with a birth rate of forty-six and a death rate of fifteen—and an annual growth rate of 3.1 percent—will double in size in twenty-three years and quadruple in forty-six years if these rates are sustained.[10]

Before the twentieth century, both birth rates and death rates were very high in the third world. Both were often about forty or forty-five per thousand; net population growth was therefore zero, or at least very small. Death rates were high because of low standards of living, pervasive infectious disease, and the absence of medical care. Birth rates had to be high to maintain the population. Consequently, cultural practices developed over the years that encouraged large families. A typical experience of a mother in the third world would be to bear perhaps eight children, five of whom might die before maturity. Perhaps one or two sons might survive to provide for her in her old age.

High fertility and mortality existed in preindustrialized Europe too. When economic growth occurred in Europe and people's incomes started to increase, health conditions improved, death rates fell, and the population began to grow. This growth spurt was relatively short-lived, however, because by the twentieth century, most Europeans (and Americans) had voluntarily reduced their fertility, having decided that they preferred small families. The evidence indicates that in most communities of the developed world, rising standards of living led people to want to reduce the number of children and to succeed in doing so, even before mechanical means of contraception were available.

The third world experienced remarkable reductions in death rates in the twentieth century—for example, from forty or forty-five per thousand people each year to ten per thousand in India, seven in China, twelve in Ghana, six in Colombia. These improvements in mortality were not set off by rising standards of living. To the contrary, they began while the great majority of third-world people were desperately poor and under colonial subjection. Death rates fell largely because the imperialists imported cheap public health technologies, including the spraying of malarial swamps with insecticides, the use of vaccinations, and later the introduction of antibiotics.

One cannot complain about the success of colonial public health measures in saving lives. It is critical to see, however, that this mortality improvement occurred without any change in the standards of living of the people. In Europe and North America, increased longevity had been an integral part of a long process of social change; in the third world, increased longevity was bestowed from outside the social system.

In Europe and North America, the social change that improved health conditions and caused death rates to fall eventually led to the reduction of birth rates as well. In the third world, however, there were few of the changes in standards of living and cultural norms that might have persuaded people to decrease the size of their families. The great majority of people have remained poor and continue to see children as material and spiritual assets—the more the better. Children can be put to work at a young age to help increase family income. If they survive, they can provide security for their parents in their old age. The cultural and religious practices of most third-world societies, developed over countless generations in support of high fertility, have been left unchallenged. Girls commonly marry at puberty, and their value in the eyes of their families and frequently themselves is determined by their success in childbearing.

The necessary result of the quickly declining death rates, combined with the sustained high level of childbearing, was a population explosion unprecedented in human history, with populations doubling each generation. This population growth occurred at the same time that land in the third world was being removed from subsistence cultivation and used increasingly for the production of export crops. More people, less land: the consequences are not hard to see. In the postcolonial decades since the 1960s, birth rates have begun to decline in a number of third-world countries, but nowhere are they approaching the low death rates.

It is sometimes argued that to focus on the population explosion as a cause of third-world poverty is to blame the victim, to hold third-world peoples at fault. This view is incorrect. The population explosion is a consequence of European imperialism. The imperialists imported cheap public health measures that lowered death rates—without undertaking the much more difficult task of economic development that might have led people with rising incomes to choose to lower birth rates. The result is population growth that has persisted long past the colonial age, threatening to overwhelm the third world's best efforts at social change.

The Legacy of Imperialism

A quick survey of the age of European imperialism easily dispels the notion that the third-world societies of today are essentially traditional, or untouched, as many in the modernization school picture them. They were transformed by five centuries of imperialism, and today they are almost as different from their former cultures as modern-day North American and European societies are from medieval feudalism. They are still poor, it is true, and they still have vestiges of traditional culture—certainly more than exist in the world's rich countries. But the languages, the political structures, the demography, and the economic systems that mark today's third world are to a large extent the result of unequal, oppressive relationships with the European empires.

Some of the motivations of the imperialists were altruistic. Many of the people on the spot—the soldiers, the administrators, and the farmers—saw themselves as aiding the local people. The missionaries saw themselves as saving them. Rudyard Kipling, the bard of British imperialism, wrote without irony in 1899:

Take up the White Man's burden—
Send forth the best ye breed—
Go bind your sons to exile,
To serve your captives' need;
To wait in heavy harness,
On fluttered folk and wild—
Your new-caught sullen peoples,
Half devil and half child.[11]

As discussed in Chapter 3, Karl Marx and many of his followers argued that imperialism was frequently a progressive force, breaking down rigid social structures and opening societies to capitalist development, which was a necessary step on the road to socialism and prosperity. There is a grain of truth in this view—for some imperialist ventures, at some times. Imperialism brought railways and roads, it brought new technology, and for some, it brought educational opportunities. For most people in the third world, however, it brought oppression and poverty.

Nowhere have the contradictions of imperialism been explored with greater force and insight than in Joseph Conrad's 1898 novella *Heart of Darkness*. The narrator, Marlow, travels to the Congo (later Zaire and now, again, Congo) with a sense of adventure and a certain idealism, a belief in the civilizing mission of imperialism. What he found were European merchants whose ideals were only self-seeking. "To tear treasure out of the bowels of the land was their desire," he says, "with no more moral purpose at the back of it than there is in burglars breaking into a safe."[12] The consequence was the destitution and murder of the Africans. Conrad's images can be seen as premonitions of the Holocaust that was to disfigure the next century: "Near the same tree two more bundles of acute angles sat with their legs drawn up. One, with his chin propped on his knees, stared at nothing, in an intolerable and appalling manner: his brother phantom rested its forehead, as if overcome with a great weariness; and all about others were scattered in every pose of contorted collapse, as in some picture of a massacre or a pestilence."[13]

The empires were central to the expanding capitalism of Europe. They were needed for their wealth and for their primary products. Without the empires, European economic growth might never have occurred, or if it had, it might have been restricted and much less impressive. Imperialism was not just an add-on; it did not occur in a "fit of absence of mind," as some thought at the time. It was an integral component of world capitalist development. Imperialism was one of the major formative movements of the modern age. It brought with it incredible cultural destruction, economic impoverishment, death, and even genocide. It opened the world to new ideas, new technologies, and new opportunities. It created the world we live in, be we rich or poor.

Notes

1. As an undergraduate history student at Queen's University in Canada, then one of the last vestiges of the ideology of the British Empire, I was enthralled by the statement of my most dignified professor, a gaunt Englishman in flowing black robes who lectured to the class in slow cadences. "The eighteenth century is a vital link," he said, "between the seventeenth century and the, er, nineteenth century."

2. J. A. Gallagher and R. E. Robinson, "The Imperialism of Free Trade," *Economic History Review,* 2d ser., 6 (1953): 9, 13.

3. C. C. Eldridge, *Victorian Imperialism* (London: Hodder and Stoughton, 1978), 122.

4. This case is reported by William H. McKellin and cited in Howard Rheingold, *They Have a Word for It* (Los Angeles: Jeremy P. Tarcher, 1988).

5. From Biko's writings collected in Donald Woods, *Biko,* 2d ed. (New York: Henry Holt, 1987), 117.

6. Chinua Achebe, *Arrow of God* (New York: Doubleday, 1969), 261–62.

7. F. Stirton Weaver, "Positive Economics, Comparative Advantage, and Underdevelopment," *Science and Society* 35 (summer 1971): 169–76.

8. Sehdev Kumar, "Third World Toils to Feed the West," *Globe and Mail* (Toronto), April 15, 1988, A7.

9. The number of years it will take a population to double is found by dividing the population growth rate (in percent) into seventy. Thus a population growing at 1 percent a year doubles in seventy years, a population growing at 2 percent doubles in thirty-five years, and so on.

10. The birth and death rates in this paragraph are found in United Nations, Department of Economic and Social Affairs, *1999 Demographic Yearbook* (New York: United Nations, 2001), table 4.

11. Rudyard Kipling, *The Five Nations and the Seven Seas* (New York: Doubleday, Page and Company, 1925), 66.

12. Joseph Conrad, *Heart of Darkness* (New York: Penguin Books, 1973), 61.

13. Conrad, *Heart of Darkness,* 45.

Suggestions for Further Reading

See Bibliography for full details.

David B. Abernethy. *The Dynamics of Global Dominance: European Overseas Empires, 1450–1980.*

Chinua Achebe. *Arrow of God.*

Joseph Conrad. *Heart of Darkness.*

Philip D. Curtin. *Death by Migration: Europe's Encounter with the Tropical World in the Nineteenth Century.*

D. K. Fieldhouse. *The Colonial Empires: A Comparative Study from the Eighteenth Century.*

E. J. Hobsbawm. *The Age of Empire, 1875–1914.*

J. A. Hobson. *Imperialism: A Study.*

V. I. Lenin. *Imperialism, The Highest Stage of Capitalism.*

Bernard Lewis. *What Went Wrong? Western Impact and Middle Eastern Response.*

Albert Memmi. *The Colonizer and the Colonized.*

George Orwell. *Burmese Days.*

Edward Said. *Orientalism.*

David E. Stannard. *American Holocaust: The Conquest of the New World.*

Chapter Five

Nationalism and Independence

Revolt is the only way out of the colonial situation, and the colonized realizes it sooner or later. His condition is absolute, and cries out for an absolute solution; a break and not a compromise. . . . For the colonial condition cannot be adjusted to; like an iron collar it can only be broken.
—Albert Memmi, *The Colonizer and the Colonized*

Political power grows out of the barrel of a gun.
—Mao Tse-tung

I, personally, would wait, if need be, for ages rather than seek to attain the freedom of my country through bloody means. . . . The world is sick unto death of blood-spilling. The world is seeking a way out, and I flatter myself with the belief that perhaps it will be the privilege of the ancient land of India to show the way out to the hungering world.
—Mohandas K. Gandhi

The nineteenth century was the age of imperialism in the third world, the twentieth century the age of nationalism and independence. Rebels and patriots fought back against the white imperialists, driving them from their lands and creating new nations in the wake of their departure. They took responsibility for their own destinies.

Nationalism represented resistance to outside rulers, pride in one's own identity, and a program for political self-determination. The nationalist movement was successful; by the second half of the twentieth century, almost all the areas of the third world that had been colonized by the Europeans achieved independence. At the United Nations,

102

the great majority of the delegates to the General Assembly were representatives of the newly emergent nations of Asia, the Middle East, and Africa, along with Latin America. It turned out, however, that the demise of the European empires and the success of the nationalist program did not necessarily lead to a solution of economic and social problems; as the twenty-first century dawns, those problems remain as acute as ever throughout much of the third world.

The Origins of Third-World Nationalism

The nationalism of the twentieth century was a new response in the third world; it was a response specifically to the experience of being controlled by the European imperialists. With few exceptions, the people of the third world had not been organized into nations before the arrival of the colonialists. Their loyalties had not been nationalist. In Africa and the Americas, people's identities had been tied to their ethnic and tribal groups, often to their villages or their extended families. Most of Asia had been organized for centuries in a shifting series of empires, dynasties, and bureaucracies. The concept of the nation-state was not a relevant one. But the imperialists were themselves nation-states, and they created administrative structures that resembled nations. So when the people of the third world fought back against their oppressors, they did so in the name of the nation, not in the name of the village, the family, the tribe, or the dynasty.

The fact that imperialism engendered nationalism is an indicator of how profound the imperialist experience was in most areas of the third world. Imperialism severely damaged, distorted, even destroyed the social structures it encountered; when the imperialists finally retreated, those traditional societies could not be brought back to life and recreated by the third-world rebels. Imperialism forced the third world irrevocably into the dominant world system, a system of nations. Furthermore, imperialism challenged the identities of third-world peoples, their senses of self-worth and dignity. The imperialists generally treated the people they encountered as inferiors, as niggers, gooks, and wogs. In response, the people of the third world needed to affirm their own value and importance; they did so in large measure by asserting their nationality.

In many areas of the third world, the nationalist movements began about the turn of the twentieth century. Resistance movements had occurred earlier, but they had not coalesced around the idea of the nation. The Indian Mutiny of 1857, for example, was a serious enough threat to lead the British to terminate the rule of the East

India Company and replace it with the direct authority of the Crown, but the rebels did not conceive of themselves as representing a unified Indian nation. Their grievances had to do with threats to their religious practices and their customs, not with the denial of nationhood. In 1885, however, the principal Indian nationalist organization was founded: the Indian National Congress. Although the Congress was open to all factions of Indian society, it was dominated by Hindus; in response, the All-India Muslim League was founded in 1906. Both organizations were nationalist, calling for an end to British rule and the establishment of a new country or countries in its place. Their nationalism was complicated by their religious identities; the eventual inability of the two organizations to resolve the contradiction between a nationalist and a sectarian vision of the future led to the partition of Pakistan from India at the time of independence in 1948. In spite of their sectarian problems, both the Congress and the League were nationalist organizations, working for the replacement of imperialism by an independent nation-state. In many other areas of the imperial world, nationalist organizations began to appear at about the same time.

It is important to distinguish the nationalist program in the third world from the revolutionary program. Nationalism occurred almost everywhere, but revolution only in pockets. The distinction is that the nationalists sought political rights for all the colonized people; they deemphasized class conflicts among their own people and stressed instead their common oppression by the imperialists. Revolutionaries, in contrast, sought the restructuring of their societies. At his trial in South Africa in 1963, the leader of the African National Congress (ANC), Nelson Mandela, summed up the difference:

> The ANC's chief goal was for the African people to win unity and full political rights. The Communist party's main aim, on the other hand, was to remove the capitalists and to replace them with a working-class government. The Communist party sought to emphasize class distinctions while the ANC sought to harmonize them. This is a vital distinction.[1]

The strength of nationalism was that it was an ideology capable of uniting an oppressed people, of drawing them together in opposition to their common enemy, the imperialist oppressor. In preindependence India, when the British talked of the difficulties the Indians would have resolving their ethnic and religious differences in an independent country, the leaders of both the Indian National Congress and the Muslim League replied that although this might be true, it was no business of the British. The British needed to leave, and following their departure, the Indians would settle their own problems in their own ways, without outside interference. It was the one proposition on which all Indians could agree.

If national unity was the strength of the nationalist program, however, it was also its weakness. Nationalist movements in the third world were willing to focus on the struggle against the common enemy, but most were unwilling to deal with the ways in which oppression was exercised within the nation. Such an emphasis would have torn apart the unity that was the movement's strength, so in most cases it was avoided.

In some areas of the third world, however, nationalism took on a revolutionary cast. Most importantly, in China, the struggle against foreign domination (in particular, against the Japanese occupation) merged into a communist revolution that completely overturned class structures and social relationships. Similarly, in Vietnam, North Korea, Cuba, Nicaragua, and Iran, nationalist movements against a foreign oppressor joined forces with revolutionary movements against local classes. One should bear in mind, however, that the revolutionary movements in the third world were nationalist as well as revolutionary. They drew strength from the patriotism of their people. Ho Chi Minh's revolutionary movement overthrew landlord and bourgeois classes in Vietnam, but it also defended itself fiercely against control by foreigners: the French, the Americans, and even the Chinese communists. Mao Tse-tung was first and foremost a Chinese leader, Fidel Castro a Cuban, Gamal Abdel Nasser an Egyptian.

Marx, and after him Lenin and the Russian revolutionaries, had thought that nationalism was a particular manifestation of capitalism. Nationalist identity, they thought, was fostered by capitalists as a way of blinding the workers to their true interest. They had expected that national divisions would wither away as the communist revolution spread throughout the world and revealed that the real conflicts between people were not in terms of their nationality or their race but in terms of their class. This did not occur in the twentieth century, however, and after the failure of international communism to achieve a worldwide revolution, the Soviet communists themselves became increasingly identified with the aspirations of the Russian nation. The sudden emergence of acute and sometimes violent nationalism that followed the collapse of the Soviet empire reveals that communism never succeeded in obliterating nationalism; it only suppressed it temporarily.

The success of the nationalist movements in the third world was inevitable, or at least very likely, in the long run. The indigenous people simply cared too much about their own dignity and oppression to allow imperialism to continue generation after generation. The speed with which the new nations won independence was, however, breathtaking.

At the end of the Second World War, the European powers confidently resumed control over their colonies. Within just a couple of years, however, China was convulsed in a revolution and India was granted independence. Although these were the two largest countries of the third world, they were thought at the time to be exceptions. Even in the 1950s, almost no contemporary observers expected the independence of the African nations to come within their lifetimes. By the early 1960s, however, almost the entire continent of Africa was under the control of its own people.

In retrospect, one can see that the timing of the successful movements for national independence was not accidental. The European empires would have collapsed eventually because of the strength of the nationalist movements, but they collapsed so suddenly because of the weakness of the Europeans themselves. The nations of Europe subjected themselves to two devastating world wars in the first half of the twentieth century. The First World War (1914–18) took a toll of life never before seen in human conflict. Scarcely had the Europeans begun to rebuild their societies and economies when they were hit by the worst economic disaster since the industrial revolution, the Great Depression of the 1930s. The depression was finally defeated only by the coming of the Second World War (1939–45), a war that was even more destructive of lives and productive capacity than the first. The continent that had emerged into the twentieth century with such verve, power, and confidence found itself in tatters at midcentury.

The Europeans did not understand at the end of the Second World War how exhausted they were. They could see that the United States was taking over their accustomed role of world leader and that a bipolar world conflict between the United States and the Soviet Union was emerging, a conflict in which their own role was secondary. What remained hidden for a time, however, was that Europe had lost both the morale and the economic strength to rule its colonial empires.

The French, in particular, were recalcitrant. Faced with a nationalist uprising in Vietnam, they engaged in a long war, with the support of the United States. They finally conceded defeat only after their spectacular military loss at Dien Bien Phu in 1954. In Algeria, they hung on even longer, eventually abandoning the settlers and the army in 1961. The British were somewhat more peaceful about their withdrawal from empire but were equally unaware that their moment of imperial glory was gone forever. Prime Minister Winston Churchill pontificated that he had "not become the King's First Minister in order to preside over the liquidation of the British Empire,"[2] but that is exactly what he and his successors did. Even in the mid-1950s in Africa, the British and French colonialists were saying that independence would take generations, because the Africans were not yet ready to assume control of their own countries. Ready or not, they did assume control in a few short years before and after 1960.

The nationalist movements in the third world originated, therefore, as responses to the European empires, and they succeeded because of the weakness of the imperialists. Without exception, they promised both dignity and material progress to their oppressed peoples. With some exceptions, they failed to deliver on these promises.

The Indian Subcontinent

The first significant area of the third world to achieve its independence after the Second World War was India, in 1947. At the end, the British left under amicable terms, having agreed to independence in return for Indian participation in the war. The struggles in the previous decades had been anything but friendly, though.

The British had ruled India directly since the mutiny of 1857. In the twentieth century, they faced increasing resistance from nationalist groups, especially from the Congress Party and the Muslim League. The great leader of the Indian independence movement was the ascetic spiritual teacher Mohandas Gandhi, who had developed his techniques of nonviolent resistance in South Africa and then returned to India in 1919.

Gandhi worked within the Congress Party—he was president from 1925 to 1934—but he was not a politician in the conventional sense. He was a man of the spirit who taught by example. In her 1938 novel *Kanthapura,* Indian writer Raja Rao showed how Gandhi was incorporated into the pantheon of spiritual leaders, how his teachings were connected to the deepest traditions of the people. The storyteller weaves this legend for the villagers, in which the sage Valmiki addresses the supreme god Brahma:

> "You have forgotten us so long that men have come from across the seas and the oceans to trample on our wisdom and to spit on virtue itself. They have come to bind us and to whip us, to make our women die milkless and our men die ignorant. O Brahma, deign to send us one of your gods so that he may incarnate himself on earth and bring back light and plenty to your enslaved daughter." . . . "O Sage," pronounced Brahma, "is it greater for you to ask or for me to say Yea? Siva himself will forthwith go and incarnate himself on the earth and free my beloved daughter from her enforced slavery." . . .
>
> And lo, when the Sage was still partaking of the pleasures Brahma offered him in hospitality, there was born in a family in Gujerat a son such as the world has never beheld! Hardly was he in

the cradle than he began to lisp the language of wisdom. You remember how Krishna, when he was but a babe of four, had begun to fight against demons and had killed the serpent Kali. So too our Mohandas began to fight against the enemies of the country. And as he grew up, and after he was duly shaven for the hair ceremony, he began to go out into the villages and assemble people and talk to them, and his voice was so pure, his forehead so brilliant with wisdom, that men followed him, more and more men followed him as they did Krishna the flute-player; and so he goes from village to village to slay the serpent of the foreign rule. Fight, says he, but harm no soul. Love all, says he, Hindu, Mohammedan, Christian or Pariah, for all are equal before God. Don't be attached to riches, says he, for riches create passions, and passions create attachment, and attachment hides the face of truth. . . . He is a saint, the Mahatma, a wise man and a soft man, and a saint. You know how he fasts and prays. And even his enemies fall at his feet.[3]

Gandhian nonviolence, called satyagraha, has been mistaken as a passive strategy, but it was not. It was an active means of focusing the world's attention on the violence and injustice of the oppressor. It was a means of changing the oppressor's acts by shaming him and calling his good sense into question. When Gandhi's followers were attacked savagely by the British, they suffered without fighting back; by bearing witness, they put the British into an untenable ethical position. Had the struggle been one of military force, imperialism in India might have lasted much longer, because the British had almost a monopoly of arms. Gandhi succeeded in turning the battle into one of conscience, however; on that basis, he and the Indians were successful.

The strategy of nonviolent resistance raised many questions in India, as it did later in other areas of the world—for example, in the southern United States during the civil rights movement of the 1960s. It was attacked by militants as being a strategy of cowardice. It was attacked by socialists as evading the central issue of class structure. It drew worldwide sympathy to the cause of anti-imperialist nationalism, however, in a way that no other strategy could have. Gandhian nonviolence succeeded in eroding the moral position of the British and driving them out of India. It was not successful, though, in solving the communal problems of the Indians. The Muslim League, under the leadership of Mohammed Ali Jinnah, refused to accept the position of being an ethnic minority within an independent India dominated by Hindus. Gandhi fought for the idea of a nonsectarian state, where all religious groups (and, within the Hindu population, all castes) would have the same rights and would be treated with equality. Throughout the 1930s and 1940s, while the Indians were uniting in their negotiations with and struggles against the British, they failed to achieve consensus about the structure of postindependence India. In 1947, as independence came, the new country collapsed into two parts: India, with a heavy majority of Hindus, and Pakistan, which was almost exclusively Muslim. Because of the geographical location of most Muslims, it was necessary to establish two sections of the Islamic state, East and West Pakistan, which were separated by 1,000 miles of Indian territory. As the two new nations were formed, a massive movement of population occurred—of Muslims out of India and of Hindus out of Pakistan. The entire subcontinent exploded in an orgy of violence. With the normal social constraints lifted, the frustrations of each religious group with the other were unleashed, and the slaughter was horrifying. Gandhi tried desperately to stop the violence by fasting almost to death; he may have had some positive impact, but he could not control it. Then just a year after independence, Gandhi himself fell victim to the subcontinent's hatred, assassinated by a Hindu extremist.

The nationalist movement of India came to its conclusion, therefore, in an incredibly contradictory manner. Indian independence was the greatest triumph of nonviolent direct action the world has seen, yet the moment of independence was one of unprecedented violence. The Gandhian spirit was one of the reconciliation of all peoples, yet the polity of the subcontinent solidified into sectarian blocs.

Postindependence India and Pakistan have struggled with this confused legacy. India became the world's largest democracy, with contending political parties vying in elections that have been, for the most part, free. At the same time, however, the prime ministership of India was handed down in succession to three generations of the same family (Jawaharlal Nehru, his daughter Indira Gandhi, and her son Rajiv Gandhi) in a dynastic fashion. More recently, the government of India has been in the control of an exclusively Hindu nationalist party. Although the official policy of India is nonsectarian, communal violence still rises to the forefront often—not only between Muslims and Hindus, but also between Sikhs and Hindus and between Hindu castes. Mohandas Gandhi, Indira Gandhi, and Rajiv Gandhi all fell victim to assassins.

The basis of Pakistan has been different; it is an explicitly Muslim state (*Pakistan* in Urdu means "land of the pure"). Religious commitment could not unify the two sections of the country, however. East Pakistan, more crowded and poorer than West Pakistan, declared independence in 1971 under the name of Bangladesh and, with Indian help, defeated a West Pakistani army at the cost of great loss of life. Bangladesh's independence brought with it another tremendous flow of refugees, this time millions of Hindus crossing from Bangladesh into the Indian state of West Bengal. Democracy has been more precarious in Pakistan and Bangladesh than in India; for most of the period of independence, the regimes of both nations have been military. In Pakistan, secular governments (both military and democratic) have been challenged by fundamentalist Islamic groups. In the period following the terrorist attacks against the United States on September 11, 2001, the Pakistani government defied the Islamists by cooperating with the Americans in their campaign against the regime in neighboring Afghanistan, but this policy led to real fury among large segments of the population. In its quarter century of independence, Bangladesh has frequently been close to collapse; it has become more dependent on international aid than any other major country.

India, Pakistan, and Bangladesh now constitute about 20 percent of the world's population and continue to share widespread poverty. None of their successive governments has been able to address the plight of the poor in a consistent way. Although there have been some areas of progress, the living standards of their people are still among the lowest in the world. The United Nations Development Programme estimates that the population earning less than a dollar a day is 31 percent in Pakistan, 29 percent in Bangladesh, and 44 percent in India. It places the three countries near the bottom of its "human development" ranking, almost as low as most African countries.[4]

China

While the peoples of the British Empire in India were struggling to forge three independent republics, the other great population group of Asia, the Chinese, were embarked on a different sort of struggle toward nationhood. China was not formally part of a Western empire, but its ports, commerce, administration, and legal system had been controlled by the European imperial powers since the middle of the nineteenth century. In the twentieth century, the Chinese went through a series of revolutions that made them masters in their own nation. The first revolution occurred in 1911, when the Manchu dynasty, which had presided over China's humiliation by the foreigners, was deposed and replaced by a Westernized military regime. This regime was in turn challenged, almost from the beginning of its rule, by the Kuomintang, or Nationalist Party, led by one of China's great revolutionary figures, Sun Yat-sen. Sun Yat-sen propounded a new vision of the Chinese nation; China in his eyes was not just a shifting series of alliances under an emperor but a unified state to which the millions of Chinese could and should show allegiance. It was critical to his strategy to terminate the imperialist control that still existed over

China. Neither the new regime in Beijing nor the Western powers were prepared to accede to this program, and a long civil war broke out.

Sun Yat-sen died in 1925 and was succeeded in the leadership of the Kuomintang by General Chiang Kai-shek. Chiang achieved considerable success in the 1920s, exerting military control over most of the country and persuading the Western powers to relinquish most of their extraterritorial rights. The seeds of disaster for the Kuomintang were sown, however, in 1927, when Chiang broke with the party's left wing, the communists. Threatened by the growing strength of the communists, Chiang purged them from the party and expelled the Russians who had been providing support and advice. In the years that followed, Chiang suppressed other groups within the Kuomintang that were challenging his leadership. Within ten years of taking over the party, he had converted it from the broad, democratic, nationalist ideals of Sun Yat-sen into an authoritarian, primarily military organization.

The communists, one of whose leaders was Mao Tse-tung, organized among the peasants in southeastern China and developed their military capacity. The Kuomintang attacked and dislodged the communists, who responded in 1934–35 by undertaking a 6,000-mile trek, later called the Long March, through the west and into the north of the country. The Long March began with 90,000 people, only half of whom survived. Along the way, the communists deepened their roots among the peasants and established tremendous popular appeal. The civil war resumed with the communists in a much stronger position. It was interrupted, however, by the Japanese invasion of northern China. The communists persuaded the Kuomintang to join forces with them to defend China from the Japanese. The alliance, although precarious, lasted for most of the Second World War.

With the defeat of Japan at the end of the war, the Chinese civil conflict resumed in earnest, this time with the United States in full support of Chiang's Kuomintang armies. But the Kuomintang had lost almost all popular support; Chiang had become indistinguishable from a long line of traditional Chinese warlords. The communists steadily gained ground, eventually driving the Kuomintang forces from the mainland to the island province of Taiwan. The communists declared the mainland the People's Republic of China in October 1949.

The Chinese revolution was the world's second great communist revolution, following the Russian Revolution of 1917. In the eyes of U.S. policymakers in the years following the Second World War, there was little difference between the two. The world appeared to be divided into two camps, with the Russians and the Chinese together representing the principal threat to the "free world." This perception was heightened by the outbreak of the Korean War in 1949, with the communist North Koreans, supported by the Chinese, fighting against the South Koreans, who were supported by the Americans. It was a naive view. The Chinese revolution was different from the Russian, and the two regimes eventually became antagonistic.

Even the theories of communism espoused by the Russians and the Chinese were different. For the Russian revolutionaries, schooled in classical Marxism, the urban workers were the revolutionary class and the peasants were prerevolutionary or possibly even antirevolutionary. The Russian Revolution, from its very inception, had an antirural cast (resulting in a relatively unproductive agricultural sector). The Chinese communist movement, in contrast, was a peasant revolution. Mao's followers had their roots among the peasantry; their most popular programs were land reform and the destruction of the landlord class. It was the Kuomintang that controlled the cities. So the Chinese revolution was in large measure the revolt of the peasants against the urban dwellers.

Although the ideology of communism was internationalist, in the end, both the Chinese and the Russian revolutions developed into deeply rooted nationalist movements. Particularly in the Chinese case, the communist revolution actually created the nation. Sun Yat-sen's ideal had been a nationalist one, but his vision of national unity had been betrayed by his successor, Chiang Kai-shek. It was left to the victorious communists to develop a program for the Chinese nation as a whole.

Chinese communism departed from the nationalist movements of many other areas of the third world, however, in that it was also profoundly revolutionary. It made no attempt to reconcile the various classes and interests in the country. The purpose of the Chinese revolution was to overthrow and destroy the oppressing classes, and it did. In particular, the hated landlords were eliminated as a class, as were independent commercial businesspeople. The history of China from the revolution to fairly recent years is an extraordinary tale of a politicized society driven at all levels—from the national to the local—by strong and shifting ideologies. Leftward movements and rightward reactions succeeded one another. The full apparatus of totalitarianism was developed, with hundreds of thousands, perhaps even millions, of arrests and deaths. Side by side with this police-state repression was the mobilization of intensive social pressure to raise the consciousness of the people and direct them toward social action.

After the victory of the Chinese revolution in 1949, two further social convulsions were promoted by the communist leaders themselves. From 1958 to 1961, the country went through the deeply disruptive Great Leap Forward, when rural communities were organized into large communes and heavy industry was dispersed in small-scale units into the countryside. The changes brought about by the Great Leap Forward were so disruptive that production fell drastically. It has been estimated that thirty million deaths were caused by malnutrition and starvation. In the respite that followed in the early 1960s, some private enterprise was allowed, and production levels recovered. Then in 1966, an even greater disruption began—the Great Proletarian Cultural Revolution, a movement begun by the aging Mao and destined to last for almost a decade. The new generation of Chinese, too young to have experienced the original revolution, were called on to create their own revolution. This they did, with remarkable thoroughness. Politics ruled above all; people with technical expertise were suspected of being insufficiently true to Maoist doctrine. Tremendous numbers of people were dismissed from their positions and purged. Many skilled people were sent to the countryside for rehabilitation. Universities were closed. The handbook of the Cultural Revolution was Mao's "Little Red Book," a collection of his sayings that was studied assiduously by workers, as the guide to correct action.

Following Mao's death in 1976, a new group of leaders took power, wresting control from the Maoist leaders, whom they dubbed the Gang of Four. They led modern China far from the ideas of the revolution's founder, deemphasizing politics as an organizing principle and stressing competition, expertise, entrepreneurship, and markets, a system hardly distinguishable from capitalism. They opened the country to foreign technology, foreign investment, and foreign ideas. In 2002, the Communist Party officially invited entrepreneurs to join its ranks. After decades of social and economic instability, the Chinese people responded actively to the new opportunities. They joined the world trading system, they raised both agricultural and industrial production, and they experienced remarkable improvements in their living standards. According to estimates of the World Bank, Chinese production grew at the extraordinarily rapid rate of 10 percent per year from 1980 through 2001.[5]

The new Chinese leaders were not prepared to relax their authoritarian political control, however. The Communist Party continued to monopolize political life, denying opportunities for dissent and opposition. When Chinese students demonstrated for democracy in the spring of 1989, they were shot down in the streets, imprisoned, and executed. In the years that followed, political control by the party did not relax, and reports of human rights abuses continued to reach the outside world.

The Chinese revolution was one of the most fundamental social movements of the twentieth century—and at the same time, it was ambiguous and self-contradictory. It completely overturned the social structure that preceded it, imposing a particularly strict and egalitarian communist system. Then it abandoned that system and hurtled headlong toward market capitalism without adopting the individual freedoms that many people believe to be essential to successful capitalism. As far as outside observers can tell, the Chinese people are divided on the question of whether the revolution has at long last fulfilled its promises or betrayed them. Only the foolhardy would presume that the Chinese have made their last sharp shift in social policy.

Vietnam

Vietnam was the site of one of the third world's most bitter and protracted nationalist struggles for independence. Lying to the south of China, Vietnam suffered centuries of foreign invasion and occupation, most often from the Chinese. As a consequence, the Vietnamese have a long tradition of resistance; Vietnamese nationalism is not just a reaction to recent European imperialism. In the twentieth century, the Vietnamese engaged in successive wars against foreigners, first against France and then against the United States.

From the late eighteenth to the late nineteenth centuries, French explorers, adventurers, soldiers, and missionaries traveled throughout the area they called Indochina, an area that consisted of the present-day countries of Laos, Cambodia, and Vietnam. They asserted control where they could, often by use of military force, but their authority was uneven and sporadic. After a century of forays, however, the French finally dominated the entire region in 1883, as part of the wider expansion of European imperialism at the end of the nineteenth century. In 1887, they created the Indochinese Union, consisting of the four areas of Cambodia, Cochin China, Annam, and Tonkin (the latter three corresponding to modern-day Vietnam); in 1893, they added Laos to the union. The French established a colonial export economy based mostly on rice and rubber. In so doing, they expropriated a great deal of the land for use by French owners and facilitated the concentration of much of the remaining land in the hands of a small number of local people. Indochina became a profitable component of the French overseas empire. French control over the area was brutal when necessary; it never fully succeeded, however, in eliminating local resistance.

The leader of Vietnamese resistance in the twentieth century was one of the most charismatic figures to come out of the third world: revolutionary, nationalist, communist Ho Chi Minh. Ho was born in central Vietnam in 1890, just as the French were establishing administrative control over the region; he died in 1969, at the height of the conflict that was both a civil war and a struggle against U.S. imperial control.

Ho spent a great deal of his life outside Vietnam. After a fairly conventional education, he left his country at the age of twenty-one as a cabin boy on a French freighter; he was not to return for thirty years. He spent his young adulthood in the West—in the United States, where he lived as a laborer in Brooklyn; in Britain, where he worked in the kitchen of an elegant London hotel; then six formative years in Paris. In Paris, the capital of his country's oppressor, he imbued himself deeply in French culture, reading widely, joining in discussion groups, and writing. He also made contact with and was influenced by French socialist and communist groups. At the end of the First World War, he tried to influence Woodrow Wilson at the Peace Conference of Versailles to include Vietnam in his vision of self-determination, but without success. He also had little success with the French socialists, as he tried to persuade them to embrace the cause of independence for Vietnam. He discovered that they were as national-ist as they were socialist, with no interest in dismembering the French empire. In the intellectual ferment that spread throughout Europe after the success of the Russian Bolshevik Revolution in 1917, Ho gradually shifted his allegiance from the moderate socialists to the revolutionary communists. He did so out of a motivation that was nationalist; he thought that the Russian Communist Party had the capacity to promote a worldwide revolution that would lead to the liberation of Vietnam. He later said, "It was patriotism and not Com-munism that originally inspired me."[6]

In the 1920s and 1930s, Ho traveled throughout the world, in-cluding Russia and China, as a revolutionary intellectual. Nowhere did he have a secure home—certainly not in China after the Kuom-intang broke with the communists. He finally returned to Vietnam in secret in 1941 to join with compatriots in the struggle against the Japanese. The Japanese had invaded Vietnam from China in 1940, driving out the French and imposing a reign of terror more fierce than even the French had contemplated. Along with Vo Nguyen Giap and Pham Van Dong, he formed a nationalist party, the Vietminh, which was to lead the country through thirty-four unbroken years of mili-tary struggle.

The end of the Second World War in 1945 and the defeat of Japan brought a moment of hope to Ho and the Vietminh that independence might be attained. Ho declared Vietnamese independence, quoting lib-erally from the U.S. Declaration of Independence, which he admired, and hoped for support from the Americans. The British and the French, however, who occupied the country at the end of the war, had no interest in Vietnamese independence. In particular, the French were committed to the reestablishment of their empire throughout Indochina. Negotiations were held in Paris, but they collapsed; consequently, the Vietminh began engaging the French militarily in 1946. Although the Americans professed an anticolonial ideology, they ended up supporting the French. By the time the French were finally defeated in 1954, the United States had given them more military aid for their Indochinese battles than economic aid for the rebuilding of their economy after the Second World War. The Americans had been persuaded to support the French against the Vietnamese because of the emergence of the cold war immediately after the Second World War and then the hot war in Korea in 1949. The Americans came to see themselves as locked in a deathly struggle for the survival of their way of life against the Russian communists. Other communists in China, Vietnam, and North Korea were seen as dupes and fellow travelers of the Russians. What might have been viewed as a local conflict was transformed, therefore, in the eyes of the Americans into a geopolitical struggle for the survival of the free world. The Americans, as citizens of the world's strongest country in the postwar era, believed themselves to have no alternative but to support their French colleagues. It was a disastrous decision for both the Vietnamese and the Americans.

The war between the French and the Vietnamese culminated in the decisive battle of Dien Bien Phu in 1954, in which the forces commanded by General Vo Nguyen Giap defeated the enemy and made the continued presence of the French in Vietnam untenable. An international conference in Geneva followed, at which the independence of all of French Indochina—Laos, Cambodia, and Vietnam—was recognized. There was a catch, however. Vietnam was to be divided at the seventeenth parallel of latitude into two parts: North and South Vietnam. The North, with its capital in Hanoi, was to be governed by the communists under Ho Chi Minh; the South, with its capital in Saigon, was to be governed by an anticommunist, Western-backed group. Under the terms of the Geneva agreement, this division was to be temporary, to be ended when countrywide elections were held in two years. The Vietminh agreed to the division, because it had no doubt that it would prevail in an election. What it had won on the battlefield, however, it lost at the conference table. In 1956, the South Vietnamese regime refused to schedule the elections. It was supported in this decision by the United States, which saw this strategy as a way of containing the global advancement of communism.

Deeply dismayed, Ho set about to continue the military struggle for the unification and independence of Vietnam. A guerrilla movement, the

Vietcong, was established in the South. In 1960, the National Liberation Front, a revolutionary political arm or government in hiding, was established for South Vietnam. The National Liberation Front, the Vietcong, and the regular army of North Vietnam were noted for their integration of women at all levels. As the communists increased their pressure against the South, the United States responded by increasing its support of the southern regime. Under President Dwight D. Eisenhower, several hundred military advisers were sent, some of whom lost their lives in skirmishes, and both military and economic aid increased. Under President John F. Kennedy, support grew, and South Vietnam increasingly became a U.S. client. The United States began to control who was in power in the South; it was implicated, for example, in the assassination of President Ngo Dinh Diem in 1963.

It was under President Lyndon B. Johnson that the United States committed itself irrevocably to a full-scale war in Vietnam. The only official authorization for the war was a congressional resolution passed during a moment of national hysteria following a military engagement involving American ships in the Gulf of Tonkin. Journalists were later able to prove that the Gulf of Tonkin incident had been consciously provoked by the United States in order to manipulate Congress. The military effort that ensued was major, with the number of American troops in Vietnam rising to a peak of 543,000 in 1969. The war pitted conventional armed power against a guerrilla foe that was able to melt into the local population. The United States and its South Vietnamese ally never succeeded in securing the allegiance of the villagers—in winning their "hearts and minds," as the phrase went—and in the end, their effort was doomed.

Because of his failure to bring the war to a successful conclusion, President Johnson declined to run for reelection in 1968 and was replaced in 1969 by Richard Nixon. Nixon was as committed to victory as Johnson had been, but after years of failing to achieve a breakthrough and facing increasing opposition to the war at home, he finally brought American involvement to an end. In 1973, most of the American troops pulled out, leaving the pursuit of the war to the South Vietnamese army. It was unequal to the task; in 1975, the northern armies marched into Saigon (renamed Ho Chi Minh City) as the last remaining American diplomats fled ignominiously by helicopter from the roof of the American embassy.

The Vietnam War left devastation in its wake. In the United States, it was responsible for the disaffection of a generation of young people from the government and for the abandonment of the once promising War on Poverty. More than 57,000 Americans died. Returning veterans found themselves both scorned and ignored for years by many of their compatriots. It was one of the few wars lost by the United States,[7] and although such a chastening experience may ultimately have been constructive, it left severe scars on the self-confidence of the nation. The war brought the morality of the country into question. Millions of people, particularly the youth, could not understand what possible interest the United States had in opposing what they regarded as the Vietnamese people's legitimate aspirations for independence.

In Vietnam, the consequences were much more severe. The loss of human life over the thirty-four years of warfare was staggering, probably in the neighborhood of two million. The economic dislocation was enormous too; formerly a major exporter of food, Vietnam became a food importer, unable to meet its own most basic needs. The scores that were settled in South Vietnam after the northern victory were not pretty. Hundreds of thousands of people who were regarded by the victors as collaborators were deprived of their property, and many were sent to punitive "reeducation" camps. Many people attempted to escape from the new regime, and the world became numbed to the stories of the boat people, some of whom were robbed, maimed, raped, and killed by pirates as they left the country. Meanwhile, rather than devote its energies to the peaceful reconstruction of the country, the Vietnamese leaders continued their military involvement by invading and administering Cambodia. (At the time of the North Vietnamese victory, Cambodia was going through its own excruciating hell, in which close to two million of its own people were killed in a genocidal orgy of purification by its Khmer Rouge faction.) Ho Chi Minh had been a man of enormous principle and vision. His successors, doubtless conditioned by more than a generation of warfare, turned out to be people of narrow views, unable to bring to their people the benefits of peace and independence.

In the 1990s, new Vietnamese leaders withdrew from Cambodia and turned their attention to the reconstruction of their country and the welfare of their own people. They followed the Chinese example, permitting private property, individual entrepreneurship, and markets and courting foreign investment, technology, and aid. The Clinton administration opened diplomatic and commercial relations with Vietnam in return for Vietnamese cooperation in attempting to account for American servicemen missing since the war. Economic growth resumed in the 1990s and continued into the new century, and the standard of living began to rise, although it is still extremely low. The Vietnamese leaders are projecting a rate of economic growth as high as China's.[8] Like the Chinese, however, the Vietnamese authorities have been unwilling to loosen their authoritarian political control.

Algeria

Algeria in North Africa was the scene of another bitter struggle for nationalist self-determination by a colonized people. The Algerian war of independence against France was fought from 1954 until 1961. Algeria had been a territory of France since 1840, when a French army had chased out the last remaining representatives of the Ottoman Empire and systematically conquered the country. France extended its control to neighboring Morocco and Tunisia as well, but only in the form of "protectorates," allowing the local governments to remain. France's relationship to Algeria was different. Incorporated directly as part of the French state, Algeria had representation in the French legislature. Most importantly, France encouraged the settlement of a white population in Algeria in the nineteenth century.

Only half of the settlers were actually French; the other half were poor southern Europeans from other countries, primarily Spain and Italy. Within a couple of generations, however, they had been molded together into a cohesive group, fervid in their patriotism toward France and in their distrust of the Arabs. By the time the war of independence broke out, one million French settlers lived in Algeria, most of whose families had been there for many generations, along with about nine million Arabs.

The white settlers owned most of the fertile land, much of which was used for the production of wine grapes. The process by which the settlers had gained ownership of the land was only partially through the use of military force. The French regime had introduced into Algeria the concept of landownership. Under the Ottoman Empire, different tribal groups had had different sorts of use rights over the land, but they did not own it. The people who tilled the land did not have the authority to transfer or sell it, except in rare circumstances. When the French introduced the foreign concept of ownership, it became possible for the settlers to acquire legal title to the land and to expropriate it from the people who had used it for centuries.

The coming of the Europeans transformed the Arab population from self-sufficiency into impoverishment. People who had once worked their own land were reduced to the status of wage laborers in a country where labor was plentiful and therefore poorly paid. Land that had once produced food to feed the local population now produced wine to delight the palates of the metropolitan French. Several revolts in the nineteenth century protested this state of affairs but failed, and no revolts occurred in the first half of the twentieth century.

Pressure for change was building, however. Hundreds of thousands of Algerians migrated to France for jobs, where they were exposed to the liberating ideas that were the legacy of the French Revolution. At home, the Algerian people were turning increasingly to Islam as a belief system that reinforced their identity and provided a form of at least symbolic resistance. The French failed to grasp the meaning of these developments, in large measure because they were used to dealing with the small minority of Algerians who did own land, wielded some authority, and professed allegiance to the French. This layer of bourgeois Algerians served to mask the growing disaffection of the majority of the people.

The fate of Algeria was sealed by events external to it. The Second World War saw the defeat of France; although the free French resisted and ultimately triumphed, the tragedy of the war sapped both their physical strength and their morale. For the Algerians, the spectacle of a defeated France gave hope that the colonizer was not all-powerful. Algerians served in the French army during the war, gaining experience and self-confidence. In the immediate postwar years, their leaders argued for concessions but were unsuccessful. The contradictions of colonial rule were becoming untenable.

The French refusal to grant concessions was based on two enormous realities. First, Algeria was the only French colony where there was significant French settlement. The mother country was willing to grant independence to its other colonies in North and West Africa but was not willing to abandon the white settlers to Arab rule. Second, after the world war, the French army had been in continuous action in Indochina, where it had ultimately been humiliated by its former subjects. Upon losing the battle of Dien Bien Phu in 1954, the French army retreated from Vietnam, and it was determined not to suffer another defeat. In Algeria, the army assigned itself an aggressive role that was extraordinary for a Western democratic country, insofar as the army was to a large extent independent of its own national government.

The Algerian revolt broke out in 1954 in the mountainous eastern region of the country. It spread two years later to the cities, in particular to the Casbah section of Algiers. It was a war of rural guerrilla action and urban terrorism directed by the Front de Liberation National (FLN), which was opposed by massive police and military action. Both sides used torture as a weapon.

From a military point of view, the French were successful. They destroyed the urban resistance in 1957 and largely succeeded in suppressing the rural movements. The Algerians were forced to develop a military capacity outside the borders of Algeria, mostly in Tunisia, while their internal forces were decimated. Although defeated in the field, however, the Algerian military forces had done their damage politically.

The French government and people were losing the willpower for continuous military engagements. They were more interested in rebuilding France economically and joining in the postwar European prosperity.

The settlers and the army found themselves fighting a rearguard action on the political front. Their commitment to a French Algeria brought about the downfall of the French government in 1958 and the ascendancy of wartime hero General Charles de Gaulle as president, but even this could not save them. Within two years, de Gaulle had decided to abandon Algeria in return for the promise of peace. The settlers turned in rage against the French government, aided and abetted by the army. The fury against de Gaulle, whom they had thought to be their savior, was fierce. The president survived an assassination attempt, and most of the army in Algeria mutinied in 1961. The mutiny was put down, and the settlers were abandoned. Algeria became an independent country in 1961, although it remained closely tied to France for aid and technology. Most of the settlers were forced out.

The ideologies lying behind the Algerian war of independence were complex. They included a resurgence of religious commitment, as well as strains of socialism, even communism. What united the Algerians, though, was nationalism—a love of their country and a grim determination to recover the lands and the dignity of which they had been robbed.

At independence, Algeria was left destitute as the French pulled out. By one estimate, the country had fewer than a dozen trained typists, for example, and the prospect of running a bureaucracy seemed hopeless. The Algerians persevered, however, and with some luck and quite a bit of support from France, they developed a sustainable economy and raised the people's standard of living fairly regularly in the early decades after independence. Algeria took the leadership in organizing the Group of Seventy-seven, a coalition of third-world countries that struggled for a "new international economic order" in the 1970s.

After several decades of fairly smooth development, however, Algeria hit a series of severe economic and political roadblocks. The economy stagnated, and average personal incomes actually fell during the 1980s and 1990s. Large-scale urban rioting erupted in 1988, with loss of life running into the thousands. The FLN lost much of its legitimacy among the people because of its economic failures and its corruption. Many Algerians transferred their allegiance to a fundamentalist Muslim party, the Islamic Salvation Front (FIS). The FIS held that Algeria's problems resulted from a lack of piety; its slogan was "to vote against the FIS is to vote against God."

The government sought to resolve the country's divisions by turning toward democracy and free elections. In 1991, however, the fundamentalist FIS won almost half the vote in the first round of national elections and stood poised to control the country when the final round was held. Faced with the prospect of a theocratic state, the government canceled the elections, banned the FIS, jailed most of its leaders, and dissolved the regional councils that were under its control. Shortly thereafter, civil disorder exploded. In response, the army overthrew the government and imposed its own control. The ensuing civil war was marked by extraordinary brutality on both sides. By one estimate, 100,000 people were killed during the decade of the 1990s. The military regime adopted an antidemocratic, repressive constitution in 1996 and won the succeeding elections. The elections have been far from true expressions of Algerians' opinions, however, because the FIS has boycotted them.

For a period, therefore, Algeria seemed to represent a distinctly positive aftermath to a revolutionary, nationalist independence movement. In recent years, however, the very basis of the Algerian state has been called into question. The possibility of a democratic society has been almost eliminated as two authoritarian systems—one military and one fundamentalist—vie for control.[9]

Muslim and Jewish Nationalism

The Algerian revolution was connected to the nationalist reawakening of the entire Arab world. The Arabic-speaking regions of North Africa and the Middle East had been a part of the sprawling Ottoman Empire, which collapsed slowly in the nineteenth century as it was confronted by the European empires. The French, British, and Italians established colonies or protectorates over the Arab world in the twentieth century, then relinquished control to independent nation-states. More than twenty countries emerged, sharing among them the Muslim faith and the Arabic tongue.

For the most part, the new Arab states were governed as autocracies; although they sometimes held elections, they seldom tolerated legitimate opposition movements. The people gradually developed national identities, but these always had to compete with supranational identities—of being Muslim and Arab. It seems curious, both to outside observers and to Arabs, that so many countries exist, because the cultures are so similar. Many Arabs actually reject the idea of separate countries and proclaim instead an "Arab nation." Numerous attempts have been made to break down the national boundaries and form larger and more powerful nations, but they have always foundered, sometimes on the competitive ambitions of the countries' rulers, sometimes on real cultural differences.

What aroused Arab nationalism more than anything was the creation of a Jewish state, Israel, in Palestine. Although foreign control
over the Arab states is a phenomenon of the past, Arabs still view the
state of Israel as an imperialist vestige, a dagger aimed at their heart.

Inspired by the ideology of Zionism (which called for Jews
throughout the world to rebuild a nation-state in their holy land),
European Jews had been migrating to Palestine since the late nineteenth century, when the area was still administered by the Ottoman
Turks. The British took control of Palestine during the First World
War and administered it as a League of Nations mandate after 1922.
They were largely responsible for the conflict that ensued, for they
promised the area twice during the First World War: to the Arabs and
also, by the 1917 Balfour Declaration, to the Zionists as a "Jewish
homeland." In the 1920s and 1930s, the British tried to restrict Jewish immigration in order to preserve the ascendancy of Arabs in the
region, but the immigration continued as Jews fled an increasingly
dangerous Europe. With the Second World War came the Holocaust,
the murder of six million Jews. Survivors fled to Palestine in increasing numbers both during and after the war, seeking a homeland in
which they could be safe from virulent anti-Semitism. The British
were hardly encouraging, but neither did they prevent the ingathering.
They attempted to work out an agreement between the Arabs and the
Jews; when that failed, they turned the problem over to the United
Nations. In 1947, the United Nations voted for a geographical partition of the area; on the basis of that vote, the British withdrew in
1948. The United Nations vote hardly resolved matters. As the British
withdrew, the Jews pronounced the founding of the republic of Israel
and the Arab armies invaded. By the end of the war, the Israelis had
doubled the territory voted them by the United Nations, and half a
million Palestinian refugees had fled the country. More than half a
century of Arab-Israeli enmity, tension, and warfare followed.

After Israeli independence, four more Arab-Israeli wars were
fought, in 1956, 1967, 1973, and 1982. The 1956 war occurred when
the British withdrew from the Suez Canal Zone; President Nasser of
Egypt moved to nationalize the canal and exclude Israeli shipping
from it. The Egyptians prevailed when the United States refused to
support the intervention of Britain, France, and Israel. In 1967, there
was a quick six-day war when the Egyptians closed the Gulf of
'Aqaba; along with their refusal to let the Israelis use the Suez Canal,
this would have cut off all Israeli commerce to the east, so the Israelis
retaliated. They scored a striking victory, taking over the West Bank
of the Jordan River and the eastern part of Jerusalem from Jordan, the
Golan Heights from Syria, and the Gaza Strip and the Sinai Peninsula

from Egypt. Their geographical expansion brought another million Arabs under Israeli rule. Although the Israelis did not incorporate the new areas directly into their state, they did encourage a number of Jewish settlements in the occupied territories, with the consequence that the return of the land to Arab authority would be much more difficult in the future. On the Jewish holy day of Yom Kippur in 1973, the Egyptian and Syrian armies attacked Israel. The fighting was much lengthier than in 1967, but again the Israelis prevailed, reoccupying the Golan Heights and crossing to the west bank of the Suez Canal. It was at the time of the 1973 war that the Arab countries instituted a boycott of oil sales to the United States—to punish it for its support of Israel—and then, a few months later, converted the boycott into a substantial increase in the price of oil.

After the 1973 war, President Anwar Sadat of Egypt made peace with Israel, to the consternation of much of the rest of the Arab population. Sadat and Israeli President Menachem Begin signed the Camp David Accords in Washington in 1979 to signify the end of thirty years of hostility. Israel agreed to withdraw from the Sinai, and Egypt agreed to recognize Israel and to permit Israeli shipping through the Suez Canal.

The 1982 war occurred when Israel invaded Lebanon to close down refugee camps from which the Palestine Liberation Organization (PLO) had been attacking Israel and to try to create some sort of orderly and friendly government in a country that had collapsed into anarchy. The Lebanese conflict proved to be too much for even the Israelis, and they eventually withdrew without accomplishing their objectives.

In the 1991 Persian Gulf War, Israel was attacked by Iraqi missiles. Under pressure from the United States not to escalate the conflict, it did not retaliate.

Throughout the existence of their country, therefore, the Israelis have never known the peace they had hoped to find when fleeing the anti-Semitism of Europe. They have developed into a military state with enormous weapons capability; they have one of the world's strongest arsenals and greater military strength than all their neighbors combined. They also have a reputation for swift, precise action, a reputation which was damaged in the 1982 incursion into Lebanon, when they permitted a Lebanese Christian militia to massacre civilian residents of a PLO refugee camp. Their military reputation was further damaged during the *intifada,* the uprising of Arab youth in the late 1980s in Israel, and again in armed conflicts, including suicide bombings by Palestinians, that began in 2000. The Israeli army was unable to suppress the attacks but responded with ferocity.

Arrayed against Israel throughout this period has been a shifting coalition of Arab nationalists. At the heart of the resistance are the Palestinian people, living both in the occupied territories of the West Bank and Gaza, and also in neighboring countries, where they have not been completely absorbed into the local populations. The Palestinians are generally a well-educated, sophisticated, and articulate people whose determination to secure a homeland for themselves has only grown in intensity.

The Arab countries surrounding Israel—Egypt, Lebanon, Syria, and Jordan—all have opposed the Jewish state but have never been able to join forces in a coherent way to achieve their ends. The Egyptians led several wars against the Israelis but then made peace so that their resources could be used to advance the welfare of their own people rather than be squandered in war. The Lebanese were the least aggressive of Israel's neighbors until their country collapsed as an administrative unit in 1975; since then, Lebanon has been the scene of almost continuous warfare and jockeying for power. The Syrians, under a militant government, have maintained their hostility against Israel and are particularly committed to the return of their territory on the Golan Heights.

Until the 1990s, the conflict seemed intractable. The Camp David Accords between Egypt and Israel stood alone and did not lead to a more general easing of tensions in the region. A glimmer of hope arose in the 1990s, however. Multilateral negotiations began among the Israelis, the Palestinians, and the neighboring Arab countries, sponsored initially by the United States and the Soviet Union. A new Israeli government, led by the Labor Party, was open for the first time to the possibility of ceding land for a Palestinian "state" that would have at least some of the attributes of sovereignty, provided that this concession would lead to a plausible peace treaty. The end of the cold war brought added pressure on the Arabs to pursue peace, because they could no longer count on Soviet support.

In this new atmosphere, the Israelis agreed to peace plans with the PLO in 1993 and with Jordan in 1994. Both accords resulted from secret and sometimes dramatic negotiations; both were announced on the White House lawn, with President Bill Clinton presiding. Israel granted a measure of autonomy to the Palestinians in the Gaza Strip and the West Bank and agreed to continue negotiations in good faith with the PLO. Under the terms of a 1995 agreement with the PLO, Israel agreed to withdraw from seven Palestinian cities in the West Bank. The most contentious case was in the city of Hebron, where the Israelis finally agreed to hand over control in 1997. In return for agreeing to peace with Israel, Jordan obtained economic concessions from the United States, including substantial debt relief. Although the terms of the agreements with Jordan and the PLO were limited and tentative, they seemed to point the way to a new era of peace.

In the beginning of the new century, however, the hopes for peace were largely dashed. Several negotiations between the Israelis and the Palestinians ended in failure. Political divisions on both sides made the negotiations extremely difficult; it became clear that many influential factions preferred a state of near-war to the concessions in which they would have to acquiesce if real peace were to be achieved. Once the Palestinians, led by Yasir Arafat, rejected a peace proposal offered by Israel's Labor government, the Israeli electorate rejected that government and installed a right-wing Likud government led by Ariel Sharon, who appeared to be much more interested in military retaliation than in serious peace negotiations. The level of violence escalated on both sides, and the prospect of peace became ever more distant.

Islamic Fundamentalism

Rage against the West—and particularly against the United States—has intensified in many Arab countries, as well as in some non-Arab Muslim areas. It finds its greatest resonance among fundamentalist Islamic groups, which, like fundamentalist sects in most other major religions, take an absolutist view of the truth of their sacred texts, reject the distinction between civil and religious life, and see people who do not share their view of the truth as the embodiment of evil. Western Europe and the United States have been targeted as enemies of the fundamentalist Islamists for a complex and varying set of reasons, including their support of Israel, their support of Arab rulers seen to be corrupt and insufficiently respectful of Islamic law, and the power of their popular culture and mores to disrupt traditional Muslim ways.

Out of this rage has come the phenomenon of modern, high-technology terrorism, the most spectacular example of which was the use of four hijacked commercial airplanes to attack and destroy prominent targets on the east coast of the United States on September 11, 2001. Recent Islamic terrorism—in many parts of the world—has led to the destruction of thousands of innocent lives and severe economic losses, and to the reconfiguration of the foreign policy of the western nations (to be described in Chapter 7). Fundamentalism has become a major force in the Muslim world, leading not just to terrorism but also to completely reconfigured nation states. The role of fundamentalism in Algeria was described above; two other countries in which it has had enormous impact are Iran and Afghanistan.

In Iran, the clash between Muslim fundamentalism and western modernization led to a radical revolution. Iran has a long history of foreign domination and of resistance to that domination. After the Second World War, the Shah of Iran, supported by Britain and the United States, overthrew a reform parliament that was threatening to nationalize the country's oil industry and thereafter ruled autocratically with the endorsement of the West. He supported the modernization of the country and the introduction of new business enterprises, as well as the growth of a westernized middle class. He was also ruthlessly dictatorial, however, ruling with the support of a brutal secret police and making massive use of torture and execution.

The opposition to the shah's regime was motivated in part by revulsion at his use of state terror but more basically by fundamentalist Islamic resistance to the westernization of popular culture. Riots and strikes led to the overthrow of the shah in 1979 and the assumption of power by a clerical hierarchy, headed by the fierce figure of the Ayatollah Khomeini. Almost in a moment, the trappings of western culture disappeared from Iranian life. Women covered their heads with the veil and were restricted from public life. Alcohol, western dress for women, mixed bathing, the western press, western music, and many other forms of foreign culture were banned. Justice was administered by stern Islamic courts. Much of the fury of the revolution was directed against the United States, which had supported the shah and was seen to be the embodiment of evil. The revolutionaries held members of the American embassy hostage. The new regime soon found itself in an eight-year war with its Arab neighbor Iraq, a war marked by the slogans of righteousness and the seemingly endless slaughter of the young. With the end of the war against Iraq and the death of the ayatollah, the Iranian authorities permitted some opposition voices and moderated their fierceness to a certain degree but did not reverse it.

Islamic fundamentalism changed Afghanistan as well. Afghanistan was destabilized by a Soviet military occupation that was followed by years of guerrilla warfare. The withdrawal of the Soviet troops in the early 1990s led to an all-out civil war between different factions in the country. In 1996, the fundamentalist Taliban movement seized control of the country and imposed a ferocious new regime. It closed schools for girls; forbade women, even teachers, to work outside the house; banned card playing and all music except religious music; and in other ways attempted to return the country to an ancient and repressive set of customs. The Taliban provided a haven to the Quaida terrorist network, led by Osama Bin Laden, and this proved its downfall. When the Taliban refused to hand over the terrorist leaders after the attacks against the United States on September 11, 2001, the United

States invaded and deposed the regime. Many Afghanis welcomed the invasion as a liberation, but many others did not, because of their commitment to Islamic fundamentalism.

Sub-Saharan Africa

Independence came to most of sub-Saharan Africa in a dazzling moment—in just a few short years surrounding 1960—and was anticipated by virtually no one. Africa had been partitioned almost overnight in the late nineteenth century; independence came to the continent in an even shorter period. Before 1957, only Liberia and Ethiopia were independent countries, but after 1964, almost all of Africa except for the southern region was composed of autonomous states. By 1994, even the Republic of South Africa was governed by its black majority.

The first African country to attain its independence, in 1957, was the Gold Coast, which took the name of an ancient African kingdom, Ghana. Thereafter, as the colonialists realized that the nationalist movements could not be defeated permanently, they made haste to withdraw from most of their possessions.

There were exceptions. Some white settlers were loath to give up political control to the Africans. As a consequence, the struggles for independence in Kenya and later in Zimbabwe (formerly Southern Rhodesia) were more protracted and difficult than they were in the areas that had simply been administered by the imperialists, without settlement. In addition, the most backward of the European imperial powers, Portugal, was untouched by the arguments for independence that swayed the other imperialists; it held on to its two principal territories, Angola and Mozambique, until 1975.

Nowhere has the promise of independence been more cruelly betrayed than in Africa. In most countries, any semblance of democracy disappeared, and one-party states became the norm for decades. Only in the mid-1990s did a significant number of African countries turn to democracy. Many are still controlled by military dictators, however. Some of the world's worst human rights abuses occurred in Uganda, principally but not exclusively under the regime of Idi Amin. The continent's most creative social programs, in Tanzania under the leadership of Julius Nyerere, did little to rescue that country from underdevelopment. The economic giant of black Africa, Nigeria, prospered in the 1970s during the world oil boom but then collapsed in the 1980s as a consequence of the oil bust. In the 1990s it was ruled by a military dictatorship that was particularly scornful of its people's aspirations. Hundreds of thousands of people have starved in the vast deserts of the north. Twenty percent of the adults live with HIV, and between three and four million people die each year as a result of AIDS-related diseases. Africa has enjoyed no sustained economic growth, and taken as a whole, the continent is scarcely better off—perhaps worse off—than it was at independence.

The greatest tragedy of Africa was for decades in the Republic of South Africa, where a white minority society became entrenched and successfully resisted whatever nationalist movements were arrayed against it. Dutch settlers had arrived at the Cape of Good Hope as early as 1652. Sternly Protestant, they mixed over the years with other Protestant settlers, most notably the French Huguenots, to form a people who eventually called themselves Afrikaners. Afrikaner mythology includes the claim that whites preceded black Africans into the southern tip of the continent, but this position cannot be reconciled with the fact that the Dutch settlers fought wars against African tribes and enslaved Africans on their farms. In 1814, the British annexed the colony as part of the settlement of the Napoleonic Wars. Eventually, the Dutch escaped what they regarded as oppressive British rule in their "Great Trek" to the interior, where they established the two independent republics of Orange Free State and Transvaal. When diamonds were discovered in Orange Free State and gold in Transvaal at the end of the nineteenth century, the British moved to annex the two republics. The Dutch, now called in some contexts Boers, resisted, and the Boer War (1899–1902) resulted. The British won the Boer War but lost the peace. The British granted full independence to the Union of South Africa. All whites, both Boer and British, were given the vote; the Africans, the Indians (who were descendants of migrants from India), and the mixed-race "coloreds" were given no consideration at all. Over the course of the twentieth century, the right-wing, religiously fundamentalist Afrikaners gradually gained power over the somewhat (but not remarkably) more liberal British.

Throughout the twentieth century in South Africa, black nationalist movements attempted to challenge the minority rule of the whites, but the principal result was to produce a long chain of martyrs and to entrench even further the white minority. The Afrikaner Nationalist Party came to power in 1948 and erected the structure of apartheid, or separateness of the races. The doctrine of apartheid was based on the pretense that the races lived separately in South Africa and that the blacks were actually foreigners in the country. In fact, however, the races have never been separate. Even most of the early Afrikaner farms used black labor, and the country's advanced industrial economy has long been completely dependent on the labor of Africans. The wealth of the white minority depended on the exploitation of black labor in the gold mines and in the factories; it was impossible for the two races to be "apart." Nevertheless, apartheid became the system of control that allowed the exploitation to continue. Independent "homelands" were established (in barren areas), and the black population was given "citizenship" in these homelands, the result being that the black labor force could be treated as an alien population, without civil or political rights.

One of the first leaders of the South African resistance was Mohandas Gandhi, who developed his nonviolent philosophy while working among South Africa's Indian population. Generations of black leaders fought the white oppression; some of the great names of recent history are Robert Sobukwe, Steven Biko, Archbishop Desmond Tutu, and Nelson Mandela. As the nationalist movements grew stronger and as the outside world paid increasing attention to the worst remaining case of colonial oppression, the white South Africans seemed to turn increasingly inward, developing their economic strength and their military arsenal while forming alliances with arms merchants and right-wing regimes around the world.

Although the military power of the government was unassailable, its commitment to white supremacy eventually collapsed—because of international political and economic pressure, because of black resistance, and also because of growing dissent among the whites themselves. In the early 1990s, South Africa embarked on a new course, leading to black majority government. In 1990, it released Nelson Mandela, the country's most famous political prisoner. It rescinded many apartheid laws, granted legitimacy to outlawed nationalist movements, and began negotiations with representatives of those movements to create a new constitution. The talks eventually resulted in a democratic constitution. In 1994, the African National Congress won the country's first open election, and Mandela assumed the presidency. The new South Africa was committed to freedom, democracy, and human rights. The challenge facing it was enormous: to form an equitable, nonracial society in a country whose very name had been a definition of racism and exploitation for generations, and to do so on a continent beset by the worst misfortunes of the third world. As a way of helping to mend the state of enmity, the South Africans set up a "truth and reconciliation commission" to identify the worst crimes of the apartheid era and, in many cases, to grant amnesty to those who admitted to the crimes. Economic development and housing for the African majority were pushed as high priorities, but the gap in living standards between rich and poor remains immense.

While South Africa was moving in the 1990s into a future that seemed more promising than anything that could have been foretold a few years earlier, other parts of Africa were suffering from previously unimagined agonies. The tragedy in tiny Rwanda was staggering. Rwanda is a former Belgian colony populated by two ethnic groups, the Hutus and the Tutsis. The Belgians did nothing to reconcile the two groups. They initially favored the Tutsis, then switched their allegiance to the more numerous Hutus before independence. A civil war between 1959 and 1963 led to the massacre of 100,000 Tutsis, the forced exile of 200,000 Tutsis to Uganda, and the establishment of a Hutu-dominated state. Tutsi resistance, under a military organization called the Rwandan Patriotic Front (RPF), continued from that time until 1994. By early 1994, negotiations seemed to have produced a tentative agreement under which the two groups would share power and the Tutsis living outside the country would be allowed to return.

In the spring of 1994, however, following the death of President Habyarimana in an airplane crash, extremist Hutus led their people in an orgy of violence against both Tutsis and moderate Hutus. The exact number of dead will never be known, but the estimates range from 500,000 to one million, mostly Tutsis, who were slaughtered over a ten-week period by their previous friends and neighbors. It was not a military operation but a frenzy of civilian violence, fueled by the Hutu-controlled radio, which urged more killing. "When you kill the rat do not let the pregnant one escape," one broadcast said. "We made the mistake thirty years ago of letting them flee into exile, this time none will escape."[10]

The Tutsi RPF was eventually victorious militarily, defeating the government army. In victory it called for reconciliation: it included moderate Hutus in its new government and promised to protect the Hutu people from retaliation. The same Hutus who had urged the slaughter now terrified their people into believing that the new government was bent on revenge. As many as two million Hutu refugees fled for their lives into neighboring countries, particularly Zaire, but also Uganda and Tanzania. Included among them were many perpetrators of the slaughter, indistinguishable to outsiders from the many others who were innocent. Conditions in the refugee camps were horrible, in spite of efforts by the American military, other countries, and nongovernmental organizations to alleviate the suffering and dying. Judicial processes have been set up within Rwanda to try the perpetrators, but the resources are completely inadequate in comparison with the number of people charged, and it is unlikely that anything resembling real justice will ever be achieved.

Zaire, one of Africa's largest countries, was completely destabilized by the Rwandan catastrophe. Previously known as the Belgian Congo, Zaire had been the victim of Europe's most brutal imperialism at the turn of the century under the personal rule of Belgian King

Leopold. For three decades, from the 1960s to the 1990s, it was headed by dictator Mobutu Sese Seko, who pillaged the country's wealth and, supported by the West as a bulwark against communism, ruled by fear. Mobutu supported the Hutus stranded in the refugee camps following the Rwandan conflict and took action against the Tutsi minority living in the eastern region of the country. In retaliation, a revolutionary alliance—dominated by Tutsis, supported by several of the surrounding countries, and led by an experienced rebel, Laurent Kabila—swept from east to west across the country, routing Zaire's army, overthrowing the government, driving the destitute Hutu refugees before them, and killing many. It was a revenge of biblical proportions: those who had slaughtered were destroyed, and with them their innocent kinsfolk. When he took over the capital of Kinshasa in May 1997, Kabila restored the country's former name of Congo. He could not, however, restore peace. The civil war continued, with Rwanda switching sides and supporting Kabila's opponents. In 2001, Kabila was assassinated. In spite of several peace conferences, and declarations of peace, the violence continued, much of it perpetrated by traditional warriors known as Mai Mai.

The most hopeful recent development in sub-Saharan Africa is the turn to democracy. The trend began in 1990, when Benin became the first African country to reject dictatorship and move to multiparty elections. By the early twenty-first century, most countries were holding regular elections. Some of the elections—for example, in Zimbabwe—were shams, in which the results cannot be held to represent the views of the people. Many of the elections, however, were honest and straightforward, often resulting in changes of government. In Kenya in 2002, the party that had governed since independence was soundly defeated in a fair election and ceded power peacefully. In one of the poorest African countries, Mali, the 2001 election was won by an opposition party. In response, the government did not mobilize the army, as it once might have; instead, it held a news conference in the capital city's convention center and conceded defeat. The event, which would have been an ordinary one in many countries, was momentous for Mali.[11] Democracy holds hope for the future, but to date the democratic regimes in Africa have been no more successful than their predecessors in bringing positive social change and economic development to their people.

Latin America

The modern history of Latin America has been different from that of Asia, Africa, and the Middle East, because almost all of Latin America has been independent since about 1820. The Spanish and Portuguese withdrew from their American empires just after the Napoleonic Wars, and they were not permitted to return. The legal independence of the Latin American countries did not imply true autonomy, however. In the nineteenth century, the British established strong trading relationships with most of the Latin American countries. To ensure the stability of their trade and also of their investments, the British developed commercial alliances with the ruling groups in most of the countries; those groups in turn kept the peace at home so that their economic connections with the outside world could continue to prosper.

In the twentieth century, the British role in Latin America was gradually taken over by the United States, as the former's relative power in the world faded and the latter's increased. The Americans maintained alliances with the ruling groups, which in turn promoted tranquillity in the local markets. The role of the United States was not always predictable; although the Americans preferred to exercise their hegemony by peaceful economic means, they were less reluctant than the British had been to resolve conflicts by the use of armed force. From the Mexican War of 1846, when the United States annexed half the territory of Mexico (securing Texas, which had previously asserted its independence, and acquiring what became the states of New Mexico, Arizona, Colorado, Utah, Nevada, and California), to the support of the contras in Nicaragua, the backing of the military government in El Salvador, the invasions of Grenada and Panama, and the quasi-invasion of Haiti, the United States has regularly been willing to make use of its military capability in Central and South America. It did not establish formal colonies in Latin America, however. Even when the United States separated Cuba from Spanish control in the war of 1898, it did not take Spain's place—rather, it allowed Cuba to be nominally independent, under American tutelage. In sum, Latin America was subjected to informal, neocolonial domination by the United States but seldom to formal control.

As a consequence, the social struggles within Latin America have had a different cast from those in the rest of the third world. The struggles have generally been internal wars in which factions within each country have sought to defeat their own ruling classes. Of course, the United States was seldom far from the minds of Latin American rebels in the twentieth century, because in most cases the ruling elites were supported by the United States. Until recently, the United States consistently supplied arms and economic assistance to right-wing regimes in Latin America, seeing them as a bulwark against communism. But the relationship between social movements and U.S. domination has been an indirect one.

Many of these themes are illustrated by the history of the Mexican revolution, which took place between 1910 and 1920. The proximate target of the Mexican revolution was the regime of General Porfirio Díaz, who had ruled the country since 1875. Díaz was a successful national entrepreneur who brought into the country huge amounts of British and American capital to develop Mexico's resources. A railway network was built across the country, mines were opened, and manufacturing industries were established. The Mexican peasants, both Indian and mestizo, lost access to the land they had tilled for generations. The hacienda system of huge commercial landholdings increasingly reduced the peasantry to the status of semifree peonage. The peasant rebellion was led by Emiliano Zapata in the south-central region of the country and by Pancho Villa in the north. Its rallying cry was "land and liberty." The peasant rebellions were successful militarily; they drove Díaz from his seat of power, and the rebels occupied the capital of Mexico City. They lacked a coherent political strategy, however, and were not able to maintain control of the country. Control passed through many hands in the second decade of the century, and the cause of the peasants slipped from center place. The 1917 constitution expropriated the oil fields from their U.S. investors and authorized the redistribution of land to the peasants. Little land reform was actually accomplished, however, until the presidential term of Lázaro Cárdenas in the 1930s.

Had Mexico actually been colonized by Britain or the United States, the goal of the revolution would have been clearer—to expel the colonizer and establish an independent nation acting on behalf of all its people. Because the United States was in the background, however, the goals of the revolution were less obvious. It was not a war of independence. Neither was it a definitive class war, as the Russian Revolution of 1917 would be. In some ways, it was the last of the pre–twentieth-century revolutions, closest in spirit to the French Revolution of a century and a half earlier—a revolution fought against a ruler perceived to be oppressive and for the rather abstract principles of liberty, but without a vision of completely restructuring the social system of the country.

The revolution is certainly the most important event in Mexican history. Despite some land reform, however, the peasantry is still largely excluded from landownership, and the distribution of income is unevenly skewed. Mexico's failure to solve its social problems was shown dramatically by the 1994 revolt of the Zapatistas, an Indian movement in the southern border state of Chiapas, led by a secretive and eloquent figure, Subcommandante Marcos. The Zapatistas challenged both the inequitable social system that exploited the Indians and the undemocratic political control of the country by the Party of Revolutionary Institutions (PRI). The Zapatista revolt was followed by the assassination of the PRI candidate for president in 1994 and then, after the election, by an economic crisis marked by the collapse of the value of both the peso and the stock market.

From the time of the revolution until quite recently, Mexico was for all practical purposes a one-party state, with politics controlled from the top down. The PRI candidates were challenged in the presidential elections of 1988 and 1994, but unsuccessfully. In 2000, however, opposition candidate Vicente Fox defeated the PRI candidate, and a new era of multiparty democracy seemed to be in place. Perhaps, after almost a century, the democracy promised by the revolution had taken hold.

The protagonist of Carlos Fuentes's great novel *The Death of Artemio Cruz* was born to poverty in central Mexico in 1889. He fought in the revolution and was captured. While in captivity, he managed to escape execution through the betrayal of a fellow prisoner, a young lawyer who was the son of a rich landowner, or *hacendado*. After the revolution, he insinuated himself into the good graces of the lawyer's father, married the lawyer's sister, and eventually took over the hacienda. A life of increasing power and manipulation followed, in which Cruz scorned any form of reciprocal love and instead pursued authority and wealth. He colluded with U.S. investors, exploiting them for his own benefit; he opened doors to Mexican resources for them to exploit. That is, he acted as the privileged go-between for the neocolonialists, just as Porfirio Díaz and his associates had before the revolution. It is a novel of the betrayal of the revolution, a plaintive, compelling reflection on the fact that the revolution changed the names and faces of the exploiters but not the exploitation.

Still, the Mexican revolution was important; more than any other event, it created the national myths by which Mexicans of today define themselves. Harriet de Onis wrote:

> During the nineteenth century the literature and art of Mexico were, for the most part, refined, sophisticated, very European. But out of the Revolution there came a new art, centering about "the underdogs"—mestizos, Indians—their problems, their aspirations, represented by the painting of artists like Diego Rivera, Orozco, Siqueiros, and the literature of the Revolution and post Revolution. . . . At the same time the mother lode of the folk revealed itself in the songs and ballads in which the people wrote their own history of the Revolution, celebrating its heroes, narrating its triumphs and vicissitudes.

When the Revolution was over, Mexico had become fused into a homogeneous whole.[12]

Mexicans have an acute sense of their nationality, of their culture, and of being both an oppressed and a revolutionary people. Living next to the colossus of the north, they can never forget their vulnerability. "Alas, poor Mexico," Porfirio Díaz may have said, "so far from God, so close to the United States." The revolution, no matter how thoroughly its aims of land and liberty for the peasants have been betrayed, remains the moment of national pride.

To the south of Mexico, in the small Central American country of Nicaragua, the Sandinista revolutionaries fought for more than a decade. In 1990, they lost in a free election to a coalition of opposition parties.

Nicaragua's was a classic revolution in the sense that it was fought on behalf of the poor people of the country against an oppressive ruling class and its military arm, the national guard. It received aid from the Soviet Union; consequently, the U.S. government tried to portray Nicaragua as a beachhead for Soviet expansionism in the Western Hemisphere, but the preponderance of the evidence is that it was a profoundly nationalist movement and, as such, refused to be put into a subordinate role by the Soviets. It was certainly an anti-American revolution, which is hardly surprising in view of the decades of American occupation of the country and the unwavering support of successive U.S. governments for the dictators who ruled Nicaragua during most of the twentieth century. It was a Christian revolution, based on the religious faith of the people and the liberation theology of many of the clergy.

U.S. involvement in Nicaragua began early in the twentieth century; President William Howard Taft sent military forces in 1909 to depose a nationalist movement. Nationalist rebellion continued, however, and the United States sent marines into the country in 1912 to "restore order," that is, to ensure the stability of a friendly Conservative government.

The marines stayed in Nicaragua from 1912 to 1933, with one temporary withdrawal in 1925–26. During this period of occupation, the United States armed and trained the Nicaraguan national guard, expecting it to be a military force that would create stability in the country and support American interests. During the American occupation, a guerrilla force under the leadership of Augusto César Sandino achieved considerable success, organizing peasants and workers and harassing the government troops.

When the marines left in 1933, power was gradually transferred to Anastasio Somoza García, the commander of the national guard.

One of his first acts was to execute Sandino, in spite of a promise he had made to protect Sandino's life. Somoza and his two sons maintained personal dictatorial rule in Nicaragua for more than forty years until the 1979 revolution drove them out. Anastasio Somoza was assassinated in 1956. His son Luis became president and ruled until 1963. After a short period of rule by puppets, Luis's brother Anastasio became president in 1967. The Somoza family ruled by the force of military power. They had no concern for the welfare of the Nicaraguan people; their style of government could best be described as rule by looting. They amassed extraordinary wealth while living conditions worsened throughout the country.

Until their last few years, the Somozas enjoyed the enthusiastic support of successive U.S. governments. The family was skilled at maintaining this support. They had all been educated in the United States; they were fluent in the American idiom and able to manipulate their benefactors with ease. They were responsive to changing currents in American thought. When President Kennedy instituted the Alliance for Progress, for example, Luis Somoza adopted some of the trappings of democracy. When the Kennedy era was over, however, Anastasio Somoza made little attempt to hide his personal and brutal control. In his last years, Anastasio Somoza finally lost the support of President Jimmy Carter's government over the issue of human rights abuses.

The Sandinista insurgency began in 1961 and gradually gained strength over the next two decades. The event that triggered the final war of liberation was the government's murder, in January 1978, of the editor of the newspaper *La Prensa,* Pedro Joaquín Chamorro. The Sandinista army engaged the national guard and finally forced Somoza out of the country in 1979, and the United States offered refuge. The conflict resulted in 50,000 deaths, or 2 percent of the Nicaraguan population.[13]

The Sandinistas, led by President Daniel Ortega, were engaged in continuous warfare after 1981. The opposition contras received financial support from the United States, and their leadership was selected and trained by the Americans. Although the contras harassed and attacked the new government and its forces, they did not have any permanent successes; they were not able to exert secure control over any areas of the country. Nevertheless, they were strong enough to divert the resources of the new government away from the urgent tasks of economic development. The U.S. Congress grew increasingly weary of supporting the contras, and in 1988, it declined to authorize additional funding. Meanwhile, a peace plan was devised by the Central American countries, under the leadership of Costa Rican President Oscar Arias Sánchez (and with the opposition of the U.S. government, which seemed to prefer a military solution).

The controversies surrounding the Nicaraguan revolution were extraordinary. The right-wing American opponents of the revolution portrayed it as dictatorial and under the thumb of the Soviets. Nicaragua became one of the two or three chief foreign policy obsessions of President Ronald Reagan. In 1985, one of his speeches on the subject began:

> The Sandinista dictatorship has taken absolute control of the government and the armed forces. It is a communist dictatorship. It has done what communist dictatorships do: created a repressive state security and secret police organization assisted by Soviet, East German, and Cuban advisers; harassed, and in many cases expunged, the political opposition; and rendered the democratic freedoms of speech, press, and assembly punishable by officially sanctioned harassment and imprisonment or death.
>
> But the Communists are not unopposed. They are facing great resistance from the people of Nicaragua, resistance from the patriots who fight for freedom and their unarmed allies from the pro-democracy movement.[14]

Supporters of the revolution saw it in different terms: as one of the most hopeful movements for the poor and oppressed ever to come out of Latin America. In contrast to the Chilean communist government of 1970–73 under President Salvador Allende, it was capable of defending itself militarily. In contrast to the Cuban revolution, it was willing to permit at least some diversity of opinion and some opposition groups. The revolution's supporters contended that any attacks on peaceful opposition groups were the unfortunate consequence of the country's being at war. President Ortega made clear statements about the regime's intention to support plurality:

> We're struggling to establish a regime that is of a democratic and pluralistic nature. . . . We seek pluralism in the sense that even though the Nicaraguan revolution is a very profound process, it does give room for participation by diverse groups. The revolution has established a framework within which different political, economic, and social forces can be active, can move about.[15]

Ortega made good on this pledge, permitting free multiparty elections in 1990. In a stunning reversal, however, the Nicaraguans rejected the Sandinistas in that election, choosing instead a coalition under the leadership of Violeta Chamorro, widow of the assassinated editor. The eleven years of Sandinista rule had brought almost universal suffering and a declining standard of living as the economy had descended into shambles. Chamorro's support apparently came from people who believed that she could end the warfare and restore friendly relations with the United States, thereby bringing a semblance of normality to the country.

She did succeed in ending the warfare. Friendly relations with the United States were more difficult to achieve, however. At home, Chamorro did her best to balance competing interests by permitting the Sandinistas to retain considerable power in the new regime. She allowed the army to remain under the leadership of Sandinista commanders, and she permitted Sandinistas to retain property they had appropriated. The U.S. government became increasingly skeptical of this strategy and greatly reduced its support of the Chamorro government. The internal affairs of this tiny country continued to be buffeted, therefore, by the global agenda of the United States, much as they had been throughout the century.

The Nationalist Identity

Many more nationalist and revolutionary movements waxed and waned in the third world in the twentieth century and into the twenty-first. They varied tremendously, from gentle to violent. One feature they all shared, however, was a concern for identity. Imperialism had shorn away the dignity of third-world peoples; nationalism was in part a yearning to recover it. Nowhere was the issue of identity more important than in black Africa, where the imperialist experience had been particularly tragic. In West Africa, centuries of the slave trade had ravaged the indigenous communities. Large migrations had shattered cultural roots. The Africans had been a people to be exploited and excluded. African nationalist movements and the cultural expressions that accompanied them have been filled with assertions of identity and self-worth, of negritude and black consciousness.

Particularly notable was the movement for negritude that accompanied the nationalism of French West Africa—an insistence that blackness was beautiful, soulful, creative, and expressive. Although treated by the imperialists as a mark of shame and slavery, blackness was in truth a badge of pride. One of the leaders of the negritude movement was Senegalese poet Léopold Sédar Senghor, a man who embodied the ambiguities of the colonial age. Senghor was educated in France and honored in French literary societies. He fought in the French army in the Second World War and then became a deputy representing Dakar, West Africa, in the French Assembly. In 1960, he led his nation to independence and became its first president. Deeply connected to French culture and at home in the salons of Paris, he nevertheless was acutely aware of race. Although he wrote in French, his images were black:

Femme nue, femme noire
Vêtue de ta couleur qui est vie, de ta forme qui est beauté![16]

Woman nude, woman black
Clad in your color which is life, in your shape which is beauty!

In Senghor's poetry, negritude was a proud proclamation, but it was not an angry one. Senghor made his peace with the French; he was almost one of them. His own experience mirrors that of most of the territories of French West Africa. When the territories became independent in 1960, all but one, Guinea, chose to remain associated with their former colonialists, hoping to benefit from French aid and technology while becoming an equal member in the community of nations. Independence as a nation was necessary because the people could not remain subject, but the independence came amicably. Negritude was a philosophy of moderation.

As such, negritude earned the scorn of Africans whose struggles were harder and whose emotions were more bitter. The angriest, most piercing cry, not only in Africa but in all the third world, came from the pen of Frantz Fanon. Fanon was born in 1925 in the French colony of Martinique in the West Indies. He studied in France and became a psychiatrist. During the Algerian war of independence in the late 1950s, he practiced medicine in an Algerian hospital and became an ally of the Algerian rebels. He wrote extensively about the psychology of the colonial relationship; his last and greatest book, *The Wretched of the Earth*, was written in a frenzied rush in 1961, as he was simultaneously working in the war effort and dying of cancer. Fanon, more than any other writer, expressed the rage of the third world against the imperialists. He deeply influenced a generation of nationalists, both in Africa and farther afield.

Fanon wrote from the context of the settler colonies, such as Algeria, where Europeans had expropriated the land and established their own farms. It was in these colonies that the anticolonialist struggles were the most bitter. The native people regarded the land they had lost as sacred and life-sustaining, and the European settlers were committed to their new homes and absolutely unwilling to give them up. Each page, each sentence of Fanon's work screams with outrage:

Every time Western values are mentioned they produce in the native a sort of stiffening or muscular lockjaw. During the period of decolonization, the native's reason is appealed to. He is offered definite values, he is told frequently that decolonization need not mean regression, and that he must put his trust in qualities which are well-tried, solid, and highly esteemed. But it so happens that when the native hears a speech about Western culture he pulls out his knife.

... In the colonial context the settler only ends his work of breaking in the native when the latter admits loudly and intelligibly the supremacy of the white man's values. In the period of decolonization, the colonized masses mock at these very values, insult them, and vomit them up.[17]

Rather than recoil from violence, Fanon relished it. After generations of suffering from colonial violence, the people of the third world could recover their wholeness by striking back:

For the native, life can only spring up again out of the rotting corpse of the settler. . . . For the colonized people this violence, because it constitutes their only work, invests their characters with positive and creative qualities. The practice of violence binds them together as a whole, since each individual forms a violent link in the great chain, a part of the great organism of violence which has surged upward in reaction to the settler's violence in the beginning. . . . Violence is a cleansing force. It frees the native from his inferiority complex and from his despair and inaction; it makes him fearless and restores his self-respect.[18]

In later chapters of his book, Fanon withdrew somewhat from the glorification of violence, but not from his anger. The imperialists had tried to pluck out the humanity of the natives, and now that they were leaving, they were establishing a native middle class to do their work for them. It was up to the people, the masses, the peasants to rise up and reassert their right to their own destiny. Fanon expressed the urgency and the fury of third-world peoples who had been subjugated.

Senghor's negritude and Fanon's anger were combined in the 1970s in the black consciousness movement led by Steven Biko in South Africa. Biko was a student leader who expressed the growing aspirations of his age group. Although Biko and the young South African blacks venerated the leaders of the previous generation, they approached their struggle against apartheid with a new urgency. The white minority had oppressed the black majority not only in physical and material terms but also in terms of their own self-image. South African blacks were a defeated people, Biko argued, and it was time for them to reassert their own worth. He and his colleagues refused to work with white liberals in the student movement, because they needed to proclaim their own pride and leadership. Journalist Donald Woods collected some of Biko's writings from his student days:

One should not waste time here dealing with manifestations of material want of the black people. A vast literature has been written on this problem. Possibly a little should be said about spiritual poverty. What makes the black man fail to tick? Is he convinced of his own accord of his inabilities? Does he lack in his genetic makeup that rare quality that makes a man willing to die for the realization of his aspirations? Or is he simply a defeated person? The answer to this is not a clear cut one. It is, however, nearer to the last suggestion than anything else. The logic behind white domination is to prepare the black man for the subservient role in this country. . . .

All in all the black man has become a shell, a shadow of man, completely defeated, drowning in his own misery, a slave, an ox bearing the yoke of oppression with sheepish timidity. . . .

The first step therefore is to make the black man come to himself; to pump back life into his empty shell; to infuse him with pride and dignity, to remind him of his complicity in the crime of allowing himself to be misused and therefore letting evil reign supreme in the country of his birth. This is what we mean by an inward-looking process. This is the definition of "Black Consciousness."[19]

The concern with pride, identity, and race was strongest in Africa, but it was evident throughout the colonized world. Everywhere that whites imposed their rule they evoked a fierce counterresponse. On each continent, the colonized asserted their worth.

The Legacy of Nationalism

The expectations created by the nationalist movements were enormous. Millions of people in the third world had come to see the imperialists as responsible for their miseries; they consequently expected their burdens to be lightened with independence. Not only would the people expel their colonial exploiters; they would assert the dignity of the nation. In place of exploitation, they would achieve sustenance for those who had suffered. In place of deceit and manipulation, they would find idealism, trust, and policies that were carefully designed to repair the damage. With the victory of the independence movements and the revolutions, there was an outpouring of enthusiasm. In country after country, the joy could be tasted; the future seemed rich with possibility. In the revolutionary countries, the task eagerly picked up was nothing less than creating a new humanity. Previously, people's personalities had been deformed by their oppressive circumstances; the new generation would be raised in a spirit of pride and cooperation.

No story is more common in history than the betrayal of the promises inherent in a revolution. The French Revolution, fought to free the people from their masters, degenerated into the Reign of Terror. The Russian Revolution culminated in a police state, purges, the murder of millions, and the gulag. Both permanently changed their countries—indeed, the world—by destroying the old order and releasing remarkable new social forces; it is hard to imagine the modern world without the French and Russian Revolutions. But the legacy of both was far more ambiguous and tortured than the participants ever imagined. What seemed at the time to be a clear-cut victory for humanity turned out to bring advances for some and disaster for others, while replacing one system of power with another.

So too with the third-world nationalist movements. We are still too close to their initial moment of victory to assess their long-term impact accurately, but there is no doubt that they share the ambiguities of the French and Russian Revolutions. They permanently ended the age of global European imperialism and thereby fundamentally altered the face of the world. They did not reverse the misery suffered by third-world peoples, however, and in some cases they added to it. Independence brought no easy solutions to the many fundamental problems facing the third world.

The economic problems all remained. After independence, as before, many of the economies of the third world were dominated by export crops that faced uncertain markets and depended on cheap labor to remain competitive in world markets. Independence hardly changed this situation at all, except that foreign faces were often replaced by local ones in positions of control.

Particularly hard to bear, however, were political developments in the third world that represented a betrayal of the nationalist movements. As local people took control, it turned out that they often had as much capacity for exploiting their compatriots as the imperialists had exhibited.

The creative literature of the revolutionary and nationalist movements shows that even during the armed struggles themselves, some of the perceptive participants could see the seeds of betrayal. One of the most remarkable predictions came from Fanon's pen at the height of the Algerian revolution. At the beginning of *The Wretched of the Earth*, he celebrated the uprising of the native, but by the middle of the book he showed how that uprising would be betrayed. In a prescient chapter titled "The Pitfalls of National Consciousness," he wrote that the imperialists would be replaced by a national middle class that would lack even the abilities of the former oppressors:

> This traditional weakness . . . is the result of the intellectual laziness of the national middle class, of its spiritual penury, and of the profoundly cosmopolitan mold that its mind is set in. . . . The national middle class which takes over power at the end of the colonial regime is an underdeveloped middle class. It has practically no economic power, and in any case it is in no way commensurate with the bourgeoisie of the mother country which it hopes to replace. . . . The

national bourgeoisie of underdeveloped countries is not engaged in production, nor in invention, nor building, nor labor. . . . Its innermost vocation seems to be to keep in the running and to be part of the racket. . . . To them, nationalization quite simply means the transfer into native hands of those unfair advantages which are a legacy of the colonial period.[20]

From a different angle, novelist Mariano Azuela foresaw the betrayal of the Mexican revolution, because the fighters themselves had such an uncertain grasp of their own goals. Azuela, a doctor, joined Pancho Villa's army and took part in military actions but then withdrew to El Paso, Texas, when Villa was defeated. In El Paso in 1915, he wrote what has become one of the major novels of the revolution, *Los de abajo,* or *The Underdogs.* It is an unromantic portrait of a band of revolutionary Indians and mestizos, drawn together by their hatred of the landlords and the *federales,* but without any clear program. The only character with a coherent revolutionary ideology is Azuela's fictional counterpart, the doctor Luis Cervantes, who abandons his compatriots at the critical moment to establish a business in El Paso. The peasants have only the ideology of continued fighting. Says one of them:

Villa? Obregón? Carranza? What's the difference? I love the revolution like a volcano in eruption; I love the volcano because it's a volcano, the revolution because it's the revolution! What do I care about the stones left above or below after the cataclysm? What are they to me?[21]

As early as 1915, Azuela could see the middle-class revolutionaries trampling over the backs of the poor, and the poor dissipating their military and moral strength in anomie and confusion.

One of the most perceptive chroniclers of the betrayal of the nationalist movements has been Nigerian Chinua Achebe. In his novel *A Man of the People,* the young, university-educated idealist Odili reflects on the process that has brought the corrupt nationalist politician Chief Nanga to power:

A man who has just come in from the rain and dried his body and put on dry clothes is more reluctant to go out again than another who has been indoors all the time. The trouble with our new nation—as I saw it then lying on that bed—was that none of us had been indoors long enough to be able to say "To hell with it." We had all been in the rain together until yesterday. Then a handful of us—the smart and the lucky and hardly ever the best—had scrambled for the one shelter our former rulers left, and had taken it over and barricaded themselves in. And from within they sought to persuade the rest through numerous loudspeakers, that the first phase of the struggle had been won and that the next phase—the extension of our house— was even more important and called for new and original tactics; it required that all argument should cease and the whole people speak with one voice and that any more dissent and argument outside the door of the shelter would subvert and bring down the whole house.[22]

In country after country, the ideals of the people's movements were abandoned by the leaders. Democracy faltered as one-party states and military regimes stifled dissent and violated human rights.

Still, the trajectory of human progress has been anything but uniform in the third world since the 1960s. Some countries have suffered from terrible human rights abuses: Cambodia, Myanmar (formerly Burma), Iraq, Rwanda, and many others. Some have gone through periods of horror but have been able to right themselves and develop political systems based on reasonable respect for different groups; Argentina, Chile, El Salvador, and South Africa are examples. Some have adopted democratic political systems, some semidemocratic systems, and some authoritarian and even brutal systems. Some have changed abruptly from one sort of system to another. In the first years of the twenty-first century, the trend seems to be toward democracy, toward human rights, away from dictatorships, and away from military regimes, but many exceptions persist.

The legacy of the nationalist movements in the third world is therefore ambiguous. They were victorious. They ended the empires, created nations where none had existed, tripled the number of independent countries, and asserted the autonomy of the world's majorities. They made third-world people responsible for third-world problems. They changed the colors on the globe. But they did not end exploitation; in many cases, they reframed it. At the core of their inability to realize the promises embodied in their movements was the intractability of the economy. With some exceptions, the new regimes could not bring about economic development or alleviate poverty.

Notes

1. Donald Woods, *Biko,* 2d ed. (New York: Henry Holt, 1987), 28.

2. Robert Rhodes James, *Winston S. Churchill: His Complete Speeches 1897–1963.* Volume VI, 1935–1942 (New York, Chelsea House Publishers, 1974), 6695.

3. Raja Rao, *Kanthapura* (London: George Allen and Unwin, 1938), 11–12.

4. United Nations Development Programme, *Human Development Report 1997* (New York: Oxford University Press, 1997), annex table A2.1 and table 1.

5. World Bank, *World Development Report 2002* (New York: Oxford University Press, 2002), Tables 1, 3, and *World Development Report 2003* (New York: Oxford University Press, 2003), Table 3.

6. Stanley Karnow, *Vietnam: A History* (New York: Viking Press, 1983), 122.

7. The others are the War of 1812, in which the United States failed in its aim of annexing the British colonies to its north, and the U.S. Civil War (1861–1865), which half the country lost.

8. Murray Hiebert and Susumu Awanohara, "The Next Great Leap," *Far Eastern Economic Review* (April 22, 1993): 68–71.

9. On modern Algerian history, see Robert A. Mortimer, "Algeria: The Clash between Islam, Democracy, and the Military," *Current History* (January 1993): 37–41. See also two reports by journalist John F. Burns in *The New York Times*, "Algeria–Remember That Name," January 2, 2000, IV, 4; and "In Assault on Islamic Rebels, a Bid to End Algeria's Civil War," January 27, 2000, A3.

10. Robert Block, "The Tragedy of Rwanda," *New York Review of Books* 41 (October 20, 1994): 3–8.

11. Among many sources on African democracy, see UNDP, *Human Development Report 2002* (New York: Oxford University Press, 2002), and Rachel L. Swarns and Norimitsu Onishi, "Africa Creeps along Path to Democracy," *The New York Times* (June 2, 2002), 1.

12. From the foreword to Mariano Azuela, *The Underdogs: A Novel of the Mexican Revolution*, trans. E. Munguia Jr. (New York: New American Library, 1962).

13. Thomas W. Walker, ed. *Nicaragua: The First Five Years* (New York: Praeger, 1985), 22.

14. Quoted in Peter Rosset and John Vandermeer, *Nicaragua: Unfinished Revolution. The New Nicaraguan Reader* (New York: Grove Press, 1986), 10.

15. Rosset and Vandermeer, *Nicaragua*, 5.

16. Léopold Sédar Senghor, *Chants d'ombre* (Paris: Edition du Seuil, 1956), 21; translation by the author.

17. Frantz Fanon, *The Wretched of the Earth*, trans. Constance Farrington (New York: Grove Press, 1968), 43.

18. Fanon, *Wretched of the Earth*, 93–94.

19. Woods, *Biko*, 130–31.

20. Fanon, *Wretched of the Earth*, 149–52.

21. Azuela, *The Underdogs*, 136.

22. Chinua Achebe, *A Man of the People* (New York: Doubleday, 1967), 34–35.

Suggestions for Further Reading

See Bibliography for full details.
Chinua Achebe. *A Man of the People.*
Manli Argueta. *One Day of Life.*
Mariano Azuela. *The Underdogs: A Novel of the Mexican Revolution.*
M. E. Chamberlain. *Decolonization: The Fall of the European Empires.*
Frantz Fanon. *The Wretched of the Earth.*

Carlos Fuentes. *The Death of Artemio Cruz.*
Mohandas K. Gandhi. *An Autobiography: The Story of My Experiments with Truth.*
William Hinton. *Fanshen: A Documentary of Revolution in a Chinese Village.*
Jean Lacouture. *Ho Chi Minh: A Political Biography.*
John Springhall. *Decolonization Since 1945: The Collapse of European Overseas Empires.*
Donald Woods. *Biko.*

Chapter Six

Economic Development

The division of labor among nations is that some specialize in winning and others in losing.
—Eduardo Galeano, *Open Veins of Latin America*

If present trends continue, economic disparities between the industrial and developing nations will move from inequitable to inhuman.
—James Gustave Speth,
United Nations Development Programme administrator

The field of economics is very complex and very boring.
—Daniel Ortega, former president of Nicaragua

The nationalist movements won independence for the third world, transforming the international political order. The age of imperialism is over. The majority of the world's population is now represented by the majority of the world's independent governments. Politically, the world has changed completely—but economically, only unevenly.

With independence achieved, the principal concern in the third world has been the economy. At the top of almost every country's priority list has been economic development. Some economic improvements have occurred, but the breakthroughs have been scarce and the disappointments many. Most people still live in poverty.

Some regions have enjoyed successes. Several East Asian countries—among them Hong Kong,[1] Malaysia, Singapore, South Korea, and Taiwan—achieved rapid growth in production over several decades and have become influential participants in international markets. They have even managed to spread some of the benefits of their growth among the poor. China has embarked on a path of steady economic growth. Some other countries have enjoyed spurts of growth that were impressive while they lasted—for example, Brazil from the mid-1950s through the mid-1970s. The oil-exporting countries of the third world—most of the Middle Eastern countries as well as Venezuela, Mexico, Nigeria, and Indonesia—had a decade of prosperity from 1973 to 1983, before slipping back to a more stagnant state. Most of the other third-world countries (with the exception of those in Africa) have experienced some modest improvements in productivity and national income since the 1960s.

After a distressing decade in the 1980s, economic performance in the third world improved somewhat in the 1990s and the beginning of the new century. Taking all the world's low- and moderate-income countries together, average incomes rose in the 1980s at the minuscule rate of just 0.8 percent a year, and even this positive rate masked huge differences. Economic growth continued fairly strongly throughout most of Asia in the 1980s, but standards of living actually fell in Africa, the Middle East, Latin America, and the Caribbean.[2] Among the causes of the decline in the 1980s were a rising debt burden, falling world oil prices, sluggish foreign markets, and economic policy mismanagement. From the 1990s through 2001, economic growth proceeded at a stronger pace, exceeding population growth in all areas of the third world except Africa.[3]

On the whole, however, for the majority of people living in the third world, the economic condition is dismal and the future unpromising. Most people are still desperately poor, with little prospect of escaping from their poverty. As Chapter 2 showed, theirs is generally not the traditional low-income life of ancient villages, a way of life supported by the tribal deities and the ancestors. For most people of the third world, that traditional way of life has been uprooted—by colonialism, by globalization, by urbanization, by commercialization, and by population growth. The modern poverty of the third world is a new phenomenon, but it does not appear to be transitory.

What Is Economic Development?

Economic development is a complex process. It happens in different ways in different parts of the world. Part of economic development is simply economic growth, which can be measured by changes in gross domestic product (GDP). GDP is a measure of output and, by conventional accounting standards, is identical to income. GDP per person is a measure, therefore, of average income or average standard of living. As we saw in Chapter 2, the differences in GDP per person across countries are staggering: measured in U.S. dollars, average GDP in 2001 ranged from $36,970 in Switzerland to $100 in Burundi.[4] As we also saw in Chapter 2, this particular comparison probably overstates the difference in standard of living between the rich and the poor countries. Income figures that are corrected for differences in the cost of living show smaller but still huge gaps.

Economic development includes more than just growth in output, however. The most serious deficiency in GDP as an index of development is the fact that almost no one in a country receives the average income. Some receive less, some much more. In some countries, the gap between the rich and the poor is growing; in others, it is narrowing. If the standard of living of the majority of the people is stagnating or even deteriorating, it hardly matters to them if their country's average income is growing.

There are numerous examples of economic changes that have increased the average GDP but at the same time have impoverished the majority of the people and can hardly be classified as economic development. A striking case is the mammoth Indira Gandhi Canal project in northwestern India.[5] Built during the 1970s and 1980s, it is much more than just an irrigation project. The main canal and its extensions are immense, covering about five thousand miles. In partnership with the World Bank, the Indian government set out to transform the desert: to move people to newly irrigated land, settle them on small plots, and convert the region from one of sparse population and nomadic herders to one of thriving agriculture. It is one of the most ambitious economic development projects ever undertaken. It required enormous capital investment and the establishment of a large new public bureaucracy to administer the project.

By some measures, the Indira Gandhi project is a success. Canals have been built, water diverted, people settled, new scientific methods introduced, and land cultivated. Agricultural production has risen dramatically. By other measures, however, the project is a catastrophe. Some of the problems are ecological. Because of inadequate drainage, some of the land has become oversaturated, and salinity levels are rising; as a consequence, the future fertility of the land is threatened. Other problems are social. The project was intended to respond to the needs of India's poorest people and to return land to the tiller. Most of the poor farmers who initially received endowments of land were, however, unable to cultivate it profitably, and they either descended into poverty or were forced to sell out to larger and more prosperous landowners. Those who sold their land became low-income wage laborers. Instead of an egalitarian community of small farmers, the project has produced a stratified capitalist system in which large numbers of impoverished people are left at the mercy of a newly prosperous landowning class. Huge expenditures of public funds and foreign aid have created a new elite and consigned the majority of the people to poverty.

Does the canal project constitute economic development? It depends on the criterion. If one looks only at GDP and the growth of agricultural production, yes. If one looks at long-run sustainability or the impoverishment of the people, no. GDP growth is part of economic development, but as the canal project shows, it is only one part. Increasingly, economists and other social scientists have directed their attention to additional indicators such as sustainability, income distribution, and basic human needs.

Sustainability of economic development was the central idea at two major United Nations conferences a decade apart: the Earth Summit in Rio de Janeiro in 1992 and the World Summit on Sustainable Development in Johannesburg in 2002. Unfortunately, a principal theme of the second conference was that not much had been accomplished since the first conference.

As economic growth has proceeded in both rich and poor countries, it has taken a major toll on the natural environment. Economic growth has been associated with water pollution and water scarcity, air pollution, problems of solid and toxic wastes, soil degradation and desertification, deforestation, loss of biodiversity, ozone depletion and other atmospheric changes, and global warming.[6]

As these effects have become better understood, some people—particularly activists in the environmental movement—have claimed that economic growth and development are incompatible with environmental preservation. If we are to maintain a thriving natural environment in the future, they believe, we will have to cut back on economic growth. This way of posing the issue—environment versus development—has not won over the proponents of economic development, because it seems to call for a halt to development and an end to the hopes of the world's majority for an improved standard of living.

Instead of an opposition between development and environment, increasing numbers of people are calling for sustainable development: development that protects its environmental base so that it can be continued into the indefinite future. According to this way of looking at the issue, economic growth that fails to protect its environment is not true development, because it cannot be sustained. The Indira Gandhi project is a prime example. Over the short run, it has raised output and incomes, but unless major changes are made in the drainage systems, the irrigation will so poison the soil that crop yields will fall. To be a genuinely successful example of economic development, the canal project would have to provide for the long-run productivity of the land. Proponents of sustainable development, who had the strongest voices at the Rio and Johannesburg conferences, argue that it is feasible to plan development projects that protect water, air, and soil quality and that can therefore be continued over the long run.

Another dimension of economic development that has become increasingly important is income distribution. In the early days of thinking about development, income distribution—the gap between the rich and the poor within a country—was given little attention. At the beginning of his seminal 1955 book, Sir W. Arthur Lewis of Saint Lucia, a Nobel Prize winner and the third world's most distinguished economist, made it clear that distribution was irrelevant to his main concern. "Our subject matter is growth and not distribution," he wrote.[7] The mainstream view was that economic growth inevitably brought with it increasing inequality between the rich and the poor, at least in its early stages. Inequality should not be regretted, because it was inevitable. Moreover, it was thought that inequality might even be helpful to economic growth, because income that was concentrated in a few hands might be more available for saving and investment than income that was widely disbursed.

Over time, this perspective has changed, at least among academic observers of the development process. Although the income gap has widened in some poor countries, it has narrowed in others. With some exceptions, incomes have become more unequal over the last several decades in Africa and Latin America but more equal in Asia, particularly East Asia. It is therefore no longer plausible to argue that an increase in inequality is inevitable. Nor can one argue any more that it is helpful. Countries such as South Korea that were able to raise the income levels of their poorer people found that these people now constituted a large internal market for their manufactured goods that could be used, along with foreign markets, to stimulate continued growth. Countries such as Brazil, where the poor grew in number but not in standard of living, eventually stagnated because their firms could not sell their goods to their own people.

The principal reason that the distribution of income, and not just its growth, is central to the meaning of economic development is that development is about people. When the Indira Gandhi Canal leaves most of the people in its region worse off, it cannot be counted as genuine economic development, even if it raises agricultural production.

Specialists in economic development have found new ways to think about their subject that highlight the impact on ordinary people. In the 1970s, "absolute poverty" and "basic needs" were posited as the standard for judging economic development, and the 1990s saw the related idea of "human development."

These ideas have influenced policies at the world's most influential center of economic development, the World Bank. Established at the end of the Second World War, the World Bank is an international lending organization, financed and controlled by the rich countries and dedicated to promoting economic change in the poor countries. In the 1970s, Robert S. McNamara, president of the bank, and his associates directed attention to the critical needs of the most destitute, the "absolute poor," as he called them. At the same time, Dudley Seers and other independent economists were calling for an economic development strategy that focused on "basic needs." According to this new way of conceiving of development, poverty—rather than low GDP—became the target.

The basic needs of each person were thought to include sufficient nutritious food, adequate shelter from the elements, decent clothing, protection from disease, and elementary education. These basic necessities were unavailable to hundreds of millions, perhaps billions, of people in the third world. The test of economic development, in the eyes of this school, was whether these basic needs were being met, not whether average GDP was growing.

In the 1990s, the United Nations Development Programme (UNDP) advanced the basic needs approach a step further by constructing a "human development index."[8] One of the components of the index is GDP per person, but only up to the world average of about $5,000. Increases in income above that level add little to basic human welfare in the opinion of the UNDP research team, headed initially by Pakistani economist Mahbub ul Haq. The other components of the human development index are health, measured by the expectation of life at birth, and education, measured by a combination of adult literacy and average years of schooling.

These broader approaches make a considerable difference in one's assessment of economic development. If one takes as the criterion for development a country's success in meeting the needs of its population rather than the growth rate of its GDP, then some countries that were once considered failures are now successes, and vice versa. China, for example, does poorly under the GDP test but quite well on the human development index. China still provides relatively low incomes for its population, but the Chinese live longer than most other people in the third world, and at last count, 82 percent of Chinese adults were literate. Sri Lanka and Nicaragua are among the other countries whose records in meeting basic needs are more impressive than their GDPs. The growth of Cuba's GDP has been slow since its revolution, but it provides basic literacy and health care to a population that once lacked them and has improved nutritional standards among the poor.

On the opposite side, some countries have been successful in increasing production but have not used their new wealth effectively to improve the welfare of their people. Brazil has a relatively high GDP but a lower life expectancy (reflecting poor health conditions) than most countries at the same income level. During the two decades from the mid-1950s to the mid-1970s, Brazil was the miracle of the third world, with a rapidly advancing industrial sector and growing productivity. The Brazilian right-wing military regimes built this miracle on the backs of destitute peasants and urban slum dwellers, however. In Algeria, Iraq, Iran, and many other Middle Eastern countries, human development has not kept up with production.

Population Control

One of the most controversial features of economic development in the third world has been population growth. Some argue that a growing population is such a threat to human welfare that fertility reduction must be considered part of the very definition of economic development. On the other side, some claim that population growth is close to irrelevant, or that there is no need to worry about it, because birth rates will decline on their own within a couple of generations. Many take more moderate positions in between.

The basic facts are overwhelming. Between 1960 and 2002, the world's population more than doubled, from three billion to more than six billion. Projections show that it will grow to more than eight billion by the year 2025—not far in the future. Some forecasters predict that the world's population will top out at about eleven billion by the end of the twenty-first century. The population growth rate in the third world has fallen since 1960, but only from about 2.3 to 1.5 percent a year. UN projections show that the third world's share of world population will rise from 77 percent in 1990 to 84 percent in 2025.[9]

Population growth is determined almost precisely by the gap between birth rates and death rates (migration can make a difference, but usually not much). Until the first part of the twentieth century, populations in the third world grew slowly, because although birth rates were relatively high, death rates were almost as high. As Chapter 4 showed, the population explosion of the second part of the century was caused by a rapid improvement in health conditions, which caused a precipitous drop in death rates; birth rates lagged behind, falling only slowly in some countries and not at all in others.

The arithmetic of growth is such that even a small annual rate of increase can lead to a large change over decades and generations. For example, Brazil had an annual population growth rate of 1.4 percent from 1990 to 2001, a rate which would lead to a doubling in fifty years if sustained.[10] In Jordan, on the other hand, the growth rate in the same period was 4.2 percent a year, a rate that would lead to a doubling in seventeen years.

The consequences of continued population growth over a long period are clear. It has proved difficult for demographers to estimate an optimal population size for a given country,[11] but no doubt there is some size that is too large, some size that puts undue pressure on limited natural resources and causes incomes to fall. Whether or not third-world countries are close to these sizes now, they will certainly approach and exceed them if population growth continues, with repeated doublings in size.

Economic calculations are almost invariably made over a short term—a presidential term, a generation. We seldom think much beyond a generation. In the case of population growth, however, it is important to think about the long run—say, several hundred years. In the long run, the growth rate of population (indeed, the growth rate of almost anything) must average out to zero. If a population growth rate is less than zero—if it is negative, if deaths exceed births—the population will decline and eventually disappear. If the growth rate is greater than zero, the population will expand beyond any fixed limit. A growing population will eventually mean standing room only, then layers of people standing on top of one another—an obvious impossibility. Long before standing-room-only occurred, the world would be ecologically incapable of supporting the population. Therefore, in the long run, the only sustainable population growth rate is zero.

The only way to achieve zero population growth is to have death rates equal birth rates. This can happen at any level: both can be high, say forty or fifty per thousand, as in prehistoric societies; or both can be low, around ten per thousand. Therefore, if the world is to enjoy the fruits of economic development and if people are to live full, comfortable lives in good health—that is, if they are to enjoy low death rates—then birth rates in the world must eventually fall to low levels. It is important to remember this truth when assessing the current debate over population.

Most of the debate is over three separate questions: Is rapid population growth an immediate threat to economic development, rather than just a long-term threat? Will fertility fall on its own, or must exceptional policy efforts be made to reduce it? What methods of fertility control are morally acceptable?

On the first question, economists, biologists, and ecologists can point to all sorts of reasons for thinking that population growth is a clear and present danger, particularly in the third world. Some economists, for example, argue that if fertility falls and the population growth rate is reduced, whatever economic growth a third-world country achieves can be directed toward improving standards of living rather than simply providing for an increased number of people at the same standard of living. If fertility falls and, as a consequence, the age distribution of the population grows older, the "burden of dependency" is reduced. That is, each adult of working age has fewer dependents to provide for and therefore has more choices—to provide more amply for the young people who remain dependent, to increase his or her own consumption standards, and/or to increase savings and thus provide for greater increases in future income.[12] Biologists and ecologists point to how much more difficult sustainable development becomes when the population is growing, because all the negative impacts on the natural environment tend to increase. For all these reasons and more, the argument is made that fertility reduction is an essential component of economic development—not far away in the future, but now.

There is plenty of dissent to this view. Empirical researchers have not been able to verify the alleged negative impact of population growth on economic development.[13] Their studies seem to show that when population growth is increased and all other things remain equal, economic growth is increased proportionately, leaving no negative effect on average incomes. Perhaps an increasing population has the resources to provide for its own needs. Some argue that the burden of dependency is a myth and that large families provide status and income for parents in the present and security for them in their old age. Some claim that because high population densities in some European countries have had no negative economic effects there, the same will be true in the third world. And some argue that although large and growing populations may put pressure on fixed resources, this is a global problem that originates in the rich countries, because rich people use, on average, much more of the earth's scarce resources than do the poor.

No resolution of this debate is in sight. Among the many barriers to a resolution is the fact that our current empirical, statistical methods are not adequate to analyze the effects of demographic changes. The fact that statisticians cannot identify any major impacts is therefore not conclusive evidence one way or the other. In spite of all the controversy, it is hard not to come back to the position that in a world of fixed physical limits, growth in the human population makes an improvement in its standard of living more difficult.

The second debate is about whether governments should embark on extensive birth-control programs or whether fertility will fall of its own accord over time. The evidence from Europe and North America is that high standards of living eventually bring low birth rates; in some European countries, the current demographic fear is one of population decline, not growth. Why prosperity should bring low fertility is a bit of a mystery, in spite of extensive scholarly investigation into the question. Perhaps the clue is the personal insurance that is thought to inhere in large families in the third world. It may be impossible to convince poor people in poor countries, living constantly on the brink of economic disaster, that their ultimate welfare does not depend on having a large family. Perhaps a prosperous society—with resources to spend on social security, unemployment insurance, medical care, and pensions—is needed before families will relinquish the idea that their security depends on their children. The argument is often made that economic development influences population growth, not vice versa. Or, to use a popular phrase, "development is the best contraceptive."

In any case, fertility has fallen in the third world, with the steepest drops generally occurring in countries where economic growth has been highest, income distribution most equitable, the basic needs of ordinary people most fully attended to, and the status of women most improved. In Asia, for example, birth rates fell precipitously to around twenty per thousand or less by the beginning of the twenty-first century in China, Sri Lanka, and South Korea. In much of Latin America, birth rates have also fallen, although not as far, to between twenty and thirty per thousand. In most of sub-Saharan Africa, however, where the economies have been stagnant or worse, birth rates are close to their historical highs, above forty per thousand. In the Arab Middle East, where economic growth has occurred but income distribution has become more unequal, birth rates are only a little lower than those in Africa.[14]

In every society, fertility is at least partly a voluntary decision, so social conditions have an impact on changes in birth rates. Yet the authorities in many countries of the third world are not satisfied with the pace of purely private, voluntary decision making and have embarked on major birth-control programs to speed the process. The programs provide birth-control information and technology to families so that they can make informed choices about the number of children they will have and so that women can take greater control over their lives and be spared the physical strain of constant pregnancy. Sometimes the programs go further by engaging in publicity and propaganda about the advantages of small families. The effectiveness of such programs is in doubt, but for those who think that population growth represents a drag on social and economic improvements, they are worth the attempt.

The two largest countries of the third world, India and China, have both made a tremendous commitment to birth-control programs. India has a large network of clinics and an extensive public relations campaign urging families to opt for fewer children. China has one of the few coercive programs. In some cases, the Chinese government has insisted that families have at most one child. In some areas of China, the government has compiled detailed information about the fertility histories of women, including their menstrual cycles and birth-control methods. People choosing to have a second child rather than an abortion can be fined large sums of money and even be demoted or fired from their jobs.[15] The Chinese authorities are convinced that their economic development efforts will be crippled if rapid population growth resumes. Although scattered evidence indicates that they may have backed off somewhat from their most severe fertility restrictions, they are still strongly committed to a continued reduction in birth rates.

The third debate is over the morality of contraception and, especially, abortion. At the UN conference on population and development in Cairo in 1994, the most heated fights arose over these questions. Some participants in the conference, particularly those from Muslim countries, took the position that most forms of contraception are incompatible with their national values and that abortion is absolutely forbidden. The Vatican, claiming to speak for the world's Roman Catholics, pushed this position strongly and refused to endorse the conclusions of the conference because of the hint that abortion might be a sanctioned practice in some countries. Other countries, however, maintained that the status of women was dependent on access to safe, effective, modern means of contraception and that this was a human right that should be denied to no one. Although the conference did not endorse abortion as a means of birth control, many countries were adamant that the availability of safe, legal abortions was a necessity for the world's women.

The many debates over fertility and population growth cut quickly to the core of human values and ethics: to people's varied religious beliefs, to their conceptions of family, and to their ideas about sex. No beliefs could be more personal or more strongly held. Belief systems, however, do not emerge in a vacuum; they develop in ways that are compatible with, and often support, the surrounding social structure. Enormous problems arise when social arrangements change quickly and belief systems lag behind. This, in my view, is the heart of the debate over population. For millennia, most human societies were poor, health conditions were threatening, and death rates were high. It is no surprise, therefore, that beliefs and moral systems arose in support of high fertility, for without it, the societies would have disappeared. Now we live in a world of improved health and declining mortality. In such a world, high fertility threatens human societies because it will lead to population growth that is out of control. In present circumstances, morality must quickly shift to support low fertility. It has shifted in some areas of the world and among some groups of people, but the shift is uneven, painful, and conflict ridden. It is essential, however, to the future of the human species.

False Paths to Economic Development

In much of the third world, the history of economic development since independence has been a history of false promises. A series of what seemed at the time to be easy answers appeared, keys that would unlock the door to riches. They have not. One by one, the fashionable answers proved wanting—in some cases because they ignored the reality of a much too complex world, in other cases because they were abandoned by the people who should have been responsible for their success. The false answers included nationalism and independence alone, socialism and government planning, industrial growth and a shift away from agriculture, foreign aid and capital investment, investment in human capital, a hike in oil prices, and the new international economic order. In the 1980s, the third world was buffeted by an unprecedented debt crisis, the lingering effects of which are still felt. In the 1990s, many third-world countries shifted their economic strategies toward the free market and aggressive participation in international trade; in the twenty-first century this may work better than the previous strategies, but a lot of evidence that is already available leads one to be skeptical.

Political Independence

To say that nationalism and independence were false paths is not to deny that they were necessary for economic progress, for they surely were; it is to deny, however, that political autonomy was a sufficient condition.

Before independence, the imperialists paid little if any attention to the economic well-being of the local people. The colonial powers had economic interests in the third world, of course. They were looking for cheap raw materials to support industrialization at home, and they also expected the colonies to generate enough income to cover the costs of their administration. These interests had nothing to do with improving the lot of the local people, however. In fact, the economic attractiveness of the colonies lay largely in the fact that labor was cheap, and labor was cheap because standards of living were marginal. The imperialists had no incentive to improve living conditions. When administrators thought at all about the welfare of the colonized, it was almost always in terms of peace, order, and efficient government. In the opinion of the imperialists, colonial administration was justified for establishing a rule of law, suppressing local conflicts, breaking down customs thought to be uncivilized, and establishing communications among different areas. Hardly any of the rulers conceived that these changes could or should bring about significant improvements in the incomes of the local people. Not until the independence movements began to be successful after the Second World War was the subject of economic development in the third world taken seriously.

As Chapter 5 explained, a spirit of euphoria accompanied the independence of the Indian subcontinent, of sub-Saharan Africa, and of the other regions of the third world that rejected their colonial status in the years following the Second World War. Independence was a mark of pride, a sign of equality in the world. It was also understood as a portent of a better life ahead. Almost without exception, the nationalists and their followers believed that by casting off the oppressive hand of the colonialists and taking control of their own economic destiny, they could vanquish the exploitation that was responsible for their poverty. To be an independent nation seemed synonymous with economic progress.

It turned out not to be so. Independence brought no automatic release of the powers of economic progress. Colonial exploitation was certainly responsible, at least in part, for the poverty of the new nations, but that exploitation did not end with independence; it continued in a neocolonial guise.

The leaders of the new nations—the Nehrus and the Nkrumahs—might have understood this better had they paid closer attention to Latin America. Almost all the Latin American countries had been independent for more than a century, since about 1820. Some of them, most notably Argentina, had actually enjoyed periods of prosperity. In the post–World War II period, however, they were all poor, or at least the vast majority of their people were. In Latin America, neocolonial exploitation was reinforced by domestic exploitation, with small groups of landholders, military officers, and urban commercial families wresting wealth from the cities and the countryside, often leaving their fellow citizens destitute. In Nicaragua, for example, by the end of their rule, the Somoza family owned fully one-quarter of the country's land. The Latin American example showed that independence might create opportunities for a local oligarchy to replace the colonialists and advance at the expense of their brethren, but this was not the promise that had led millions to dance in the streets throughout Asia and Africa as independence was proclaimed.

Independence was a precondition of economic prosperity, because it removed the imperialists from direct authority over the third world. By itself, however, it could not lead to significant economic improvement, because it changed very few of the conditions that created the poverty. It did not change the fact that most people pursued agricultural tasks with primitive technology or produced low-priced commodities for export to the (former) colonial centers or were crowded into urban slums. Frantz Fanon's predictions proved chillingly accurate in many countries: the nationalist leaders settled simply for independence, for replacing foreign exploiters, but they lacked the vision and ability to replace the exploitative system. For many of those who thought that independence would bring automatic improvements, the subsequent decades were devastating.

Socialism and Government Planning

A large part of the promise of independence was thought to be that the governments of the new nations would be able to intervene forcefully in the economic and social structures of their countries, changing their direction, casting aside the elements that were exploitative and stagnant, and replacing them with a new order that addressed the needs of the people. To assert the people's control over the economy, some countries turned to socialism, to a social revolution that was intended to replace greedy capitalist classes with public ownership of the means of production. Other countries were more moderate in their approach, but even the countries that intended to retain a capitalist framework with private enterprise invariably saw government planning at the center of a national commitment to economic development.

The turn to government planning was influenced strongly by the various versions of dependency theory. The planners thought that to rely on the free market would be to remain vulnerable to a system dominated by the rich countries, a system that was responsible for world poverty in the first place. If governments did not intervene to alter the path of economic growth, the world's poor countries would just continue the way they were currently going. In a free-market system, producers make goods for which the market demand is strongest—and the strongest market demand was coming from the rich countries, with their insatiable need for cheap primary commodities. So the free market was pushing the third world deeper and deeper into a swamp. Unless governments intervened to change the pattern of production, the planners argued, the populations of the third world would be trapped.

The common wisdom was that the third world needed to develop its manufacturing and service sectors to complement its mining and agriculture. A complex economy needed help from the government to get started. If a third-world economy were left unprotected against the market, its manufacturing sector could never compete with cheap imports from the developed countries. Manufacturing needed tariff barriers against import competition, and it probably also needed subsidies, licenses, low-interest loans, and many other forms of government support.

Even economists in the mainstream modernization school believed in government planning. Although their ultimate faith rested with private enterprise, they thought that third-world economies needed a plan, an overall blueprint prepared by the government to show the expected path of growth. In the decades after independence, economic plans proliferated throughout the third world. Many of them showed in great detail the growth that was expected in each sector and the government policies that were needed to ensure that growth.

Among observers of the development process in the rich countries, there were a few cautionary dissenters to this consensus as early as the 1950s. Conservative British economist P. T. Bauer argued strenuously for a free-market approach to economic development, saying that individual entrepreneurs, risking their well-being in the pursuit of profits, were the most effective possible force for economic development. Government planners, he believed, would invariably make the wrong choices because they had nothing to lose. In the United States, Albert O. Hirschman, a student of Latin American economies, argued for unbalanced, unplanned growth. A typical third-world country lacked the managerial resources to plan the myriad components of a manufacturing sector. It would be better, said Hirschman, to proceed without integrated planning, to allow bottlenecks to emerge and then to trust that someone would find it profitable to break the bottleneck by providing either the input or the market that was needed. These dissenting views titillated the academics in the developed countries, but they had little influence among the politicians and bureaucrats of the third world. The predominant opinion in the third world was that the unconstrained private sector was incapable of producing real economic progress. The debate within the third world was different. It involved those who favored government economic planning in partnership with private-sector capitalism versus socialists, communists, and revolutionaries who wanted to replace the private sector altogether. The goal among the latter was to change the national class structure, to eliminate the upper, property-owning classes that had used their privilege to exploit the ordinary people. No possibility of partnership with the privileged classes existed, they thought, because the interests of those classes were utterly at odds with those of the majority. In China, Burma, North Korea, Cuba, and other revolutionary socialist countries, the path to progress was to replace private enterprises with public ones that were controlled by the government and operated for the benefit of the people.

The socialists argued that if private enterprise dominated the economy, the government could plan all it wanted but would lack the authority to implement the plan. Even more fundamentally, if private enterprise dominated the economy, the rich capitalists would dominate the government, and the government would have no interest in planning to benefit the majority of the people. So private corporations should be expropriated, and the government, acting on behalf of the people as a whole, should own and operate industries.

The two giants of Asia exemplified these two approaches to economic planning. India, although socialist in ideology throughout most of the period since independence, has remained stubbornly capitalist in fact. Not coincidentally, the strongest third-world contributors to the modernization school of social science have come from India. Although India has published a series of five-year plans showing in detail the expansion that is expected in each region and sector, the main initiative in the economy has remained in private hands. The plans served mainly to delay and disrupt economic development.

In revolutionary communist China, the guesswork was taken out of the planning process. A centralized planning office in Beijing set overall goals for the entire economy, and a series of regional planning offices was responsible for their implementation. Because the manufacturing plants were owned publicly, the planning offices were in a position to issue instructions and to set quantitative goals for each plant. Plant managers were given bonuses for meeting or exceeding the production goals that were set for them. The primacy of centralized control over the economy was intensified during the period of Chairman Mao's Great Proletarian Cultural Revolution (1965–75), when political ideology ruled over all other considerations, expertise was shunned, and many people with skills were thrown out of work and worse.

Although heated debate ensued for decades between proponents of the Indian and the Chinese models, virtually no one in the third world thought that government direction of the economy might be part of the problem rather than part of the solution. Remarkably, in recent years, the consensus in favor of government control has collapsed. Economists and politicians have retreated both from central planning and from socialism. The "monetarist" economists, who favor free-market solutions to almost every problem, have found themselves with new influence.

The consensus in favor of central planning collapsed for several reasons, the most important of which was that planning failed to produce economic development with any consistency. Why this was so is a debated question, with many contending explanations. One of the stronger explanations is that government control of the economy tends to create a "rent-seeking" society.[16] According to this idea, government planners set quotas and licenses, establish monopolies, and in many other ways restrict the free pursuit of economic gain by their citizens. Those who are favored by the government, those who get the licenses, monopolies, and other privileges, are in a position to make a lot of money. It is therefore in their interest to spend money in order to obtain those privileges—through political contributions, bribery, and other means. It is, of course, in the interest of the government officials to accept the money. The process comes to dominate the economy. The planners become reapers of illicit gains, and the country's entrepreneurs devote their ingenuity to obtaining official privileges rather than to increasing production. In the eyes of the rent-seeking theorists, therefore, government control of the economy leads to economic stagnation, not development. In the retreat from central planning, theories such as rent seeking have largely replaced the ideology of government control and dependency theory.

The most startling retreat from central planning came in the world's two greatest communist countries, China and the Soviet Union, both of which abandoned socialism as an economic system. After the death of Chairman Mao in 1976, the Chinese under Deng Xiaoping set out on a rightward path, leaving behind much of the central planning and the collective ideology that marked the first decades of the revolution. The new direction represented an explicit and profound reaction against the excesses of the Cultural Revolution. The Chinese reasserted their traditional respect for learning. They rehabilitated most of the people who had been disgraced in the previous decade, recalling them from the menial tasks and prisons to which they had been consigned. Private enterprise was introduced into both the farming sector and industry. Farmers were encouraged to cultivate individual plots of land and were allowed to profit individually from their productivity. Urban markets flourished, with the prices of many goods set by the forces of supply and demand, not centrally by a planning agency. The Chinese solicited foreign investment and looked for export opportunities. The changes in the Chinese economy occurred gradually, first in one sector, then in another. They were guided by the Communist Party, which retained rigid political control of the country. For the most part, however, socialism was abandoned in the economy.

The Soviet Union's retreat from economic centralization was more precipitous. It began later and culminated in the complete collapse of the country as a political entity. The Soviets had enjoyed remarkable successes in the twentieth century in heavy industry and military technology, but they did not do nearly as well at improving the quality of life of their citizens. Premier Mikhail Gorbachev and the reformers he gathered around him became convinced that the heavy hand of the bureaucracy was responsible for much of the stagnation. They called for *glasnost*—openness and free discussion—and for *perestroika*—a restructuring of the economy to make more use of the market. The Soviet encouragement of *glasnost* was the opposite of the Chinese policy of suppressing free expression.

As it turned out, *glasnost* could not be contained by the Soviet rulers. Once people could express their views openly, they rejected the entire apparatus of the Soviet state and its empire. First the satellite countries of eastern Europe were released from Soviet control, then the constituent republics of the Soviet Union exerted their independence. A short-lived coup against Gorbachev in the summer of 1991 failed, but in surmounting the coup, Gorbachev put himself under the control of Russian nationalists and democrats led by Premier Boris Yeltsin. The Russians administered the final death blows to the Soviet Union before the year was out, with the resulting independent republics aligning themselves in a loose confederation.

The downfall of the Soviet Union brought with it the collapse of centralized economic planning and socialism. It did not, however, bring with it a well-articulated market system. The economies of the former Soviet Union descended into a certain chaos, with sharp cuts in production, rampant inflation, and serious threats of starvation. Some entrepreneurs emerged with new products and more efficient ways of doing things, but without an effective legal system, many of them turned to crime. The economy was trapped in a downward spiral. What in China had been a gradual evolution toward the market, directed by the strong hand of a centralized party, was in Russia a quick abandonment of the failed socialist economic system, with no clear vision of what was to replace it.

Some voices in Russia responded to the turmoil by urging a return to centralized and dictatorial control, but it is unlikely that a socialist economy will be re-created in that country. In much of the third world as well, the turn away from central planning by the government appears to be profound and not easily reversed.

Industrialization and Agriculture

It is now clear that one of the consequences of the heavy hand of government economic control in the third world was an overwhelming bias in favor of industrialization and urbanization and against agriculture. The origins of the bias are understandable, because the economic development of the rich countries entailed urbanization. Two hundred years ago, most of the people in Britain, France, Russia, and the United States worked the land, providing for their own families' needs and perhaps producing a little surplus. As those countries became richer, people left the land and entered the cities to find employment in factories and urban services. The migration out of agriculture continues to this day; less than 2 percent of the U.S. population now works the land, for example. This shift from rural to urban, from agriculture to industry and services, has been so universal that it almost constitutes the definition of economic development. Third-world countries have attempted to follow this pattern, but for the most part, they have failed.

The secret behind the urbanization of the now rich countries was that it depended on almost miraculous improvements in farm productivity. It was this part of the process that the third-world planners missed. In western Europe and North America, technological progress in agriculture has outstripped progress in factory production. In the middle of the nineteenth century in the now developed world, one farm family produced enough food to support itself and one other family. In the early years of the twenty-first century, one farm family produces enough food to support itself and more than fifty others. As a result, hardly anyone is needed in farming, and more are leaving every day. The fact that the population of the rich countries has moved out of farming is a testament, strangely, to the unprecedented success of the farming sector.

The Soviet Union, under communist control, took a different path. Its leaders regarded rural people with suspicion. Rather than supporting the agricultural sector, they murdered its leaders and converted independent plots into vast collective farms, thereby destroying the initiatives and rewards that seem to be essential to successful farming. The Soviets' failure to stimulate agricultural production was the most important reason for the failure of the economy and the low standard of living of most of the people. One clear lesson that emerges from a comparison of the economic histories of the West and of the Soviet bloc is that it is all but impossible to enjoy an urban economy with a high standard of living unless that economy is based on high-productivity agriculture.

Typically, third-world countries followed the Soviet example rather than the western European and North American. Under government direction, they tried to industrialize without establishing a productive agricultural base. The result was a perpetuation of poverty, both rural and urban.

An example may indicate the difference in approach and the consequences. In North America and western Europe, farming communities have more than their share of political power and, as a result, are able to secure price supports, subsidies, and all sorts of other benefits from their governments (that is, from the nonfarmers). Government regulations keep the price of food relatively high, and the high prices provide an incentive to farmers to produce more food than is actually needed. Except during occasional periods of drought, the farm problem in those areas is one of surplus—too much food for too few customers.

In contrast, in many countries of the third world, governments respond to the evident distress of poor urban people by enacting legislation to keep the price of food artificially low. In some cases, the political future of the government depends on continuing these price ceilings on food; without them, the urban poor might overthrow the government. By keeping food prices low, the governments are, in effect, confiscating farmers' incomes. As a consequence, rural people frequently find that it is not worth their while to invest in agricultural improvements, because the low price of the food that they sell will not cover the cost of those improvements. Food production therefore stagnates. The typical farm problem in the third world is shortages—insufficient food to go around. These shortages are not God-given; in many cases, they are the logical consequence of well-meaning but wrongheaded government policy.

This is only one example among many. What it reflects is a stronger political influence from the cities and a relative powerlessness of the countryside—not in every third-world country, but in many. Nothing has been more harmful to the poor countries than the neglect of their agricultural sectors.

The agricultural problems of the third world are different from those of the developed countries because the third world is, for the most part, tropical.[17] Although tropical ecosystems differ from one another, they all lack a winter season that stops growth. The year-round heat in the tropics results in continuous biological growth and reproduction and therefore tremendous competition among species for survival. Any new plant or animal introduced into the ecosystem by human beings is immediately attacked by biological predators; its chances of survival in a healthy state are low. Again and again, attempts to innovate with new agricultural crops in the third world have failed because of the unrelentingly hostile climate.

Poor countries need agricultural research to develop species that will survive and that will improve farm productivity. Some successes have already occurred. With the help of the Rockefeller Foundation, research stations invented high-yielding types of wheat in Mexico and rice in the Philippines, and these new seeds have had considerable success in other parts of the third world, particularly in South Asia. This "green revolution" brought with it its own problems, however. The need for increased irrigation, increased fertilizer, and more precise timing of cultivation sometimes resulted in the displacement of small peasant farmers by large landowners who had better access to loans and other resources.

New agricultural research stations are slowly being established throughout the third world, but the discoveries that have been made so far are only a small fraction of what is needed. Attention also has to be paid to packaging green-revolution technology in such a way that it can support rather than displace poor people.

Economic development certainly implies industrialization and urbanization, but pursued by themselves, they are dead ends. The major cities of the third world are being stifled by migrants forced out of the countryside. By the early twenty-first century, more than half the population in the middle-income third-world countries live in cities, while in the low-income third-world countries the proportion is about one-third.[18] Everywhere in the third world, the cities are growing faster than the national population, but they are not providing decent jobs and housing. Urbanization can proceed successfully only if it follows agricultural progress, so that the people can be fed. Learning this lesson has cost the third world dearly, and it still has not been effectively learned in many countries.

Savings, Foreign Aid, and Capital Formation

In the 1940s, 1950s, and well into the 1960s, most observers believed that the clue to economic development was capital formation. Low-income countries needed massive new investments in factories, equipment, irrigation networks, transportation, and communications in order to raise the productivity of their labor forces. Economists believed that countries were poor because their people were working with primitive equipment. Economic development was thought to depend on an increase in capital investment in the third world, a rapid substitution, for example, of mechanized earthmovers for shovels.

That capital formation was the key to growth was the lesson of economic theory at the time; it was also the apparent lesson of post-war European reconstruction. After the Second World War, the European economies were in shambles. A few years later, they were back on their feet again, with the help of American foreign aid through the Marshall Plan, which provided funds for rebuilding the factories.

In the 1950s, politicians, bureaucrats, and academics alike thought that this European experience could guide third-world development. With international cooperation, generous foreign aid, and some government planning, European productivity had bounced back. The common wisdom was that the same sort of concerted effort could set the less developed countries on a path of self-sustained economic growth. They simply needed to construct capital goods—factories and machines—and their problems would be solved. To buy the capital goods, however, they needed investment funds. The funds could come from two sources, foreign or domestic, and each bears some discussion.

Resources for investment could come into the poor countries from abroad in a variety of ways. The most obvious, following the example of the Marshall Plan, was foreign aid.[19] After decades of experience with foreign aid, we have now grown accustomed to rather cynical analyses of its uses, understanding that foreign economic aid is often indistinguishable from foreign military aid and that both are frequently used in support of geopolitical aims that have little connection with humanitarian purposes. Still, the basic justification for foreign aid, and some of the actual practice, is that it should be used in support of economic development. Aid comes to the third world from individual governments among the developed countries, as well as from multilateral international organizations such as UN agencies, the World Bank, and regional development banks. Some aid is in the form of grants, and other aid is in the form of loans at subsidized interest rates.

Some foreign aid should properly be called "relief," because it is used directly to feed the hungry or to supply the basic needs of the poorest. Although this kind of aid has saved lives, relief is not the real point of aid. The objective is to provide third-world countries with the resources to increase their capital—to finance projects, build factories, reclaim land, process fertilizer, and so on. The hope is that foreign aid will be used in such a way as to increase the country's productivity so that relief-type aid will not be needed in the future.

A second foreign source of capital is the private sector, providing loans and investments to the third world. This source of capital has become even more controversial than foreign aid. Private foreign capital enters a third-world country in one of two ways—as equity capital or as loans. What equity means is that foreign investors buy an asset in the third world—a company, for example, or a factory. The investors may actually build the asset. They may own the asset completely on their own or jointly with a local partner. In either case, the foreign investors own a piece of the third-world economy. The flow of equity capital into the third world has led to a controversy over the role of multinational corporations.

Much of the equity investing is done by enormous international companies—the biggest in the world—that own operations in dozens of countries. They frequently tower over the countries in which they operate. The Aluminum Company of America (Alcoa), for example, has worldwide sales greater than the entire GDP of Jamaica, the country in which it mines most of its bauxite. The multinational corporations provide capital and technology to poor third-world countries. The criticism of them is that they tend to dominate and distort the countries in which they operate, imposing their own standards and displacing the local ones. They are sometimes so rich and powerful that they can secure favors for themselves that are not available to local companies. When they send the profits they have earned back to their home countries, they may actually drain capital out of the third world.

The alternative way for private foreign capital to come into the third world is in the form of loans. In this case, the ownership of the companies stays in the third-world country. The disadvantage is that a loan is a fixed obligation. No matter how well or how poorly the borrower does, it is still faced with the obligation of making regular payments back to the lender, usually a large bank.

During the 1960s and 1970s, when multinational corporations were spreading quickly throughout the third world, critics were vehement in their attacks on them. They called instead for more loan financing, so that the foreign capitalists would stay at arm's length from the third-world societies and allow them greater autonomy. In the 1980s, however, as loans to the third world increased dramatically and many of the poor countries were trapped by impossible repayment obligations, there were reverse pleas for more equity financing, calls for foreigners to take a greater stake in the fortunes of the third world.

The Marshall Plan, under which the United States had financed European recovery, turned out to be a poor model for providing capital to the third world. Governments of the rich countries sent foreign aid to the poor, but on the whole, they have not been generous. The United States and Britain, in particular, have reduced their commitment to aid, expressed as a percentage of their GDPs. The distribution of American aid has been remarkably skewed, being heavily directed to countries that have strategic and military importance to the United

States rather than to countries where the need is greatest. The multi-lateral agencies such as the World Bank have done better, but they are constantly strapped for funds. In the private sector, banks and corporations have provided quite a lot of capital to third-world countries, but the process has been continually surrounded by controversy and bad will, whether because of local economies' domination by multinational corporations or because of the debt burdens. One by one, third-world countries have discovered that foreign capital is not the principal answer to their problems and that they must look internally for most of their capital investment.

To understand the process of internal capital formation, it is useful to think of a country's production as being divided between two uses. It can be devoted to present uses—that is, to consumption—to provide for current needs, or it can be devoted to future uses, meaning that it can be used for investment in capital. These two uses compete with each other. Resources that are directed toward capital investment cannot also be used to meet today's pressing needs. Put differently, any decision to invest in future productivity implies a sacrifice, a reduction in the resources available today. This is the case whether the decision is made by individuals, by companies, or by governments—and whether it is made under a capitalist system or a socialist one. It is one of the truths of economics that cannot be avoided: resources devoted to capital investment must be taken away from current consumption (unless borrowed from abroad).

Investment that uses domestic resources requires sacrifices that are particularly difficult for a poor country to bear. Until the mid-1960s, however, economists were convinced that an increase in savings and the capital investment that went with it were absolutely essential to economic development. Because increased capital produced increased output, there was no substitute for the raising of investment and savings. Arthur Lewis wrote, in a widely quoted paragraph:

> The central problem in the theory of economic development is to understand the process by which a community which was previously saving and investing 4 or 5 per cent of its national income or less, converts itself into an economy where voluntary saving is running at about 12 to 15 per cent of national income or more. This is the central problem because the central fact of economic development is rapid capital accumulation (including knowledge and skills with capital).[20]

The famous Lewis model put savings and capital formation on center stage. Practically every serious attempt to understand the process of economic growth postulated capital formation as the main issue.

The actual experience of third-world countries turned out to be more complicated than these economic models suggested, however. It is no longer obvious that the central issue in economic development is how a country changes from a 5 percent saver to a 12 percent saver. Some countries with relatively high rates of saving and capital formation have had low rates of economic growth, and vice versa. Furthermore, the growth of production has not always brought with it significant improvements in the quality of life of ordinary people.

The fact that investment in capital is not the principal determinant of economic growth was first discovered in the developed countries. Economic historians, attempting to apply the abstract models of the growth theorists, came up with the startling result that capital formation could account for only a small proportion of the growth in production. Try as they might to refute their findings, they consistently discovered that a great deal of economic growth was the result of some unknown and unmeasured factors. New attention was therefore directed to such subjects as education, entrepreneurship, managerial capacity, even spiritual energy and enthusiasm, but the strongest candidate to take the place of capital as the engine of growth was technology.

The message arrived quickly in the third world—that technological advancement was important. But that led immediately to a quandary: what technology? The great research and development efforts were in the developed countries, not in the third world. Should the third world devote itself to copying the advanced countries' technology—to reading their journals, copying their blueprints, importing their machines, and courting their multinational corporations? That was certainly a cheaper and more feasible course of action than attempting to do the research and development work themselves. The suspicion arose, however, that the technology of the developed countries might be inappropriate for the less developed. The developed countries faced high wages and labor shortages; therefore, a great deal of their industrial research went into labor-saving technology—automation, robotics, computerization, and the like. In the third world, the economic problems were different. Most countries of the third world had lots of workers, many of them underemployed, most of them living on very low incomes. The technology they needed was labor-using, not labor-saving. Another sort of problem arose in agriculture: the unique environmental conditions in the third world meant that the rich countries' technology could not simply be transferred.

So technology transfer from the rich countries to the poor is part of the answer, but only part. The new emphasis on technological development as a central component of economic change implies that the third world has to do its own research. Research and development are expensive and risky: there are no guarantees that money invested will yield useful results. It is guaranteed, however, that an absence of investment in research and development will yield no useful results. So third-world countries are increasingly facing up to the need for technical education and applied research.

Investment in Human Capital

At the same time that the role of capital formation was being questioned, new attention was being paid in the third world to the importance of the human beings whose life task it is to labor and produce. The early models of development had been constructed by economists in the modernization school around the simple but bizarre assumption that labor was a homogeneous commodity, like a series of interchangeable hands, one much the same as the next, and that the only way to improve the productivity of labor was to provide workers with more and better machines. This is nonsense. Some workers are healthier and stronger than others; some are better educated and more skilled; some are better motivated. The quality of the labor force has a great deal to do with its productivity.

The idea of investment in human capital gained currency in the 1960s and 1970s. Economic theorists proposed that just as a country could invest in its stock of physical capital—its machinery and its factories—so too could it invest in its human capital by increasing the skills and capacities of its workers. In what seemed like a mere moment, health, nutrition, literacy, and technical training became issues that transcended relief and welfare; they appeared to be the key to economic development.

Third-world leaders came to understand that although wages were low in their countries, labor was not cheap. Labor was actually expensive, because it lacked education, training, and energy and was therefore relatively unproductive. In fact, a considerable amount of good work has been done to improve labor quality in many low-income countries, but the initial flash of excitement—that somehow this was the answer—has faded as the problems of widespread poverty have proved intractable even to this strategy.

The new approach to human capital made it clear that improvements in health care were not only a matter of providing for the welfare of the sick and disabled, although that was important. Recent planning documents in many third-world countries insist that expenditures on health care be thought of as an investment in the future of the country, an investment that will pay off in a stronger and more capable working population.

As noted in Chapter 2, some countries have made significant progress in the period since independence in extending public health, sanitation, mosquito eradication, and paramedical care. The achievements of China are remarkable, as are those of India. In other areas, however, health care is still primitive. Most African countries have few doctors, the majority of whom tend to live in the cities and cater to a middle-class clientele. They are often ignorant of the sorts of tropical diseases that afflict the majority of the people.

For poor countries, fancy high-technology Western medicine cannot be the answer, because expensive care cannot be made available to most of the people. The Chinese have shown that well-organized teams of public health workers can make a remarkable difference to the health of a population and to its longevity—and that as these improve, the economic productivity of the workers improves as well.

Basic to the health of a third-world population is its food and nutrition. Although most developing countries are predominantly agricultural, with most people living on the land, nutritional standards are often inadequate. Food deficiencies are actually more prevalent in rural areas than in urban, because rural people are, on average, poorer. Diets are typically deficient in two separate ways: caloric shortfalls and lack of specific nutrients. Calories in food are converted by the body into energy; nutritionists have established levels of calorie intake that appear to be necessary for people involved in daily physical work. In many areas of the third world, these standards are not met even on average; because the distribution of food is unequal, a high proportion of the population lacks sufficient food to work a fully productive day. Muscle strength is reduced, as are coordination, speed, and attention span.

Deficiencies of various specific nutrients are responsible for widespread diseases in the third world, including kwashiorkor (resulting from protein deficiency), which produces characteristic bloated bellies, and anemia (resulting from a lack of iron). The most harmful deficiency in much of the third world is in protein intake, a particularly serious problem in fetal development and infancy, when brain cells and intellectual capacity are developed. Malnutrition at this stage of human growth probably leaves physical and mental deficiencies that cannot be reversed at later ages, even if nutrition is improved. Of course, nutrition generally does not improve at older ages. The nutrition of children, for example, once they are weaned from their mothers' milk, is frequently worse than the nutrition of infants. Improvements in nutrition are therefore urgently needed, not just for the welfare of the people living in the third world but for their future prospects. The elimination of hunger could increase the population's capacity for productive labor tremendously.

Human capital means education in all its dimensions—from basic literacy through technical training and on-the-job skill enhancement to higher education. Third-world educational systems have frequently failed the people, however, because they have been too meager and badly conceived. Just like the decision to invest in physical capital, the decision to invest in human capital involves a present sacrifice in favor of anticipated future gains. Education requires an out-of-pocket expense, and because it keeps the students out of the labor force, it also lowers their current earnings. The tradeoff is a particularly difficult one for poor people: a family often sacrifices a great deal by keeping a son or daughter in school.

The most important educational issue in most low-income countries is basic literacy. Close to a billion people in the third world cannot read or write. This is a tremendous personal handicap, as it restricts them from interaction with much of the rest of the world. For economic development, it is a formidable barrier. People who cannot read cannot follow written instructions; in villages, they are condemned to subsistence methods, unable to understand new technologies. Several years of primary education are frequently insufficient to ensure basic literacy. Most children learn to read after a few years of schooling, but once they leave school, two things happen. The most ambitious leave their rural communities; unsatisfied with the prospect of the poor subsistence life they see around them, they hope for improved prospects in the cities. Many of those who stay behind lose their reading skills in a few years because they have no opportunity to continue reading. As a consequence, it is common to find villages whose inhabitants are, for the most part, illiterate, although they have been to school.

One of the most creative responses to the problem of illiteracy was pioneered in Latin America by Paulo Freire, who taught reading skills to adults using materials that gave them power and had a practical effect on their lives. The point of literacy, in Freire's philosophy, is to allow poor people to take control of their lives and to confront the power structures that are oppressing them. So instead of using "Dick and Jane" readers, the peasants decide what works they need to learn to read, such as legal contracts. They learn the language of organizing, and they develop a political analysis through talking about their lives—an analysis that leads them to social action. This approach to adult literacy has been highly effective in countries such as Cuba and Nicaragua, although other countries have found it too threatening to adopt.

In many respects, the secondary and higher educational systems in third-world countries have been a waste of resources. The systems are often inappropriate to the pressing economic needs of the countries.

Educational philosophies that were adopted from the colonialists are in some cases the last vestige of colonialism. The most glaring colonialist legacies have largely been eliminated: French-speaking African schoolchildren no longer memorize facts about "our ancestors, the Gauls." The overall approach to education remains, though.

In much of the former British Empire, schools still use the grading and examination systems left to them by their masters as a way of keeping standards high. The imprint of colonial education is a curious one. During the colonial period, the top British military and civilian administrators were graduates of exclusive schools and of Oxford and Cambridge, where they were educated in history, literature, philosophy, and classical languages. Such a course of study was thought to be the best background for the generalists whose responsibility it was to govern a far-flung empire—and it may well have been. It is not, however, the best curriculum for the majority of students in the third world today. The conviction frequently remains, however, that the best education is a general one, an education that deals with great ideas and significant literature, not one that immerses students in technical detail. As a consequence, higher educational systems in the third world often turn out a surplus of teachers and lawyers but leave their countries with a significant shortage of technically trained people: engineers, scientists, economists. Many parts of Africa and the Indian subcontinent have seen the startling phenomenon of significant unemployment among the highly educated—people whose training and aspirations are inappropriate for the urgent needs of their countries.

The insight that human capital is critical is correct. Skilled, capable, energetic people are central to economic development—certainly as important as physical capital. Human capital is not a magic key, however. Countries that have made significant progress in health, nutrition, and education have benefited, but they have not automatically made the transition to prosperity. Most alarmingly, the level of investment in human beings is still extremely low in most of the third world. Many governments that were struggling with huge debt burdens actually reduced spending on health and education in the 1980s and have been unable to restore the cuts in the period since then. Health and education may be important determinants of economic development, but they are equally consequences of development. A desperately poor society simply cannot afford to invest the resources that are needed in its own people. If it could, it would not be desperately poor. Many third-world countries have made significant improvements in health and literacy in the last several decades, but these improvements have not come cheaply or easily. So the discovery of the concept of human capital did not lead to a transformation of the human condition.

Oil Prices and the New International Economic Order

In the decade from 1973 to 1983, the most promising development for the third world seemed to be the increase in oil prices masterminded by the international cartel called OPEC (the Organization of Petroleum Exporting Countries). The price increases transformed the economic prospects of the oil exporters. It was welcomed by the oil-importing third-world countries as well, because although it caused immediate hardships for them, it seemed to promise a transformation of the entire international economic system that could benefit them in the long run. The third world united around the hope that the oil price increase would be the precursor to a "new international economic order" (NIEO). As events unfolded, however, the price increase proved to be only a temporary advantage, and the NIEO proposals collapsed.

Petroleum reserves are found in many parts of the world, but the largest fields are in North Africa and the Middle East. Until the early 1970s, the great multinational oil companies, based in the United States and western Europe, produced most of the Middle Eastern oil. They paid royalties to the host countries, sold the oil for an average price of about U.S.$3 a barrel, and made substantial profits. The oil-producing countries, joined together in OPEC, were powerless to get a better deal from the oil companies.

In the 1970s, this situation changed dramatically. The cataclysmic event occurred in 1973 when the Saudis and the other major OPEC countries decided to use oil as a political weapon. Determined to punish the United States for its support of Israel in the October war, OPEC reduced overall production and then instituted a total boycott of exports to the United States and some (not all) of its Western allies. This was only a short-run strategy: OPEC soon discovered a tool more powerful than the boycott. It took control of oil pricing away from the oil companies and, within a few months, quadrupled the price to about $13 a barrel. By March 1974, the boycott was suspended, and the westerners were invited to buy oil at the new high price. Over the next few years, the OPEC countries went further and actually nationalized the oil production facilities that were held by the companies.

The price increase was easily the biggest shock the international economy had sustained since the Second World War. Oil is, after all, the world's most important commodity, the basis for almost all world industry and much of its agriculture. The shock was repeated in 1979 when OPEC raised the price again, this time to more than $30 a barrel. This action had a tremendous impact on all the world's countries, both rich and poor. Some of the most important effects were still being played out at the beginning of the twenty-first century.

Many of the long-run results were unforeseen and actually harmful to the oil exporters. In the immediate wake of the OPEC action in the mid-1970s, however, the exporters were jubilant. A group of third-world countries had finally succeeded in turning the tables on the rich countries. Rather than seeing their own countries sucked dry by low-priced exports that went to fuel Western industrialization, the OPEC countries were now bleeding the developed countries, showing that their former masters were vulnerable, that their prosperity depended on the resources and the cooperation of the oil exporters.

The price increases led to inflation, recession, and unemployment in the developed countries, and to an extraordinary accumulation of wealth by the oil-exporting countries. The OPEC countries used their new wealth to import consumer goods, to raise living standards among their populations, and to embark on ambitious programs of industrialization.

The rest of the third world used the example of the oil prices to call for a complete restructuring of the international economic order. Calling themselves the Group of Seventy-seven, they argued that the prices of all their commodity exports, not just oil, should be kept high and stable. They knew that they were not strong enough, and their commodities not critical enough, for them to get away with imposing unilateral price increases—hence the demand that the rich countries join them collectively in a new international economic order. The NIEO contained proposals besides commodity price increases: a restructuring of the international monetary system, new controls on multinational corporations, increased foreign aid, and tariff preferences on manufactured goods. The heart of the proposal, however, was a "common fund" to be paid for by the rich countries and used to keep the prices of third-world exports high.

By a decade after the first oil price increase, the OPEC strategy had failed, and with it the NIEO proposals. OPEC had initially been able to raise oil prices because it controlled so much of the world supply and could cut back on that supply to create shortages. The industrialized countries were so addicted that they could not reduce their use of oil significantly. By the mid-1980s, however, when the world had gotten used to ten years of high oil prices, the easy advantage of the oil exporters disappeared. OPEC could no longer restrict the supply of oil. The individual OPEC members actually cheated on their agreed quotas, seduced by the high prices into producing more and more. Only Saudi Arabia was willing to restrict its exports significantly, and eventually even it refused to play the patsy. Outside OPEC, the high prices made it profitable for other countries and companies to explore for oil in risky circumstances and to produce it even when the costs were high. Tremendous new resources were exploited—for example, on the north slope of Alaska and in the North Sea between Scotland and Norway.

At the same time that new supplies were finding their way to market, the consumption of oil was falling. Over a period of years, the oil-consuming countries learned how to conserve, how to be energy efficient. The result of the declining consumption and the expanding quantity of oil supplies—both caused by the high price—was a worldwide glut. As a consequence, the price fell precipitously. From highs of just less than $40 a barrel, the price fell to $9 in 1986, then rebounded in recent years to between $20 and $30. This might seem to be a high price compared with the pre-1973 period, except for one thing: the last three decades have seen a significant worldwide inflation of all prices—brought about, ironically, by the oil price increases in the first place. Prices have risen on average about five- or sixfold. In real terms, therefore, in terms of the amount of other goods and services for which a barrel of oil can be exchanged, the price of oil is just slightly above what it had been before 1973. The oil market has come full circle; the exporters have lost their entire advantage.

The lesson was long and painful and may be repeated. The prospects for future oil prices are naturally uncertain, but high prices could lead once again to temporary wealth among the oil exporters and to both recession and inflation in the rest of the world. The industrialized countries are vulnerable because the relatively low prices since the 1980s have lulled them into abandoning their energy-conservation policies. There may be cycles of conservation and profligacy if oil prices move up and down in cycles. It is now obvious, however, that a group of third-world countries, even a group as powerful as OPEC, cannot manipulate world prices to solve their economic problems on a permanent basis. That hope has disintegrated.

With the collapse of oil prices, the hopes for the NIEO vanished as well. If a monopolistic oil cartel could not succeed in the long run, what hope was there for cartels in other primary commodities produced by the developing countries? As the OPEC boom turned into a bust, third-world enthusiasm for the NIEO subsided and disappeared.

Development in the 1980s: Waylaid by the Debt Crisis

In the 1980s, economic development slowed to a snail's pace in most areas of the third world, particularly in Latin America and Africa; in some cases, it went into reverse. The principal culprit was a wholly new problem: the debt crisis.

The origin of the third-world debt crisis was the OPEC price increases of the 1970s. The price increases produced a tidal wave of change in international monetary relations. Billions upon billions of new funds flowed into OPEC's coffers. The oil exporters used some of these funds to increase their imports of goods and services from abroad, but their imports could not absorb all their new earnings. They were left with a huge volume of liquid cash. What to do with this cash became known as the "recycling" problem.

Much of the surplus cash was invested by the OPEC countries in the great banks of the developed countries. The banks, awash in funds and looking for opportunities to lend those funds at a profit, discovered eager borrowers among the governments of the oil-importing third-world countries. These oil-importing countries were in ideological solidarity with OPEC but were stretched to the limit by the high prices. Unlike the developed countries, they could not reduce their consumer use of oil—for private automobiles, home heating, and the like—because little of their oil went to consumer uses. Almost all the oil imported by third-world countries was used to support industry, so any attempt to cope with the crisis by reducing oil use would have crippled their manufacturing sectors—the very sectors that they saw as the leading edge of their economic development programs. Third-world governments borrowed money from the great banks largely to cover the cost of the imported oil. They also borrowed to pay the bills on imported consumer goods for their new middle classes. Amazingly, once the oil boom was in full swing, even some of the oil exporters, such as Mexico, began to borrow large amounts to cover their growing consumption.

Foreign borrowing by a developing country is not always a bad idea. In the nineteenth century, the United States built its railways with funds borrowed from the British and benefited from the transactions. To be beneficial, however, the loans must be invested in productive new projects. For example, a third-world country may borrow money from abroad to construct a new irrigation network. If the project is successful, it will generate new jobs and higher incomes. A portion of the new income is used to pay back the principal and interest on the loan, and income still remains from the project to improve the living standards of the local people. If the loan is used simply to purchase consumer goods or other goods that are already being imported from abroad, however, no new productive activity is begun and no new revenue is generated. The repayment of the debt then becomes a burden: the borrowers have to lower their living standards in order to come up with the funds to repay the loans.

This is the story of the third-world debt crisis. Both the borrowers and the lenders conspired to make some of the worst loans in the history of international finance. The borrowers were desperate for the funds because of their high oil bills. The lenders were desperate to make the loans, because they owed interest payments to the OPEC countries. Neither side had an incentive to look closely at the true picture, which was that few of these loans were actually going into the financing of new, productive, financially sound projects in the third world.

In the late 1970s and early 1980s, the crisis hit. Country after country—particularly but not exclusively in Latin America—found itself committed to debt repayment schedules that it could not possibly meet. In 1980, Mexico's debt repayments amounted to 50 percent of the value of its exports; Brazil's, 63 percent; Argentina's, 37 percent; Peru's, 47 percent; and Chile's, 43 percent. They and many other third-world countries were in over their heads. The crisis was exacerbated by rising world interest rates and by declining prices for third-world exports. If the loans were to be repaid, the people's standards of living would collapse.

The search for a solution to the debt crisis dominated thinking and negotiations about economic development in the 1980s. It was a crisis that at times threatened not only the economies of the third world but also the stability and prosperity of the entire international economic system. Worst-case scenarios were not hard to imagine. For a few years, the third-world debts were actually greater than the net worth of the lending banks. In other words, if the debtor countries had refused to honor their debts, the banks would have collapsed as business entities. The specter of the collapse of the world banking system was frightening, threatening another world depression that might have been worse than the one in the 1930s. By the late 1980s, however, this danger receded as most of the banks succeeded in accumulating enough reserves to buffer themselves against the danger of third-world loan defaults.

For the developed countries, the debt crisis was only a potential danger, but for the third world, it was a monumental present disaster. In 1981, there was a net positive flow of funds from the rich countries to the third world of $42.6 billion; by 1988, there was a net reverse flow, from the poor countries to the rich, of $32.5 billion, most of the shift occurring because of debt servicing.[21]

Third-world countries simply could not afford to pay off their debts. To grasp the problem, one must understand that to pay off debts to the United States, Mexicans must have U.S. dollars. U.S. banks will not accept Mexican pesos; if they would, the debt crisis would be easily solved, because the Mexicans would just print more pesos—but the U.S. banks won't. Where can the Mexicans get dollars? They cannot just buy dollars with their pesos, because if they tried to do this, the value of the peso would collapse: foreigners do not want to hold pesos. So the Mexicans must export more goods to the United States and other countries (thus earning dollars) than they import from those countries (spending dollars); they must run an export surplus. This is easier said than done, though. It is not simple for Mexico to increase its exports. Mexican industries find it difficult to compete in international markets, and the rich countries protect their own industries against the threat of foreign imports. Because the Mexicans must run an export surplus in order to make payments on their debt, they are therefore forced to reduce their imports. There are many complex ways of doing this, but what they all amount to in the end is reducing the incomes of the Mexican people so that they are unable to buy so many goods from abroad. In other words, the debt crisis led directly to a staggering drop in the standard of living of Mexicans and of other third-world peoples facing the debt burden. In the six-year term of Mexican president Miguel de la Madrid (1982–88), real wages (that is, money wages corrected for changes in the cost of living) fell by 40 percent. Poverty increased extensively, and whole sections of the middle class were wiped out. In just two years, from 1985 to 1987, Nigeria's per capita income fell by more than half, from $800 to $380; the fall was caused by both the debt crisis and the collapse of oil prices. No wonder economic development in the third world seemed to take a backseat in the 1980s. The struggle was no longer for economic development in many countries; it was to resist massive deterioration in living standards.

In the 1990s and early 2000s, the debt burden remained a serious problem for many countries, but the crisis had passed for most of them. Discussions involving all the participants—the governments of the developed countries, the lending banks, the International Monetary Fund, the World Bank, and the governments of the borrowing countries—led to solutions that relieved many of the debtors of their worst burdens. Under some of the plans, third-world countries were permitted to reduce their debt payments in return for agreeing to restructure their economies in such a way as to put greater emphasis on the market and less on government control. The banks were willing to acquiesce in the plans; although they had to write off some of their loans, they were reasonably assured that the remainder would eventually be paid off. With the agreements in place, international lenders and investors had renewed confidence in third-world economies, particularly in Latin America, and funds began to flow once more from the North to the South. As a result, the pace of economic growth began to pick up again in the 1990s.

The debt crisis made it clear that the world's poor countries were enmeshed in an increasingly globalized economy. They had never been isolated from the rich countries, of course, but in the 1980s, and to an even greater extent in the 1990s, they became more and more connected to global economic processes. They were susceptible to massive and rapid flows of capital, both into and out of their countries. If international investors and bankers lost confidence in their economies, they could pull out great sums of money at a moment's notice, leaving the poor countries gasping for breath and crying for mercy. In the 1990s, these sorts of crises hit a number of East Asian and Latin American countries several times. If third-world countries were to enjoy economic success in the new age of financial globalization, they would have to play by the rich countries' rules, not their own.

Into a New Century:
Rediscovering the Market and Exports

Third-world economic growth recovered in the 1990s and early 2000s—not everywhere and never smoothly, but in most countries. The recovery was associated with an extraordinary shift in strategy, away from government control, protectionism, and planning and toward the free market and export promotion. Government intervention came to be seen as the source of the economic problem in the third world and private initiative as the solution, rather than vice versa. In country after country, especially in Latin America and Asia, controls were dismantled, subsidies abolished, and tariffs reduced. In place of the rejected state-centered economy, private entrepreneurs were encouraged to compete against one another at home and against foreign producers in international markets.

The new affection for the market entailed a remarkable reversal in ideology. What only yesterday had been regarded as falsehood was now seen as truth.[22] To cite a few examples:

Private entrepreneurs. Once they were thought of as exploiters pursuing their own interests, which were unlikely to correspond to the interests of the majority of the people. The new ideology is that entrepreneurs, risking their own money, are the best judges of productive economic opportunities. They have a far greater incentive than do government bureaucrats to choose sectors and technologies for investment in which markets are likely to be growing and new enterprises successful. They are therefore the most effective engines of economic growth.

Profits. Once seen as a mark of exploitation, profits are now seen as the inducement and justifiable reward for successful risk taking.

The state. Once seen as a disinterested body, concerned with improving the welfare of all the people, the state is now seen as a self-serving hierarchy that is as likely as not to rob the people.

Prices. Formerly, it was thought that prices were set by powerful institutions and had the principal effect of transferring wealth from the poor and weak to the rich and powerful. In the new market-oriented ideology, free prices are seen as reflecting real scarcities in the economy and therefore as giving people the proper incentives to use resources efficiently. If the government were to change market prices through subsidies, price supports, or price controls, it would send the economy in an inefficient direction.

International markets. According to the dependency school, international capitalist markets were the source of underdevelopment. The market-oriented ideology sees them instead as opportunities for aggressive third-world countries to use them to their own advantage.

Self-sufficiency. The old view was that poor countries should block out the influence of the outside world so that they could concentrate on the needs of their own people. The new view is that self-sufficiency is a prescription for stagnation, because it cuts a country off from the dynamic pressures and opportunities of the outside world.

The shift toward this new ideology was strongest in Latin America and China but was present to some degree almost everywhere. In part, it was a genuine intellectual shift, occasioned by the evident failures of the state-centered approach to economic development in most third-world countries. The collapse of socialism in the Soviet bloc and in China deprived the advocates of a state-centered approach of their principal models.

The most impressive models of economic development since the early 1980s have been ones in which the role of the government was distinctly reduced. The startling news has been the success of four proudly capitalist societies in Asia: Taiwan, Hong Kong, Singapore, and South Korea—the newly industrializing countries (NICs). Each achieved rapid economic growth through an aggressive strategy of export promotion—not the traditional primary commodity exports, but new manufactured exports. Manufacturing in each society began with textiles and then moved on to products embodying higher technology, including electronics and automobiles. The initiative for this growth came from the private sector, from individual entrepreneurs. The governments were not passive in these four countries. They directed resources, licenses, and finances where they were most needed. Rather than controlling the economy and planning the interrelationships in it, however, the governments concentrated on creating an economic environment in which private firms could thrive. The NICs faced some serious setbacks toward the end of the 1990s, but then recovered almost completely.

In addition to leading to fast overall economic growth in these four countries, capitalism without a controlling government plan produced at least some benefits for the poor. The NICs still suffer from poverty, but the share of income going to the poorest has risen sharply. The continuing success of the NICs showed the rest of the third world that it need not reconcile itself to perpetual stagnation.

The shift toward the market was a consequence not just of third-world countries' observing the evident successes and failures around them but of international power politics as well. The rich countries insisted on the shift as the price to be paid for their support in an era of financial globalization. Third-world countries were particularly vulnerable during the debt crisis. The rich countries had it in their power to relieve the poor of at least some of their debt burden, and they agreed to do so, but only at a price. The price went by the name of "conditionality" or "structural adjustment." Both terms refer to the conditions required by the rich countries and by the International Monetary Fund (which is controlled by the rich countries) before they will step in to help a poor country with debt or balance-of-payment problems. Typically, the third-world countries are required to lower their tariff barriers against imports, reduce if not eliminate subsidies to favored companies, eliminate price ceilings on food, cut back licenses and other barriers that restrict entry into different markets, reduce the government deficit, and lower the growth of the money supply in order to reduce inflation.

The rich countries take the position that these sorts of reforms are in the interest of the poor, that the reason they insist on them is to ensure that the poor countries give themselves the best possible chance at economic growth. With the reforms, third-world countries are likely to succeed economically, the rich countries argue; without them, they will fail, and the financial help from the rich will be wasted. It is not hard to discover a more self-interested motivation, however. The structural-adjustment reforms make possible greater economic connections between the rich countries and the poor: more opportunities for foreign investment and more markets for exports from the developed world. The shift toward the market is, therefore, at least in part an indicator of a loss of autonomy by third-world countries, an admission on their part that they must play by the rules of the rich countries if they are to have a chance of economic success.[23]

Most of the leaders of third-world countries are ambivalent about structural adjustment. It almost always causes great hardship, as sectors of the economy and society that were previously protected are left to fend for themselves in an unprotected and uncaring market. Yet the adjustments may be needed in order to help the countries take advantage of international markets. For example, government licenses and tariffs that are designed to protect local manufacturing plants may result in their costs being so high that they cannot compete effectively against foreign producers. Only if they are forced to fend for themselves will they be able to produce efficiently enough to compete.

International trade is increasingly seen as the leading sector that will drive economic growth. The NICs have competed aggressively abroad with modern manufactured goods. Now many other countries are trying to follow their example and break into the markets of the developed countries with industrial products. The new ideology rejects the fear that the third-world countries cannot compete and therefore need to protect their home markets against rapacious foreigners; rather, it embraces the idea that they must become productive and efficient enough to compete against all challengers.

A serious problem with this new strategy is that to the extent that third-world countries are successful in exporting to the rich markets of the North, they threaten jobs and industries in the North, and their exports are likely to face increased barriers to entry. Hence the importance of international agreements for lowered barriers and even for free trade becomes obvious; they hold open the promise that third-world growth will not be stifled if the export strategy proves successful. In recent years, two comprehensive agreements that reduced, but did not eliminate, trade barriers have proved very controversial: the North American Free Trade Agreement (NAFTA) and the Uruguay round of the General Agreement on Tariffs and Trade (GATT). NAFTA, implemented at the beginning of 1994, provides for free trade and the elimination of tariffs among Mexico, Canada, and the United States. The Uruguay round of GATT, negotiated over a seven-year period and adopted at the end of 1994, provides for the reduction of many tariffs and other restrictions on trade around the world. It also provided for the end of GATT as an organization, and its replacement by the World Trade Organization (WTO), an institution with more power to disallow restraints on trade by member countries. Opponents of the agreements in the developed countries feared that they would lead to a loss of jobs at home because of increased imports and that they would hamstring domestic laws regulating labor and the environment. Proponents countered that the residents of the developed countries would gain both jobs and income because of increased exports and that social legislation would be protected. Time will provide the answers, but in any case, the relative impact of the agreements on the world's major economies is likely to be small.

In countries such as Mexico, however, the more open trading rules of NAFTA and the WTO could have a major impact. The agreements have been controversial in the third world too, but there the controversy centers on the overall strategy of market capitalism and export promotion. While their countries have been moving aggressively in those directions, many groups of people have become convinced that it is a fatal error to allow weak economies to become more vulnerable to international competition. The most dramatic response to NAFTA occurred on January 1, 1994, the day the agreement was implemented, when a group of Indians in the southern Mexican state of Chiapas, calling themselves Zapatistas in honor of the revolutionary hero, declared war on the Mexican government. The uprising was put down, but it captured the imagination of Mexicans and many outside of Mexico. It was a dramatic example of popular resistance to the new economic strategy of letting the market dominate. It was not alone; resistance movements arose in Venezuela, Bolivia, Argentina, and other countries. Dissidents in the rich countries lent their support, arguing against globalization and the free market, and saying that the new arrangements were largely designed to facilitate the exploitation of the poor by the rich.

The move toward the market in the third world has been successful, for the most part, in generating economic growth; the biggest question is whether it will also be successful in alleviating poverty. So far, the record is mixed. The NICs have done quite well for their poorer people; as their economies have prospered, the relative gap between the rich and the poor has narrowed. In Latin America, however, the opposite is true. Most of the new income has accrued to a small proportion of the population, and poverty is not falling. The success of the NICs in narrowing the income gap may be due to the programs of land reform and agricultural development that preceded the phases of intensive capitalist growth. In most of Latin America, in contrast, the peasants have never been favored, and as a consequence, both they and the urban poor lack the power to secure some of the benefits of the new prosperity. In many Latin American countries, the growing gap between rich and poor is, once again, threatening economic and political stability.

One of the consequences of the move toward the market has been the increasing importance of nongovernmental organizations (NGOs) in many low-income countries. As governments have left their people more open to unpredictable price fluctuations and to unemployment, and as they have withdrawn their protections and safety nets in order to let the market operate with fewer constraints, they have left large segments of their populations at greater risk. To meet this challenge, many NGOs expanded the scope of their operations greatly in the 1990s.[24]

NGOs are of many types and functions, from large international organizations based in the rich countries, such as the Red Cross and Save the Children Fund, to small grassroots organizations that have grown up among poor people, and countless others in between. David C. Korten divides them into "Voluntary Organizations (VOs) that pursue a social mission driven by a commitment to shared values, Public Service Contractors (PSCs) that function as market-oriented nonprofit businesses serving public purposes, People's Organizations (POs) that represent their members' interests, have member accountable leadership and are substantially self-reliant, and Governmental Nongovernmental Organizations (GONGOs) that are creations of government and serve as instruments of government policy."[25]

NGOs perform many tasks, including the provision of emergency aid, instruction and education, village-based economic development, and microcredit programs. The microcredit programs are particularly interesting. Based on the pioneering experiments of the Grameen Bank in Bangladesh, they have swept into most areas of the third world. The programs provide modest business loans to poor people, often to small groups or "circles" of people who become responsible for one another's business success and for the repayment of the loans. The microcredit programs thus help to create small communities of people who work with and support one another.

The NGO movement has typically been infused with enthusiasm and idealism. The NGOs have been willing to take risks where governments and for-profit businesses have declined to enter. They have often situated themselves as defenders of the poor, in opposition to what they have regarded as exploitation by third-world governments. Some observers now see a danger that NGOs will lose their idealism and political independence and become coopted by governments. This may happen because governments of both third-world countries and donor countries are increasingly turning to NGOs and funding them more generously, in the hope that they will be able to blunt the damage caused to those who are most vulnerable to the market system. With increased funding comes increased accountability and control, however, and the distinctiveness of NGOs may be eroded.

At the beginning of the twenty-first century, the market was king and all else fell before it. It is unlikely to retain this ascendancy forever. Unless the market can produce a decent life for all the people of the third world, not just a chosen few, it will come under attack in the future. Reliance on the international market may well join the long list of nostrums—including socialism, state control, capital formation, foreign aid, and the new international economic order—that were once thought to be the key to economic development but that eventually proved unequal to the task.

Notes

1. Hong Kong, a British colony, was ceded to China in 1997.

2. World Bank, *World Development Report 1992* (New York: Oxford University Press, 1992), Tables 2, 26.

3. World Bank, *World Development Report 2003* (New York: Oxford University Press, 2003), Tables 1, 3.

4. World Bank, *World Development Report 2003*, Table 1.

5. On the Indira Gandhi Canal, see Michael R. Goldman, "'There's a Snake on Our Chests': State and Development Crisis in India's Desert," Ph.D. dissertation, Board of Studies in Sociology, University of California, Santa Cruz, 1994.

6. For a comprehensive treatment of the relationship between economic development and the environment, see World Bank, *World Development Report 1992*.

7. W. Arthur Lewis, *The Theory of Economic Growth* (London: Allen and Unwin, 1955), 9.

8. The United Nations Development Programme has published a *Human Development Report* annually since 1990.

9. UNDP, *Human Development Report 1990* (New York: Oxford University Press, 1990).

10. World Bank, *World Development Report 2003*, Table 1. As noted in Chapter 4, the number of years required for the population to double is found by dividing the annual percentage growth rate into seventy.

11. For a full discussion of the attempts to identify an optimum or maximum world population, see Joel E. Cohen, *How Many People Can the Earth Support?* (New York: Norton, 1995).

12. This way of looking at the economic consequences of population growth, by concentrating on changes in the growth rate and the age distribution rather than on the absolute size, was proposed in Ansley J. Coale and Edgar M. Hoover, *Population Growth and Economic Development in Low-Income Countries: A Case Study of India's Prospects* (Princeton, N.J.: Princeton University Press, 1958).

13. For a good summary of the empirical problems in this field of inquiry, see National Research Council, *Population Growth and Economic Development: Policy Questions* (Washington, D.C.: National Academy Press, 1986).

14. A rich source of world demographic data is United Nations, Department of Economic and Social Affairs, *Demographic Yearbook* (United Nations, New York: annual).

15. In 1988, in a publicized case, the United States gave political asylum to six Chinese who fled from their country's birth-control policy, which would have required abortion to prevent the birth of a second child. The Chinese government, naturally, protested.

16. The term may have been used first by Anne O. Krueger, "The Political Economy of the Rent-Seeking Society," *American Economic Review* 64 (June 1974): 291–303.

17. For an excellent discussion of this neglected aspect of economic development, see Andrew M. Kamarck, *The Tropics and Economic Development: A Provocative Inquiry into the Poverty of Nations* (Baltimore: Johns Hopkins University Press, 1973).

18. UNDP, *Human Development Report 2002*, Table 5.

19. For a discussion of the ethics of foreign aid, see John Isbister, *Capitalism and Justice: Envisioning Social and Economic Fairness* (Bloomfield, Conn.: Kumarian Press, 2001), Chapter 10.

20. W. Arthur Lewis, "Economic Development with Unlimited Supplies of Labor," *Manchester School of Economic and Social Studies* 22 (1954): 139–91.

21. UNDP, *Human Development Report 1990*, 5.

22. For a comprehensive discussion of the change in view, see Anne O. Krueger, "Trade Policy and Economic Development: How We Learn," *American Economic Review* 87 (March 1997): 1–22. For a cautionary warning that an effective state is still a precondition for economic development, see World Bank, *World Development Report 1997*, whose subtitle is *The State in a Changing World*.

23. For a spirited polemic against structural adjustment and other policies of the International Monetary Fund by a Nobel Prize winner and former chief economist of the World Bank, see Joseph E. Stiglitz, *Globalization and Its Discontents* (New York: W. W. Norton and Company, 2002).

24. On the importance of NGOs, see David C. Korten, *Getting to the 21st Century: Voluntary Action and the Global Agenda* (West Hartford, Conn.: Kumarian Press, 1990). On the growing relationship between NGOs and governments, see David Hulme and Michael Edwards, eds., *NGOs, States and Donors: Too Close for Comfort?* (New York: St. Martin's Press, 1997).

25. Korten, *Getting to the 21st Century*, 2.

Suggestions for Further Reading

See Bibliography for full details.

Tim Allen and Alan Thomas, eds. *Poverty and Development into the 21st Century.*
H. W. Arndt. *Economic Development: The History of an Idea.*
John Feffer, ed. *Living in Hope: People Challenging Globalization.*
Thomas L. Friedman. *The Lexus and the Olive Tree: Understanding Globalization.*
Robert Gilpin. *The Challenge of Global Capitalism: The World Economy in the 21st Century.*
William Greider. *One World, Ready or Not: The Manic Logic of Global Capitalism.*
David C. Korten. *Getting to the 21st Century: Voluntary Action and the Global Agenda.*

Kusum Nair. *Blossoms in the Dust: The Human Factor in Indian Development.*
Amartya Sen. *Development as Freedom.*
Kathleen Staudt. *Policy, Politics and Gender: Women Gaining Ground.*
Joseph Stiglitz. *Globalization and Its Discontents.*
Michael Todaro. *Economic Development.*
Daniel Yergin and Joseph Stanislaw. *The Commanding Heights: The Battle for the World Economy.*

Chapter Seven

Foreign Policy

As the Cold War fades away, we face not a "new world order" but a troubled and fractured planet.
—Paul Kennedy, *Preparing for the Twenty-First Century*

We need bread for the hungry rather than weapons in space.
—Willy Brandt, "North-South: The Task Ahead"

States like [North Korea, Iran, and Iraq] and their terrorist allies constitute an axis of evil, arming to threaten the peace of the world. By seeking weapons of mass destruction, these regimes pose a grave and growing danger. They could provide these arms to terrorists, giving them the means to match their hatred. They could attack our allies or attempt to blackmail the United States. In any of these cases, the price of indifference would be catastrophic.
—President George W. Bush,
State of the Union Address, January 29, 2002

On the whole, the rich countries have not been helpful to the world's poor people. The existence of widespread world poverty is not solely their fault; it is a much bigger problem. Still, the countries of the North, absorbed by their own problems of security and economy, have turned their backs on one of the great moral challenges to face the globe; in countless ways, big and small, they have acted to make the problems of poverty and exploitation worse, not better.

From the end of the Second World War through the decade of the 1980s, the foreign policy of the rich countries was dominated by the cold war, the struggle for dominance between the communist and capitalist worlds. In this struggle, third-world countries were treated largely as pawns. With the collapse of the Soviet Union and the disappearance of the cold war in the 1990s came a glimmer of hope that the rich countries might consider the alleviation of the world's poverty to be a compelling objective of their foreign policy. That hope was probably destined to be disappointed in even the most favorable of circumstances, and since September 11, 2001, it has been extinguished. American foreign policy is now dominated by the so-called "war on terrorism," not the war on poverty. Meanwhile, the Europeans, although unwilling for the most part simply to fall in line behind American leadership in the war on terrorism, nevertheless lack the resources and will to formulate a more constructive foreign policy.

The End of the Cold War

The cold war—the confrontation between the United States, western Europe, and their allies on the one hand, and the Soviet Union and its allies on the other—colored almost every aspect of public life. In the United States, generations of politicians were judged by their anticommunist credentials and their commitment to stand up against the Soviet threat. In the Soviet Union, the foreign threat was used as a justification for dictatorship. The Europeans were exceptionally vulnerable, geographically located as they were between the two superpowers. An arms race squandered untold sums of money that might otherwise have been used to improve the human condition. Then the cold war ended for the most unexpected and dramatic of reasons—the complete collapse of the Soviet Union as a political entity. Of the former cold war rivals, only one remained.

By the 1980s, the Soviets had become fatally overextended abroad, and their domestic economy was deteriorating. Premier Gorbachev made a series of what in retrospect appear to be desperate, futile efforts to salvage the Soviet state. He pulled back radically from foreign involvement. The Soviets withdrew from their war in Afghanistan in 1988 and drastically cut economic aid to Cuba and other dependent countries. They permitted the client states of their eastern European empire—Poland, East Germany, Czechoslovakia, Hungary, Bulgaria, and Romania—to break away from their control in 1989. They stood by powerless as Germany was reunited in 1990. At home, Gorbachev's regime permitted freer political expression and attempted to restructure the failing economy. It was all in vain. The end of the Soviet Union came in 1991 when, following an abortive coup by communist hard-liners, Gorbachev was forced to accept the independence of all the Soviet republics and the repudiation of communism.

The successor state in Russia, led by the democratically elected Boris Yeltsin, faced enormous domestic problems. The economy deteriorated rapidly. Politically, the adherents of the old guard fought Yeltsin for power at every turn, trying to turn the country back from economic and social reform. Regional, ethnic, and national conflict spread. Yeltsin ventured into a disastrous military encounter in the breakaway region of Chechnya. Eventually his control weakened so much that he yielded power to his chosen successor, Vladimir Putin. Russia turned to western Europe and North America for aid. Although some tensions remained between the former enemies—over policy toward Iraq, for example—Russia was transformed into something between an ally and a client of the West. The bipolar conflict that had lasted for almost half a century disappeared.

Foreign Policy During the Cold War: Globalism

During the cold war, the countries of North America and western Europe formed a political, military, and economic alliance for the purpose of protecting their security and confronting the Soviets. The United States took the leadership position in this Western alliance. In comparison to its allies, it adopted the strongest and most rigid anti-communist position. The Canadians and the Europeans remained under the protection of American might and generally supported the United States, although they frequently toyed with somewhat more liberal or conciliatory policies toward the Soviets. Throughout this period, however, it was the foreign policy of the United States, not that of its allies, that was predominant. The United States built an enormous nuclear and conventional military arsenal to counter the Soviet threat. Its geopolitical policy was one of "containment," keeping the Soviets and their allies penned up to the maximum extent possible.

Both the United States and the Soviet Union extended the cold war struggle to the third world. Each viewed its interest as being to secure the allegiance of third-world governments and to prevent its foe from extending its influence.

During most of the cold war period, U.S. foreign policymakers viewed the third world from what is sometimes called a globalist rather than a regionalist perspective. A regionalist perspective would have taken the local conflicts seriously; it would have seen the Nicaraguan revolution as the struggle of an oppressed peasantry against a dictatorial military regime and the South African conflict as a movement for racial justice. The globalist perspective was to see almost all third-world societies as pawns in an enormously complex chess game being fought by two master players—the Soviet Union and the United States—the stakes being the freedom of the people in the Western alliance. In the globalist perspective, the regional issues were secondary and unimportant. The globalists had no difficulty in embracing authoritarian dictators if they took the right stand against the Soviets: "He may be a son of a bitch," the saying went, when referring to third-world dictators, "but he's our son of a bitch."

The contrary policy, regionalism, was actually attempted for four years in the late 1970s, during the much-maligned presidency of Jimmy Carter. The Carter administration put human rights, rather than anticommunism, in the place of honor in its third-world policy, the consequence being that the United States offended a number of its allies. The Carter policy was less than completely successful. Although it gave hope to the victims and the oppressed in poor countries, it did not produce many concrete changes. The administration underestimated the military determination of the Soviets in Afghanistan, and it was drawn into a humiliating hostage crisis in Iran. Carter's critics on the right were sharp, arguing that he was giving up the historic American role of opposing Soviet expansionism. In the end, it was Carter's ineffectiveness in foreign policy more than anything else that led to his defeat after one term.

With Ronald Reagan's victory in the 1980 presidential election, the philosophy of globalism returned. Reagan came to office with an explicit mandate to restore U.S. power, to recover from the decline the country was seen to have suffered. Reagan and his supporters saw the world in bipolar terms, with the United States leading the free world against the "evil empire" of godless Soviet communism. The central thrust of American foreign policy in the 1980s was to reassert U.S. power throughout the world and to confront the Soviets at every turn. In Central America, in the Middle East, in southern Africa, in the Pacific—in fact, throughout the third world—U.S. policy became to support those who opposed the communists. Other considerations mattered little.

The U.S. government under President Reagan downplayed the issue of human rights in the third world. The United States supported a series of military regimes in Latin America, even against the centrist democratic governments that eventually replaced them. In South Africa, the U.S. policy of "constructive engagement" was perhaps intended to pressure the white ruling regime away from apartheid, but it was perceived as a proapartheid policy working against the freedom of the black majority, all in the name of anticommunism. In El Salvador, the United States supported a right-wing government against what it saw as a Marxist rebel movement; in Nicaragua, it supported the rebels against what it saw as a Soviet-dominated revolutionary government. In both cases, the purpose was to deny the Soviets a foothold in Central America. In the Philippines, up until the very last moment, the United States supported the dictator Ferdinand Marcos because he was a bulwark against communist rebels.

The tragedy of this policy was that in country after country, it put the Americans squarely against the aspirations of poor people. It was not a necessary policy, because the great majority of third-world peoples and their governments had only a marginal interest in the great cold war power struggle. One can see in hindsight that the Americans actually created geopolitical problems for themselves where none needed to exist. In Vietnam, Ho Chi Minh explicitly sought American friendship at the end of the Second World War, long before he looked to the Soviets for help. In southern Africa, black resistance movements tolerated communist influence only because they saw the Americans' support of the white minorities. In Central America, peasants would have preferred to live in peace and friendship with the United States; their leaders turned to the Soviets for help only because the Americans supported the landowning factions.

The regionalist perspective was kept alive principally in the foreign policies of some of the United States' allies. Once the British were reconciled to their withdrawal from empire, they generally supported the American position. Other allies, however, dissented somewhat. The Canadians and the Scandinavians tried to establish relationships with third-world countries that promoted economic development. The Germans and the Japanese cautiously began to create new bridges to poor countries. The French maintained unique connections to their former colonies, particularly in Africa, often supporting dictatorships for their own reasons. The impact of all these slightly different policies was much weaker than that of the American policy, however.

The New American Hegemony

The United States emerged from the Second World War as the globe's strongest power. Although it had fought in the war, its economy had suffered no war damage; in fact, its economy was vastly stronger in 1945 than it had been in 1939. In contrast, the economies of most of the other war participants—Britain, continental Europe, the Soviet Union, Japan, and China—were shattered.

That moment of American pre-eminence was short-lived, however, as the rest of the world recovered from the war. By 1960, Europe was back on its feet again—partly with the help of American aid. The separate western European countries formed the European Union and increasingly cooperated in economic and financial affairs, and to some extent in political and military affairs as well. Japan embarked upon a long period of economic growth, led by high-technology exports that penetrated markets throughout the world. Most importantly, the Soviet Union concentrated on the expansion of heavy industries and the military, and quickly began to challenge the dominance of the United States.

In the cold war decades—roughly 1950 to 1990—quite a lot of evidence existed that American hegemony was declining. The share of world output produced by the United States fell, and many other countries caught up to it and even surpassed it in terms of average standard of living. In 1971, the American dollar lost its position of unquestioned world currency when the international system of fixed exchange rates was abandoned. Most importantly, the United States lost the Vietnam War, the only war it had lost in its history, with the ambiguous exceptions of the War of 1812 and the Civil War. The United States had gone into Vietnam in the 1950s and 1960s as the world's strongest military force; it emerged apparently severely weakened, with serious questions about its ability to exert its authority on a world scale.

In the years since the end of the cold war in 1990, however, it has become clear that American dominance in the world has been reestablished. Indeed it has been more than reestablished: the relative power of the United States is greater now than it ever has been. Today there is no dimension of power in which the United States is even challenged. For example, at the latest reckoning, the United States spends more on its military forces than do the next twenty biggest spenders combined, and it does so with only 3.5 percent of its gross domestic product. It has by far the world's largest army, air force, and navy, and its superiority in nuclear weapons is overwhelming. Not only does it have more military forces, it has by far the best military forces in terms of technology, because it spends three times more on military research and development than the next six countries combined. Its superiority in military technology is matched by its superiority in technology in general, because it spends more on overall research and development than the next seven richest countries combined. No other country, or even combination of allied countries, can come close to challenging its position of dominance.[1]

Will this new dominance last for long? Perhaps not. Several observers of the current scene have developed arguments predicting that American hegemony in the world is temporary. Historian Paul Kennedy, in his provocative book *The Rise and Fall of the Great Powers,* argues that the United States, like all previous imperial powers, will overextend itself militarily in the protection of its far-flung interests. Meanwhile, countries that are protected by the American military umbrella, but relieved of the necessity of spending on their own military forces, will concentrate on technological progress and overcome American economic superiority. Political scientist Chalmers Johnson, in *Blowback: The Costs and Consequences of American Empire,* argues that Americans are and will be so arrogant in their exercise of power that they will provoke the opposition that will in the end overtake them.

No one can predict the future with any degree of confidence, of course, but still, reasons exist to doubt that the end of American dominance is around the corner. Political scientists Stephen Brooks and William Wohlforth argue that the United States is so far ahead of its potential challengers in all aspects of global power that the latter have no chance at all of catching up. The European Union, even if it had the will to challenge the United States, would face an almost hopeless gap in technology. And no signs point to its having the will. The Japanese, the Russians, and the Chinese are all much weaker.[2] For now, and likely for the immediate future, we live in a world in which the United States is the dominant political, economic, and military power.

This is not to imply that the United States can control world affairs, or that it is safe from danger. Obviously, it cannot and it is not. A good example of its inability to control affairs outside its borders is the continuing conflict between Arabs and Israelis in the Middle East. During the cold war, this conflict was part of the global power struggle, with some of the Arab states receiving considerable support from the Soviet Union while the United States protected the interests of Israel. Now that the Soviets have disappeared and the Russians have only a minor influence in the region, the violence between the combatants has increased rather than decreased, and the United States is further away than ever from being able to impose even a temporary peace.

Because of the huge gap in power between the United States and all other countries, any account of the foreign policy of the rich countries toward the third world must emphasize the American role. The Canadians, Japanese, and western Europeans are not always completely happy with the policies of the United States, but they lack the power to undertake a completely different set of policies. They almost always fall in behind the Americans, at least eventually.

Because of its enormous strength, the United States need not worry about military attacks from states seeking to displace its position of dominance. This hardly means that it is free from danger, however, as the terrorist attacks of September 11, 2001, demonstrated.

The War on Terrorism

Terrorism is the classic weapon of the weak. Terrorists cannot win wars or defeat established states. Even when successful—and they often are unsuccessful—they kill relatively small numbers of people and they destroy minimal property, at least in comparison to full-scale warfare. The unpredictability of terrorism and its random destructiveness can, however, have a major impact, because terrorism captures imaginations and headlines around the world, and creates enormous fear among millions of people. The rich and powerful have always been susceptible to terrorism.

The scale of terrorism took an enormous jump when nineteen members of the Quaida network, apparently under the direction of its leader Osama bin Laden, hijacked four American passenger jetliners and crashed them: two into the twin towers of the World Trade Center in New York, one into the Pentagon near Washington, and one (probably intended for another high-profile target on the American east coast) into a field in Pennsylvania. The loss of life still has not been established exactly, but was in the neighborhood of three thousand.

President George W. Bush's initial response was to promise that the perpetrators would be arrested and punished, but within a day, his response changed fundamentally. The attack was quickly understood not as a crime but as an act of war, and the appropriate response to it was seen as a war: a war on terrorism. According to reports in the *New York Times* of September 13, 2001, the president vowed to "end" states that sponsor terrorism. His secretary of state, Colin Powell, said, "First we're going to cut it off, and then we're going to kill it. We will go after that group, that network, and those that have harbored, supported and aided that network, to rip the network up. When we're through with that network, we will continue with a global assault against terrorism in general." The war on terrorism had begun.

The first campaign of the war was an invasion of Afghanistan, a country that, under its radical Islamist Taliban government, had provided safe haven and training facilities to bin Laden's Quaida network. The United States was joined by several other allies, including the Canadians and the British. The bombing began in October, and by December the Taliban were routed and a new government, friendly to the western powers, installed. The Afghan campaign was successful in dislodging the Taliban, but unsuccessful in capturing bin Laden.

President Bush made it clear that the war on terrorism was to be the dominant principle of American foreign policy. Relationships with foreign states were now to be judged in terms of their impact on that

war. The most important early example was in Pakistan. At the time
of the terrorist attacks, Pakistan was in considerable disfavor with the
Americans and subject to some sanctions because of its testing of
nuclear weapons. After the attacks, the only relevant question was
whether Pakistan would support the United States and its allies in
their attack against the Taliban government of Afghanistan. This
demand placed the Pakistani government in a serious dilemma,
because the Taliban had a great deal of support among the Pakistani
population. Nevertheless, the government quickly agreed to provide
the invaders whatever assistance was requested, following which the
United States dropped all its previous objections to Pakistan's policies.

Once the Afghan campaign was completed, the Americans and
their British allies turned their attention to Iraq, ruled by the dictator
Saddam Hussein. Although the Americans and British tried for a time
to connect Iraq with the Quaida, and to use this alleged connection as
a reason for going to war against Iraq, the connection was never
established and probably does not exist. Instead the allies focused on
Iraq's attempts to develop weapons of mass destruction—biological,
chemical, and nuclear—and argued that unless Iraq were forced to
disarm, it would pose a distinct terrorist threat in its region and in the
world more broadly. They advanced the doctrine of the "preemptive
strike," the idea that the rest of the world was justified in declaring
war, without having previously been attacked, in order to disarm a
state whose intentions to commit terrorism were feared.

Terrorism is a serious threat, and any responsible government of
a developed country must advance a coherent policy to combat it.
What is remarkable about the current war on terrorism, however, is
that (at least as of the time of writing) it completely dominates all
other aspects of American foreign policy. Other issues, if they are
dealt with at all, are seen through the lenses of the war on terrorism.
In this respect, the war on terrorism has replaced the cold war as the
dominant theme of international affairs. Just as in the previous era,
regional issues cannot be seen in their own terms, but rather in terms
of their effect on terrorism.

A good example of this distortion exists in the relationship between
Mexico and the United States. Before the September 11 attacks, two
new presidents, George W. Bush of the United States and Vicente Fox
of Mexico, had renewed their personal friendships and had promised
a number of initiatives to improve relations between the two countries. It was particularly important for the United States to support
Mexico at this time, because Mexico was emerging from an eight-
decade period of being virtually a one-party state. One of the most
sensitive issues had to do with Mexican citizens living in the United

States, many of them without legal documents, and the presidents had agreed to work for an amnesty and a regularization of their immigration status. Immediately after September 11, these initiatives were abandoned. The reason apparently was that the terrorists had been immigrants, so the United States was now determined to reduce the flow of immigration and subject existing immigrants to closer scrutiny. It mattered not at all that no Mexican or Latino immigrant had been implicated in the terrorism; they were immigrants and therefore suspicious. Once again globalism replaced regionalism, this time because of the war on terrorism.

The Illusion of the North-South Dialogue

As the former colonies became independent, they attempted to challenge the idea that the dominant issue in world affairs was the East-West conflict of the cold war. They tried to shift the axis ninety degrees, proposing that the most important international issues were North-South ones, the relationships between the rich and the poor countries. In international organizations and at a series of conferences spanning decades, the poor countries tried to negotiate with the industrialized world in order to reshape the international order and secure some economic advantages for the poor.

The North-South axis traces its origins to the April 1955 meeting of the leaders of twenty-nine independent African and Asian countries in Bandung, Indonesia, at the First Conference of Afro-Asian Solidarity. The leaders considered their countries to be "nonaligned," and they used the term *third world* in that sense, meaning that they were allied with neither the Eastern nor the Western bloc in the cold war. At a later meeting in 1961, with more participants, they adopted the name Non-Aligned Movement (NAM). The NAM supported decolonization and noninterference by the former colonizers in the affairs of the third world.

The first impulse of the new third-world countries was to declare their neutrality in the great East-West power struggle. Soon, however, neutrality ebbed as an organizing principle, and they turned to partisanship in their own behalf—the cause of the South. For many years, they confronted the governments of the developed countries in what became known as the North-South dialogue, demanding fundamental changes in world economic and political relationships.

The cause was pressed in many arenas. As each colony became independent, it joined the United Nations; by the 1960s, that organization was dominated by third-world countries. They were able to control the UN General Assembly, where each country has one vote, as well as the affiliated UN organizations that are created by the General Assembly. The third-world countries made development, decolonization, and North-South relations the principal agenda of the United Nations.

In 1964, the United Nations sponsored the first UN Conference on Trade and Development (UNCTAD) in Geneva. UNCTAD became an institution, with its own secretariat, and thereafter sponsored international conferences every several years. At these conferences, the South pressed its case for concessions from the North and the restructuring of international economic relationships. Its first secretary-general was Argentinean economist Raúl Prebisch, and its ideology was that of the dependency theorists.

The North-South dialogue reached its height in the 1970s, with the comprehensive proposals from the third world for a new international economic order (NIEO). In 1973, the fourth NAM summit, in Algiers, created the Group of Seventy-seven and announced the program for the NIEO. Then, in December 1974, the UN General Assembly adopted the Charter of Economic Rights and Duties of States, a document incorporating most of the NIEO platform. The vote adopting the charter was lopsided, with only six nays and ten abstentions. Significantly, however, the nays included the big three of the North: the United States, Britain, and West Germany. Following the adoption of the charter, a whole series of new negotiations was undertaken.

A UN commission chaired by Willy Brandt, the former chancellor of West Germany, and composed of representatives from all parts of the world was established in 1978. Its purpose was to suggest ways of promoting adequate solutions to the problems involved in development and in attacking world poverty. It reported in 1980, endorsing most of the proposals for the NIEO.

Throughout the 1970s, the governments of the major Northern powers were willing to engage in discussions about the issues raised by the South. For the most part, they were not willing to endorse the Southern platform, but they studied it and proposed alternatives. Some of the governments of the smaller Northern countries—for example, the Scandinavian countries—were enthusiastic in their endorsement of the NIEO. There was reason to think that good-faith negotiations were under way. Even if a full NIEO were not adopted, there might be some movement in the direction proposed by the South.

These hopes came to naught in the 1980s. One reason was the victory of Ronald Reagan and the Republican Party in the 1980 general election in the United States. Far more than his predecessor Jimmy Carter, Reagan espoused a free-market, private-sector solution to economic problems, one that was quite incompatible with the NIEO proposals of the South. This became crystal clear at the Cancun, Mexico, meeting of twenty-two representative heads of state in 1981, called to consider the proposals of the Brandt Commission. Reagan and the Americans listened politely to the third-world platform but made no commitments whatsoever; as a result, the conference came to no conclusions.

After Cancun, little was heard of the NIEO. As explained in Chapter 6, the collapse of the OPEC (Organization of Petroleum Exporting Countries) oil cartel and the worsening debt burdens of the 1980s led third-world countries to concentrate on their own crises at home and to lose hope for a restructuring of the international economy.

With the collapse of the South's agenda, it became obvious that the third world had little bargaining power in international politics and that almost all the power resided in the North. For a few years in the 1970s, it had seemed that North-South issues might compete with the East-West confrontation for the honor of the principal theme in international politics, but that turned out to be an illusion. From the 1980s to the present, it has been clear that the policies of the rich countries toward the poor are determined principally by their perceptions of their own self-interest, not by the demands of the poor.

A Constructive Foreign Policy

The war on terrorism has given new coherence to the foreign policy of the industrialized countries, particularly the United States and Britain. It is a coherence that had been lacking since the end of the cold war. In the decade of the 1990s, foreign policy was distinctly incoherent, without any overriding principles. At the end of the Persian Gulf War in 1991, President George Bush had called for "a new world order," but he was not articulate about what this phrase meant, and he did little to follow up on it after the war. As a result, each separate action by the great powers seemed unpredictable and unconnected to other actions. With the dawning of the new century, however, a new purpose has come to dominate foreign policy: fighting terrorism.

In the wake of the terrorist attacks, the isolationist tendency in American foreign policy has all but disappeared, at least for the time being. Isolationism—a withdrawal from active involvement in international affairs—has often been a strong tendency in American thinking about foreign policy. The country's first president, George Washington, warned against foreign entanglements. The possibility of isolationism has been a luxury granted to Americans by virtue of their insulated location between two great oceans; it is a luxury unavailable to the Europeans. American isolationism did enormous damage to the entire world in the period after the First World War, when the United States declined to join the League of Nations and thereafter refused to take the threat of German, Italian, and Japanese totalitarianism seriously, right up to the moment when its fleet was bombed at Pearl Harbor. Isolationist thinking enjoyed a remarkable resurgence in recent years. The debacle in Vietnam led many Americans to think that foreign involvements could lead only to disaster; the end of the cold war led even more to think that American security was no longer threatened from abroad. The isolationist tendency spanned the political spectrum. The principal leftist argument in its favor was that the United States has consistently been a force acting in favor of elites and against the aspirations of ordinary people, particularly in the third world. The hope for progressive social change in poor countries would therefore be immeasurably improved if the United States were to withdraw militarily and diplomatically. The right-wing argument was that American prosperity and business success are hampered by foreign military involvements that withdraw resources from more important uses. Less ideologically, many Americans simply came to believe that nothing that happened in foreign countries, or to foreign people, was worth the slightest risk or sacrifice by Americans. One of the results of the September 11 attacks is that hardly anyone today advances these arguments. It is completely clear now that the United States is not, and cannot be, isolated from international events and that it must therefore have an active foreign policy. No doubt American isolationism will revive in the future, but not when the war on terrorism is the principal theme of foreign policy.

The disappearance of isolationism does not mean that unanimity or even consensus exists in the formulation of foreign policy. The principal dispute today is between a "conservative" or "realistic" foreign policy on the one hand, and a policy on behalf of democracy, economic development, and human rights on the other.

The war on terrorism, as it is currently being waged, is consistent with a conservative or realistic approach to world affairs. This approach is based on the assumption that the world is a dangerous, anarchic environment and that the first duty of any country's foreign policy is therefore to protect its own security. Governments of democratic states are responsible to their own people, it is asserted, not to people outside their borders. Countries must use their military muscle in defense of their own people when their economic or military security is seriously threatened. They are entitled to make preemptive strikes when a possibility of aggression exists and not just wait to respond until they are attacked. In a world dominated by such an approach, the rich countries have little interest in foreign aid or in the economic development of poor countries. They are, however, strongly committed to free markets throughout the world, so that they can trade and invest abroad with maximum profitability. They are drawn naturally into alliances with elites in the third world, people who control economic resources and are willing to go into partnership with multinational corporations. In such a view of the world, the rich countries are wary of popular movements that threaten existing international economic networks.

The Persian Gulf War of 1990–91 fits well into this sort of conservative scheme. The enormous American and allied military commitment was surely not for the benefit of the population of tiny Kuwait, nor was it in defense of human rights or on behalf of Saddam Hussein's victims within Iraq (because the United States largely abandoned them after encouraging their opposition to the Iraqi regime). It was a war intended to protect the flow of oil from the Persian Gulf to the North. It is unlikely that President George Bush would have agreed to a war against foreign aggression had the vital economic interests of the United States not been at stake. A little more than a decade later, the war on terrorism fits this scheme as well. The attack against Afghanistan occurred not on behalf of the human rights of the Afghani population, but to deny safe haven to the terrorists who had attacked the United States. Similarly, the argument that the United States, Britain, and their allies have against Iraq has little to do with the regime's treatment of its own people and everything to do with its threatening posture internationally.

An alternative foreign policy would take the threat of terrorism seriously, but it would see the interests of the industrially advanced countries in broader terms. It would advocate democracy, economic development, and human rights in the world, as well as the more traditional goals of security and prosperity. The developed countries should pursue such a policy, I believe, partly because it is the right thing to do, and partly because it would advance their own long-term interests. The rich countries will find it much easier to prosper in a world marked by democracy, economic advancement, and the respect for basic human rights. For example, prosperity at home is enhanced by prosperity abroad, because the rich countries depend so heavily upon expanding foreign markets for their exports. Health at home depends upon health abroad. The AIDS virus originated in Africa and has caused enormous loss of life in the North; other infectious diseases may follow the same route from the third world unless public health standards are raised throughout the world.[3] The military security of the rich countries begins long before a direct attack; it has its roots in a just, democratic world system.

According to this understanding of foreign policy, the forces of the developed countries should upon occasion intervene in international theaters. They should do so not to further their narrow economic interests, but rather to advance values such as democracy, justice, human rights, and meeting the needs of the disadvantaged. Except in very unusual circumstances, they should do so collectively, under the aegis of an international organization such as the United Nations or the North Atlantic Treaty Organization (NATO).

The 1990s saw some examples of foreign policy by the United States and its allies that were consistent with these principles. The dispatch of American troops to Somalia helped reduce starvation, although it was not successful in helping that nation rebuild its political structure. Troops were sent to the borders of Rwanda to alleviate the death and anarchy in the refugee camps. American intervention in Haiti was at least partially for the purpose of restoring democracy and ending human rights abuses. The bombing of Serbia was intended to promote human rights—although it was an ill-conceived policy that ended up causing great harm to the innocent, and if anything exacerbating the human rights abuses. In each of these cases, a careful observer could detect other purposes that were not so humanitarian, but at least on the face of it, the rich countries were taking action to promote the welfare of the downtrodden.

The principal objection to such a philosophy of foreign policy is that it neglects the security and economic interests of the rich countries. The objection has some merit, but in the end it is not fully persuasive. The causes of terrorism are complex, but there is little doubt that terrorism will find less fertile ground in a world characterized by justice rather than oppression and deprivation. The United States is overwhelmingly the most powerful nation in the world. It can act in ways that are heedless of other peoples' concerns if it chooses, but it need not. Because it is so powerful, as Brooks and Wohlforth state, "it can afford to reap the greater gains that will eventually come from magnanimity."[4] The next sections consider the chances of an active, progressive foreign policy in terms of the military, human rights, and the economy.

Military Spending and Policy

From a global perspective, military expenditures represent an enormous loss. They do not make the world safer but more dangerous. At the beginning of the twenty-first century, world arms spending amounted to more than U.S.$850 billion a year, or almost 3 percent of world production. The United States spends far more on its military than any other country. Remarkably, at last calculation, the United States accounted for almost two-thirds of total world arms exports.[5] Had a significant portion of the funds spent worldwide on the military been directed to the basic human needs of the world's most destitute, they could have transformed the human condition.

For decades, the principal justification for military expenditures was the cold war. If the Soviets and their allies were arming, so must their enemies, it was thought. This reasoning was not transparently obvious, because the stockpile of weapons, both nuclear and conventional, was already sufficient to obliterate the entire human population many times over. Nevertheless, with the end of the cold war, that debate was closed, and during the 1990s overall military spending fell. Those who were expecting a "peace dividend"—military expenditures redirected to peaceful uses—were disappointed, though, at how little the expenditures fell. The countries of the former Soviet Union and its allies cut their military spending roughly in half, but spending in the western alliance fell only slightly. The failure to cut military spending significantly after the cold war represents one of the most important unkept promises. In any case, with the new war on terrorism, all talk of a peace dividend has now disappeared; military spending is rising sharply in the United States and moderately in most European countries.

The failure of military spending to fall very much in the 1990s makes one think that deterrence and protection were not the only causes of the extraordinary expenditures during the cold war. The social systems in the western alliance are quite dependent on military spending, and defense contractors have considerable political power. Everywhere defense spending is cut, the government risks losing electoral support. In Russia, where the social system was just as dependent on the military, the drastic cut in spending was part and parcel of the collapse of the state and the transformation of social relations.

In the third world, military spending has continued to grow since the end of the cold war.[6] Spending in the third world has been abetted by increasing competition among arms producers in the rich countries; facing shrinking markets at home, they have redoubled their efforts to expand their sales abroad. Total expenditures on arms are naturally lower in the poor countries than in the rich, but as a proportion of total income, they are higher. The waste represented by military spending in the third world is greater, because the human needs are so much more compelling.

What sort of military policy should the rich countries pursue, if they are to take seriously the promotion of democracy, economic development, and human rights in the world? The lesson of the Second World War is that they cannot simply withdraw; the failure of the democracies to force Hitler to back down, at a time when they could have done so, led to the greatest military and humanitarian catastrophe the world has known. The lesson of that war is obvious. At times, democracies have to use their military power to oppose fascism, aggression, and genocide. At times, they have to call on their young people to make a sacrifice, perhaps the ultimate sacrifice.

The decision to use military force should not be taken lightly, of course. It is the most terrifying decision a country and its leaders can make. Simple rules, however, will not do: neither the rule to be the world's police force under all circumstances nor the rule to refuse to engage unless under direct attack. The consequences of following either simple rule could be incredibly destructive. Rather, if the purpose of the rich countries' foreign policy is to promote democracy, development, and human rights in the world, as well as their own security and prosperity, then each case has to be considered intensively and separately before a decision can be made.

A brief review of recent interventions shows how difficult it is to decide when military action is wise. In fact, the last decades are replete with dreadful decisions. U.S. force should never have been used in Vietnam; both Vietnam and the United States paid a shocking price. It should never have been used to support the landowning classes of Central America, as it so often was. Americans should not have gone into partnership with white South Africans in supporting the UNITA faction in Angola. A long list can be drawn up. None of it can be used to demonstrate, however, that military intervention is never justified.

Some of the conflicts of the 1990s—in Iraq, Somalia, Rwanda, Bosnia, Haiti, and Kosovo—demonstrate the sorts of options that are available. One of the cases in which the United States led an alliance in armed conflict was against Iraq in the Gulf War of 1990–91. That war was fought to dislodge the Iraqis from their occupation of Kuwait, an occupation that followed the eight-year war between Iraq and Iran for regional dominance. In the Iraq-Iran conflict, the United States had tilted somewhat toward Iraq, hoping to constrain what it regarded as the virulent anti-American policies of Iran.

Iraq's dictator, Saddam Hussein, built up one of the third world's largest arsenals of military hardware and maintained an army of about a million soldiers. By the end of the Iran-Iraq war, he had accumulated a series of complaints against his allies, Kuwait and Saudi Arabia. He opposed his neighbors' policy of selling large quantities of oil, increasing world supplies, and thereby lowering the price. He argued that Kuwait should cancel the debts that Iraq owed it. Further-more, Iraq had long considered Kuwait to be one of its provinces.[7]

In August 1990, the armed forces of Iraq invaded and occupied Kuwait, claiming it as Iraq's nineteenth province. President George Bush immediately organized an international coalition against the Iraqi invasion and secured twelve resolutions from the UN Security Council. Troops were sent to Saudi Arabia to prevent an incursion into that country. When the Iraqis did not withdraw from Kuwait, Bush ordered an attack. A month of air strikes beginning in January 1991 was fol-lowed by four days of ground incursions, which produced an Iraqi retreat and considerable loss of life among the Iraqi troops.

The American invasion was controversial at home and was just barely approved by Congress. The most important reason for its authorization was to secure the free flow of oil from the region. Although the president justified the invasion in more abstract terms, as being the appropriate response to aggression against a sovereign nation, it is doubtful that the United States would have made such a major commitment had its economic lifeblood not been in such danger.

Was the Gulf War justifiable according to the sort of foreign pol-icy proposed here—an activist approach in defense of democracy, eco-nomic development, and human rights? Perhaps it could have been, but as it was pursued, it was not. The Iraqi regime of Saddam Hussein is one of the most brutal in the third world. It is based on military force and police terror, and it is merciless toward its ethnic foes within the country, the Kurds in the north and the Shiite Muslims in the south. During the brief period of the invasion, Iraqi troops treated many Kuwaitis terribly. The war could have been positioned as a war in defense of human rights, but it was not. Right up until the inva-sion, the Americans were trying to curry favor with Iraq, in order both to isolate Iran and to keep the international supply of oil stable. The American ambassador even hinted that the United States would look the other way in the event of an invasion. Then, once the Iraqis were expelled from Kuwait, the Americans took only ineffective action to depose Saddam Hussein and to protect the internal victims of his excesses. The policy in the succeeding years of imposing a trade embargo against Iraq produced great distress among the population but had little discernible effect on Iraqi policies and no success at all in persuading the Iraqi people to overthrow their dictator, with the result that the world was faced, more than a decade later, with an increasingly dangerous Iraqi regime. The Persian Gulf War was a war in defense of the oil supply, and as such, it was completely successful.

The sending of troops to Somalia in 1992 and their dispatch to the Rwandan border in 1994 were the clearest examples of the use of the military in support of human rights. In neither case were outside troops involved in a war. The United States and other western countries entered Somalia in order to slow down if not prevent starvation. Civil authority had completely broken down following a period of internal conflict. Droughts had destroyed crops, but the more important cause of starvation was anarchy. Competing militias were uprooting civilians from their homes and forcing them into camps where they had no resources. The militias were diverting emergency supplies of food and medicine from the outside world to their own use, and they were attacking humanitarian workers. Television crews managed to film the ongoing catastrophe, bringing the face of starvation into the living rooms of the developed countries.

The television coverage was particularly important. Somalia was not the only country suffering from anarchy and starvation. A short distance away, conditions in Sudan were worse. The Sudanese factions succeeded in keeping most journalists out of the country, however, so popular outrage was not fed by the nightly news. In the case of Somalia, public opinion in the rich countries demanded a response, so troops were sent. Although they did not succeed in solving Somalia's political problems, they created safe centers for the feeding and treatment of the people, then handed their task over to an international force under the United Nations. Public opinion in the United States turned against the Somalian operation to a certain extent when some American troops were killed.[8] In all, however, the mission must be judged a success in terms of its goal of halting starvation.

The Rwandan genocide was described in Chapter 5. In ten short weeks in 1994, half a million people, most of them Tutsis, were slaughtered. When Tutsi military forces prevailed, about two million Hutus fled the country to refugee camps in Zaire and other neighboring countries, where health conditions quickly became life-threatening. The United States and other countries sent troops to provide emergency medical, public health, and food aid to avert further deaths. As in Somalia, the immediate mission was successful; death rates in the camps fell. The presence of the troops did nothing to resolve the political and social problems that had led to the killings in the first place, however. Eventually the troops of the Tutsi-led revolution in Zaire closed the refugee camps. Some of the refugees returned to Rwanda, but others were pursued across Zaire, where many died of exhaustion and disease; others were massacred.

The response of the Americans and the Europeans to the conflict in Bosnia is a 1990s example of an isolationist policy—although eventually the United States had no choice but to be the honest broker of a peace agreement. Bosnia, now an independent state, was formerly a province of Yugoslavia. Yugoslavia was a multiethnic country: the province of Serbia was populated predominantly by Eastern Orthodox Serbs, Croatia by Roman Catholics, and Bosnia by Muslims. The different ethnic groups were and are found in all areas, however. As Yugoslavia disintegrated, the constituent ethnic groups and their states engaged in deadly struggles with one another. Although plenty of blame can be placed on all sides, the principal culprits were the Serbs, who attempted to create a greater Serbia by annexing areas of adjoining provinces, now independent countries, that had predominantly Serbian ethnic populations. The ethnic conflict was particularly destructive within Bosnia, with the Muslim population suffering the worst harm. Genocide was revisited, this time under the terrifying name of "ethnic cleansing." Rape on a vast scale was used as an instrument of policy, particularly—although not exclusively—by Serbs against Muslims.

That this catastrophe could have happened in Europe, where within living memory the Jews had been exterminated, seemed incredible. It was as if nothing had been learned from the Holocaust. The promise at the end of the Second World War that genocide would never again be permitted turned out to be hollow. For years, the powers of Europe and North America took no effective action to stop the killing. Interminable conferences were held, resolutions passed, and threats made, with only limited restraining effect. Dutch peacekeeping forces were revealed as impotent in 1995, when they passively allowed the slaughter of more than seven thousand Muslim men and boys in the city of Srebrenica, previously designated as a protected "safe haven."

The western Europeans and the Americans argued continuously about how to deal with the conflict but accomplished little. The Europeans sent troops but then argued that the presence of troops precluded the international community from taking military action in the area, because the troops would be held hostage. The Americans argued for military action by outside forces but declined to commit their own troops. Although one cannot be sure, there is a reasonable possibility that just the threat of overwhelming force from the outside would have been sufficient to effect a peaceful solution in Bosnia. The world was not willing to try, however. The great powers did not see their interests sufficiently threatened, and their fear of a Vietnam-like quagmire was too strong. Up until 1995, Bosnia was the principal example of the failure of the western allies to use force in defense of human rights when it probably would have been effective.

In 1995, the American government finally succeeded in bringing the warring parties to the peace table in the improbable location of Dayton, Ohio. The Dayton Accords brought peace, but it was a precarious peace.

Bosnia remained on the map as a country, but it was divided in two parts—one controlled by the Bosnian Serbs, and one controlled jointly by the Muslims and the Croats. The agreement provided that refugees could return to their former homes, but this provision has not been honored. The most positive outcome of the accords was the agreement to prosecute war criminals at the International Court in the Hague. The trials were slow in beginning, but eventually took place; the most prominent defendant has been former Serbian president Slobodan Milosevic.

When the conflict in the Balkans moved south into Kosovo, the western allies were willing to use greater force, but in retrospect one can see that the force was not used wisely. Kosovo is a province of Yugoslavia, occupied predominantly by ethnic Albanians. For years, the Albanians suffered persecution and the denial of civil and human rights at the hands of the Serbs. As the human rights violations grew worse, the Americans and western Europeans tried to broker a peace accord. Eventually in 1999 the ethnic Albanians accepted it, but the Serbs did not. There followed a month of allied bombing against Serbia, whose leaders eventually conceded and withdrew their forces. The Americans were willing to bomb, but not use ground troops, because they did not want to risk a single American life in the conflict. The consequence of this decision was disastrous. Enormous human and economic damage was caused to Serbs, most of whom were in no way responsible for their government's policy in Kosovo. Meanwhile, the Serb forces and population on the ground in Kosovo—safe from attack where they were—greatly intensified their attacks against the ethnic Albanians, eventually expelling almost all of them, at least until the end of hostilities. Outside intervention was intended to protect human rights, but it ended up creating conditions in which they worsened.

The Clinton administration was willing to use force in Haiti. In the end, it did not have to engage in armed conflict, but it came close. Invading aircraft had already taken off from their U.S. bases in 1994 when former President Jimmy Carter and his delegation secured a peace agreement from the Haitian military junta.

Haiti has a long history of misrule, terrorism, dictatorship, poverty, and exploitation. To its shame, the United States frequently supported the Haitian elite and their rulers, even when massive human rights violations were clearly occurring. In the 1990s, however, the United States encouraged a democratic solution to the Haitian crisis. A relatively free and open presidential election in 1991 resulted in victory for Jean-Bertrand Aristide, a young populist priest. Shortly after assuming office, however, he was deposed by a military junta, and

Haitian rule by terrorism resumed. The United States and other countries, acting through the United Nations, established an economic embargo against Haiti and secured a diplomatic agreement that the junta would surrender power. The agreement was later rejected by the junta.

American motives in Haiti were complex. They included humanitarian concern for the plight and the rights of Haitians and pressure from African-American groups, particularly in Congress. The administration was also concerned about a major influx of immigrants from Haiti, fleeing both the economic collapse of the country and the terrorism.

Controversy exists about whether the economic embargo might have succeeded in overturning the junta had it been applied more systematically and longer. In any case, the Clinton administration lost patience; the junta agreed to turn power over to Aristide only when it knew that an assault was under way. As it turned out, the troops arrived peacefully, without opposition, and Aristide was restored to power. The results were mixed. Democracy became more firmly embedded in the country than ever before; in 1996, five years after his election, Aristide handed over power to his popularly elected successor, Rene Preval—the first time such a peaceful transition had ever occurred in Haiti. In 2000, Aristide came back to power in a disputed election, and his rule since then has been marked by chaos. The desperate poverty and enormous social cleavages are as threatening as ever. Most foreign-aid donors have suspended payments until such time as an administrative system is in place that can be trusted to spend the funds effectively. The Haitian state remains tenuous in the extreme.

Was the United States justified in sending its troops to Haiti? It is too early to know. The incident is the first time in modern American history that U.S. troops have gone south of the border in support of the aspirations of ordinary, poor people and against the power of the oligarchies that ruled them. The real test is whether the United States and other outside powers stay committed to the welfare of ordinary Haitians and help them progress, while respecting their autonomy and not turning the Haitian government into a puppet. If so, the use of U.S. troops in Haiti will have marked a genuine turning point in American foreign military policy: the use of force in support of democracy, economic development, and human rights, not against them.

As long as democratic values are under attack in the world, a justification exists for maintaining military capabilities in the western democracies that can respond when appropriate. Because the United States is by far the world's strongest military power, it is the only country that can take the leadership role. The Americans must be careful, however, to use this position of leadership as wisely as possible. They should intervene only when they have a good chance of being successful: of actually promoting democracy, economic development, and human rights. They should be careful to plan how to disengage from conflicts before they engage in them. They should not, however, adopt an isolationist policy.

As a corollary to this policy, they should act whenever possible in concert with their allies, under the authority of the United Nations. When the United Nations was founded in 1945, it was seen primarily as an instrument for collective security. The goal was that the great powers, acting through the Security Council, would join together to prevent aggression such as Hitler's. The United Nations could seldom operate in this way in the succeeding decades, however, because the cold war rivalries led one side or the other to veto any collective action. As the cold war faded and as the Soviets began to cooperate with the Western countries, the war-preventing and peacekeeping missions of the United Nations became viable. The turning point came in 1987, when the permanent members of the Security Council (Britain, China, France, the Soviet Union, and the United States), each of which has veto power, agreed on a resolution demanding a cease-fire between Iran and Iraq. In the years that followed, the Security Council passed more resolutions, brokered peace treaties, sent peacekeeping troops, authorized the use of force by its members, and imposed trade embargoes in such places as Namibia, Cambodia, Central America, Libya, Bosnia, Haiti, and Iraq. One of the payoffs from the end of the cold war is that the United Nations can now take the sorts of actions that its founders envisioned.[9]

This is not an argument in favor of the level of military spending that currently exists. Earlier paragraphs gave at least a hint of the terrible waste involved in maintaining current spending levels. With the cold war over, military spending could be greatly reduced, particularly in the area of nuclear deterrence, without compromising any country's ability to defend itself or to respond occasionally to international crises.

Human Rights Policy

Can the rich countries have a coherent policy in support of human rights in the world? The answer depends somewhat upon the country that is under discussion. In recent decades, Canada and most European countries have developed human rights policies that have had some, if not complete, coherence. A policy in support of human rights may come into conflict with their narrowly conceived national interests, in some cases, and may consequently be applied only imperfectly. On the whole, however, these sorts of contradictions have not been major. The United States, on the other hand, has an extremely checkered history of supporting human rights. Part of the reason for this may be a simple failure of will, but part is certainly the responsibility that American policy makers have felt to maintain order in the world, a responsibility that falls inevitably to the world's strongest power. In any case, the subject of foreign policy in human rights is dominated by the American experience.

In the United States, most Republican administrations since the Second World War have shown either no interest in international human rights, or cynicism. The Democratic administration of Jimmy Carter (1977–81) tried to make human rights the cornerstone of its foreign policy but was immediately engulfed in contradictions. At best, the Clinton administration was ambivalent about international human rights, and the administration of George W. Bush seems to focus on human rights only when convenient as a support to the war on terrorism.

During much of the cold war, American initiatives in the area of human rights were distorted and nullified by an anticommunist bias.[10] A vignette will illustrate. On Human Rights Day, December 10, 1984, President Reagan welcomed to the White House twelve foreign victims of human rights abuses, but not one came from a country that was friendly to the United States. They came from the Soviet Union, Poland, Iran, Cuba, Nicaragua, Afghanistan, and Cambodia, but there was no citizen of South Korea, Iraq, the Philippines, South Africa, Argentina, El Salvador, or Guatemala.

Beginning with the UN charter adopted in 1945, a series of treaties has established international law on human rights. The principal precedent for these agreements is the Nuremberg trials after the Second World War, which convicted Nazi leaders of war crimes and crimes against humanity. The Universal Declaration of Human Rights was adopted in 1948. Pacts now ban war crimes, racism, torture, genocide, political prisoners, and religious and gender discrimination. This is a startling and potentially transforming development, for the signatories to these agreements are proclaiming that there is an international law that stands above national policy. A government may be found guilty of human rights violations in terms of international law, even though it acted legally under its own laws. The International Court of Justice—as well as regional human rights courts in Europe, Latin America, and Africa—hears cases and renders judgments. The execution of the judgments is still dependent on the voluntary compliance of the country that is found guilty, but in some cases, this compliance has been forthcoming. The United States, however, protecting its own national autonomy, has refused to sign most of the human rights treaties and has thereby weakened its moral authority as a voice for decency in the world.

Human rights violations are not the invention of the third world. The most terrible attacks by states against their citizens occurred in Germany during the Nazi period and in the Soviet Union under Stalin and some of his successors. Six million Jews and unknown numbers of others were destroyed by the Nazis. Even that horror is exceeded by the victims of Stalinism, thought to number between forty million and sixty million.

Nevertheless, violations of human rights in the third world in the last several decades have been massive. The Nobel Prize–winning organization Amnesty International documents the status of political prisoners around the world and organizes campaigns for their release. Restricting itself only to those who do not espouse violence, Amnesty International estimates that there are hundreds of thousands of political prisoners. Military regimes in the third world, whether of the left or the right, are much more apt to violate human rights than are civilian and democratically elected governments.

For years, terrible human rights abuses occurred in Latin America. The imprisonment and torture of political prisoners were extensive during the years of military government in Argentina; the number of the "disappeared" in that country is estimated at fifteen thousand. In Chile, under the military dictatorship of General Augusto Pinochet, critics of the regime and supporters of former communist Premier Salvador Allende were tortured and killed—probably numbering twenty thousand. In Guatemala, Honduras, El Salvador, Peru, Paraguay, Haiti, and Colombia, there was state-sponsored violence against citizens and, in some cases, pillage against innocents perpetrated by insurgent groups. The victims included old women, pregnant women, and teenagers. In Cuba as well, an unknown number of political prisoners have been held in wretched conditions.

By the 1990s, most Latin American countries had rejected their military and dictatorial governments, with the result that human rights improved markedly. In Argentina especially, the process of coming to terms with the excesses of the past has been painful. Some young adults, for example, have discovered that the people who raised them were not their real parents but the murderers (or associates of the murderers) of their parents.

Africa as well has experienced a shift to democracy and a corresponding improvement in human rights. Within very recent memory, however, the human rights violations have been enormous, and some persist. In Asia and the Middle East, too, there are widespread practices that constitute infractions of the human rights treaties—in

China, Pakistan, North and South Korea, Afghanistan, Bangladesh, Burma, Indonesia, the Philippines, Iran, Iraq, Syria, Libya, Israel, and other countries. The majority of the world's people are still not secure from state retaliation in the expression of their political and religious beliefs. Sometimes they are attacked not for their alleged beliefs at all but simply because of their ethnicity.

One might expect that the United States—with its Bill of Rights embodying the protection of speech, religion, the press, and political dissent—would proclaim human rights throughout the world as the foundation of its foreign policy. It could, and there was a brief moment when it did. The Carter presidency represented the high point of U.S. commitment to human rights. Carter came into office in 1977 and announced that human rights would be the centerpiece of U.S. foreign policy—that he would recommend that the United States ratify the human rights treaties, that the United States would investigate and publicize human rights violations throughout the world, and that it would divert foreign aid and trade concessions away from countries that were in serious violation. The commitment to human rights as a central component of foreign policy struck a responsive chord with Americans. Even Henry Kissinger, President Nixon's secretary of state, who had not placed human rights very high on his own agenda, applauded the new policy:

> The aim of the Carter administration had been to give the American people, after the traumas of Vietnam and Watergate, a renewed sense of the basic decency of this country, so that they may continue to have the pride and self-confidence to remain actively involved in the world.[11]

Carter and Secretary of State Cyrus Vance understood that instituting an effective international human rights policy was no simple matter. The policy would come into conflict with international relationships that were important to the United States for a variety of strategic and commercial reasons. If the United States regularly compromised its stance with countries that were important strategically or economically, however, it would end up with a human rights policy that applied only to poor, weak countries—not a tenable position. Because the contradictions were never fully worked out, Carter's human rights policy remained somewhat incoherent during his four years in office.

Whatever its failings, it was a serious attempt to insert some morality into international affairs; it stands in revealing contrast to the rather cynical policy of the administrations that followed it. In Reagan's view, and in the views of his principal foreign policy advisers, the

Carter human rights policy had been a disastrous episode for the United States. Jeane Kirkpatrick, a professor from Georgetown University who became Reagan's UN ambassador, wrote in *Commentary* magazine that Carter's policy had led to "the alienation of major nations, the growth of neutralism, the destabilization of friendly governments, the spread of Cuban influence, and the decline of U.S. power" in Latin America.[12] She drew a distinction between "authoritarian" regimes, with which the United States should have friendly relations, and more extreme "totalitarian" regimes, which it should shun. By no coincidence, the authoritarian regimes were all on the U.S. side of the cold war curtain, the totalitarian regimes on the other.

When Reagan came into office, his principal goals in foreign policy were to contain Soviet influence and to reassert American strength. These priorities implied that if human rights violations were committed by governments friendly to the United States, they would be ignored; if committed by unfriendly governments, they would be publicized for propaganda purposes. In country after country, Reagan's State Department hastily removed whatever constraints had been imposed by Carter's State Department on account of human rights violations. His administration was tone-deaf to the issue. His bewilderment at the public outcry when he chose to visit the Nazi SS graveyard in Bitburg, Germany, in 1986 symbolized the betrayal of the values that many Americans thought were at the heart of their country.

In Reagan's second term, political pressures in the United States, along with changing events in the third world, forced the government to make some concessions in the area of human rights, for example, in South Africa and the Philippines. These actions were minimal, however. The United States had next to nothing to do with the overthrow of oppressive military regimes in Latin America—in Brazil, Argentina, Uruguay, Peru, and Ecuador—and their replacement by democratic, elected governments. The dramatic turn to democracy in Latin America was due not to the United States but to the Latin Americans, helped to some extent by European countries.

The first Bush administration (1989–93) was no more sensitive to human rights. It resisted attempts by Congress to impose sanctions of any kind against China for its use of force against its own people demonstrating for democracy in Tiananmen Square in 1989. It refused to criticize Iraq for the use of chemical weapons against its own Kurdish population; only after the invasion of Kuwait did Iraqi human rights violations become an important issue for the U.S. government. The closest the Bush administration came to taking human rights seriously was the sending of troops to Somalia in response to starvation.

In his campaign for office in 1992, Bill Clinton tried to position himself as being more committed to human rights than Bush. He gave several speeches discussing human rights as a factor—but only one factor among others—in the formulation of foreign policy. He was particularly critical of Bush's refusal to allow fleeing Haitians to even make a case to U.S. officials that they were political refugees entitled to entry. As it turned out, however, Clinton's human rights policy was inconsistent and little different from Bush's. After the election, he refused to discomfort the citizens of south Florida by changing the Bush policy on Haitian refugees. The sending of troops to Rwanda and Haiti can be seen as instances in which the president used U.S. force in support of human rights, similar to Bush's use of troops in Somalia. These were all cases in which no other pressing American interests were at stake, however, and in which the United States could achieve humanitarian goals fairly safely and cheaply.

The principal interest of George W. Bush's administration in human rights has come in Afghanistan and Iraq, where the ghastly treatment of women and ethnic minorities has been highlighted. It is clear, however, that these pronouncements have much more to do with the war on terrorism than with a genuine concern for global human rights. The real test of a human rights policy comes when it is in conflict with other competing interests, not when it is a footnote to grand strategy.

Perhaps it is unsurprising that successive American governments, whether Republican or Democratic, have continued to put national interest above human rights in foreign policy. That choice is no doubt the one that would be made by most Americans. Only the doomed Carter administration seriously pushed the limits of what it could do to protect the world's defenseless. The rhetoric is inconsistent with the practice, however. The first President Bush's encouragement of the Iraqi Kurds and Shiites to rebel against Saddam Hussein in defense of their rights seems, in retrospect, to have been completely cynical, because the United States was not willing to protect them when the dictator turned on them in fury. Clinton's use of troops in Haiti was accompanied by grand, even moving, statements about the U.S. role in protecting democracy and the victims of abuse, but those sorts of statements were nowhere in evidence when the same administration decided to expand its trade with China.

America's failures in the human rights arena are matched by those of Europe. The most glaring recent European failure was its refusal, until very late in the game, to take effective action to prevent ethnic cleansing in the Balkans. Human rights advocates once hoped that the end of the cold war rivalries would permit the great powers to direct their attentions to human rights in the world. Although there are promising signs from time to time, on the whole that hope must be abandoned now. The principal protection of human rights will come from democratic governments in the third world that replace military and dictatorial regimes, not from foreign pressure.

Foreign Economic Policy

In their economic policies as well, the rich countries, led by the United States, have largely rejected the idea of partnership with the world's poor. In 1968, World Bank President Robert S. McNamara appointed a distinguished international panel, with former Canadian Prime Minister and Nobel Peace Prize winner Lester B. Pearson as chair, to make recommendations about international cooperation for development. The Pearson report, titled *Partners in Development,* made a plea for extensive participation by the rich countries in the solution of the development problems of the poor. Perhaps the report was naive, but it was not laughable in 1968 to expect the developed countries to devote a significant fraction of their national incomes to foreign aid and to do so in sensitive and intelligent ways that would promote the advancement of the world's poor. With the Vietnam War, the OPEC crisis, and the worldwide recession of the 1970s, however, aid was cut back. What survived was used mostly for political purposes and not to alleviate poverty.

A decade later, a second international commission, this one under the leadership of another Nobel Peace Prize winner, Willy Brandt, was appointed by the United Nations to report on the state of international development. The Brandt report, titled *North-South: A Program for Survival,* paid little attention to foreign aid, tacitly acknowledging that aid had failed to contribute much to development. Brandt called instead for cooperation in trade, investment, industrial policy, and monetary relations, an overall package similar to the new international economic order. Like the Pearson report, the Brandt report was probably naive, but there was some cause for optimism at the end of the 1970s that the world was ready for some major structural economic changes that would promote development.

These hopes came to little. The United States cut back its aid in the 1970s, and it took no steps to reform the international economy in ways that would make development easier in the 1980s. The record of some of the other Western developed countries was marginally better, but with the United States in full retreat from a sense of responsibility for world poverty, the actions of these other countries were not enough to make the difference.

In recent years, American economic policy toward the third world has consisted principally of encouraging the adoption of free-market capitalism and the reduction of barriers to open trade. As Chapter 6 showed, many third-world countries have moved in these directions, reducing government controls and expanding their exports. They have done so for a combination of reasons—partly because their leaders have been persuaded of the wisdom of these changes, and partly because they had no choice but to acquiesce to outside pressure. It is possible that the new policies will be successful and that the pressure from the United States and the other rich countries for economic restructuring in the third world will turn out to have been constructive. It should be understood, however, that in contrast to a policy of increasing foreign aid or implementing a new international economic order, this new policy thrust requires no sacrifice from the developed countries. It is consistent with the modernizationists' concept of partnership: everyone can rise together.

The following subsections consider economic policy toward the third world in the areas of aid, fiscal policy, and foreign investment and trade.

Foreign Aid

Foreign aid has declined so much in both quantity and quality as to be almost irrelevant to the economic development of the third world. The Pearson Commission in 1968 called for the rich countries to devote 0.7 percent of their national incomes ($7 out of every $1,000) to development aid. At the time, the United States was contributing almost 0.4 percent, and some of the other developed countries were contributing more, although none was at the 0.7 percent level. In 1970, the United Nations adopted the 0.7 percent target in its Strategy for the Second Development Decade. In the intervening decades, however, the aid proportion has fallen and continues to fall. In the United States, the figure for 2000 was 0.1 percent, by far the lowest of any industrial country, and down from 0.21 percent in 1990. The United States no longer gives the highest absolute amount of aid; that honor is now held by Japan. A few donor countries—Denmark, the Netherlands, Norway, and Sweden—have reached or exceeded 0.7 percent. In 2000, Britain gave 0.32 percent, up from 0.27 percent a decade earlier. On average, however, the twenty-three richer countries of western Europe, North America, and Japan reached less than one-third of the goal in 2000, just 0.22 percent of national income.[13]

The cause of foreign aid was not helped by the end of the cold war. Aid was once seen as a weapon in the cold war, an instrument for securing the allegiance of third-world countries in the struggle against communism. Even people who had little interest in economic development or the alleviation of world poverty supported aid because of its strategic importance. In the absence of a compelling strategic rationale for aid since the cold war, political support for it has plummeted, particularly in the United States. A former chairman of the U.S. Senate Foreign Relations Committee, Jesse Helms, is well known for his view that foreign aid is "throwing money down a third world 'rat hole.'"[14]

Ironically, public opinion seems to have a higher regard for aid than do the politicians. A 1993 Harris poll found that Americans think that the federal government spends 20 percent of its budget on aid and that this is too high; a more appropriate figure, they think, would be 5 percent. The actual spending on aid is much less. In the same poll, three-quarters of the respondents said that the United States should help the poorest countries, and two-thirds said that the United States has a moral obligation to the world's poor.[15]

Quantity is only one of the problems of foreign aid.[16] Aid amounting to only 0.22 percent or even 0.1 percent of the rich world's national income could make a significant impact on third-world development if it were skillfully directed where it is needed most. In the case of U.S. foreign aid, however, little of it has to do with economic development. One obvious indicator of this is that it does not go to the countries that need it most. Only about a quarter of American aid goes to the poorest countries, and almost half goes to two middle-income countries, Israel and Egypt. Much of the aid to Israel and Egypt is for military purposes.

A small portion of American foreign aid is in the form of food, and some of this is essential. Some is allocated to famine relief, and it saves lives. It is revealing, however, to understand the motivation for most of the United States' food aid. It is not to save lives but to support the market price for American farmers. The government buys surplus grains and other food products from American farmers, helping in small measure to reduce the excesses that threaten ruin in the American farm states. More than half the food shipped overseas is sold to third-world governments and paid for in their currency. The funds generated are normally used by the United States to contribute to the country's development effort, and this is sometimes helpful. Once the recipient government has bought the food, however, it sells it rather than gives it away. The people who get the food, therefore, are the people with the money to buy it, not the truly poor. The program does affect the rural poor in one way, however. Because it adds to the supply of food in the country, it contributes to a lowering of the overall price of food and therefore reduces the incomes of poor farmers.

It is obvious that the world's rich should contribute to famine relief when droughts strike in order to save lives. Beyond that, however, it is hard to construct a good argument for continuing food aid. Food aid in normal times may seem to be an expression of generosity, but it really perpetuates dependency. Third-world countries should be able to feed themselves. If they cannot, they may need assistance in producing food. Foreign aid should be directed toward improvements in agricultural technology. It should also be directed toward helping the poorest farmers keep their land and get access to the other resources they need in order to be productive. That is how foreigners can help alleviate hunger in the third world, not by providing handouts.

A curious consensus against foreign aid exists today among political leaders in both the rich countries and the poor; aid has almost no supporters. Critics on the right in the rich countries, particularly the United States, see no reason to give away their hard-earned resources, and they fear that aid will divert the recipients from reliance on the private market. Critics on the left have no faith in foreign aid, because they see it being used primarily for ideological purposes rather than to bring about fundamental changes in the lot of the world's poorest. In international meetings, third-world governments deemphasize aid, because it seems to place them in a subservient position. Particular aid programs have their lobbies—aid to Israel and aid to French West Africa, for example—and liberals have some residual faith in aid channeled through multilateral organizations such as the United Nations, the World Bank, and the regional development banks. The contrast with the opinion of the 1960s is striking, however. The Pearson Commission report, published in 1969, saw foreign aid as the essence of the relationship between the rich countries and the poor, and it argued in the strongest terms for more of it. Today, foreign aid for economic development is an afterthought.

Whatever the weaknesses of foreign aid, it is hard not to see it in the way that the respondents to the Harris poll cited earlier do: as an expression of the moral obligation of the rich toward the poor. The withdrawal from their aid commitments is simply selfishness on the part of the world's rich—another unkept promise.

Trade

People in the rich countries worry about foreign trade. The continuing high trade deficits (the excess of imports over exports) in both Britain and the United States, the refusal of the Japanese to open their markets as fully as their trading partners would like, the North American Free Trade Agreement (NAFTA), and the power of the World Trade Organization (WTO) all make front-page headlines. Although they believe that trade is a problem, it is an obscure and difficult problem that they do not fully understand. Emotions run high. Americans blame the Japanese for not being more open to imports, for example, but they are suspicious of plans to make the United States more open.

Trade certainly is difficult to understand. People in trade-deficit countries like the United States and Britain often put the blame on foreigners, for example the Japanese, for refusing to buy more of their exports. They think the appropriate response may be retaliation, that is, refusing to buy imports from the offending countries. It is almost impossible, however, to eliminate a trade deficit by unilaterally cutting imports. Both economic theory and economic history clearly show that if a country imposes tariffs and quantitative restrictions on imports, it will cut its exports as well. Other countries will not stand idly by if the United States, for example, reduces its openness to international trade. By erecting a protectionist shield, the United States could reduce its overall reliance on foreign trade, but it would not likely restore the balance between exports and imports. Protectionism hurts the citizens of the countries that rely upon it by raising the cost of the goods they buy and reducing their ability to compete in export markets.

Although the pressure for protectionism has been growing in the rich countries, the principal policy thrust of foreign economic policy in both the United States and Britain has been in the direction of freer trade. Two initiatives have been particularly controversial: NAFTA and the establishment of the WTO, both described in Chapter 6.

NAFTA—the free-trade agreement between Canada, Mexico, and the United States—went into effect in 1994 after long, arduous negotiations and contentious debates in all three countries. It eliminates most tariffs and other restraints on trade within the North American region. Many Americans were opposed to NAFTA because they feared that it would allow Mexico to take advantage of its cheap labor and flood the United States with its goods, thereby eliminating American jobs. Many Canadians opposed NAFTA because they thought they would lose the last remnants of control over an economy already dominated by the Americans. Mexican opposition was strongest of all, on the grounds that many of their domestic industries would just be swept away by the force of American competition. Nevertheless, the agreement was ratified by the governments of the three countries, all of which took the position that their economies would be strengthened in the long run by having free access to the markets of their neighbors.

The WTO is the international body that requires countries to adhere to the rules of open international trade. Protests against the WTO and its authority have been growing. Each time the WTO meets, it is confronted by a sea of angry protesters, some of them in opposition to particular rules of the WTO, others in opposition to the very fact of increased economic integration in the world. The protesters are particularly upset by what they regard as the harmful effects of the WTO rules in the areas of environment, labor standards, and human rights. In spite of these protests, the developed countries have for the most part maintained their commitments to freer trade and the rules of the WTO.

Most economists argue that free trade has at least the potential to contribute to the growth of incomes and higher standards of living in both the developed and the developing countries. In rich countries like the United States and Britain, it is likely to cause the transfer of workers from low-productivity, low-wage occupations to high-productivity, high-wage sectors. As it does so it causes dislocations in the labor markets, as some workers lose their jobs, and it therefore will always provoke some opposition. Nevertheless, they argue, free trade is to the benefit of the country as a whole. The best way for a country to respond to the dislocation caused by international trade—in particular, to the disappearance of jobs in some industries that can no longer compete with imports—is by providing generous compensation and retraining assistance to those affected, not by reducing participation in international trade.

More open trade is of central importance to the third world. This is particularly true at the beginning of the twenty-first century, when so many countries have rejected their former inward-looking, autonomous economic policies and have cast their lot with the free market and export promotion. The residents of the rich countries should not forget that third-world countries have adopted this new policy at least partly in response to unrelenting pressure from the rich countries to do so. Now, more than ever, poor countries need to expand their exports to earn foreign currency so that they can make their debt payments, import capital goods for development, and buy consumer goods from abroad.

As we have seen, the developed world has moved away from a commitment to foreign aid and has rejected demands that the international economy be restructured to give the poor countries an advantage. In place of these two policies, the rich have recommended that the developing countries adopt the current rules of the international economic system and promote their exports more aggressively. For them to turn around and block those exports would represent a betrayal. At the beginning of the new century, there are some signs of betrayal. The huge farm subsidies in Europe and the United States have the effect of blocking the agricultural exports of the third world. President George W. Bush's imposition of a tariff on imported steel in

2001 blocked the development of an important industry in a number of other countries. Fortunately, these restrictive actions are so far exceptions to a general rule in the rich countries of promoting more open trade.

This is a very important issue. Even people on the liberal left in the rich countries frequently come out against increased imports from third-world countries. They see domestic factories shutting down in sectors such as textiles, steel, and electronics, then reemerging in the third world and selling their goods in the rich countries' markets. They complain that businesses that relocate abroad are motivated by greed and that third-world exports can compete against American products only because of "cheap wages." The truth, however, is that wages are "cheap" in the third world because people there are poor and because their productivity is low. If we are ever to have a more equitable world in which labor is not cheap, it will occur in part because manufacturing is distributed more evenly over the globe's surface, not just in the rich countries. For that to happen, industries must move from the rich countries to the third world, and the third world must have markets in the rich countries.

Trade is an area in which win-win solutions are possible. The rich countries can stimulate their economies by expanding their exports, and so can the poor countries. For this to take place, however, countries must be willing to buy the imports of foreign producers, even when imports drive domestic producers out of business.

Can the Rich Cooperate with the Poor?

The foreign policies of the North were dominated until recently by a globalist, anticommunist, geopolitical perspective that blinded people to the real aspirations of the world's majority. The world was dangerous, of course: there was conflict between the West and the Soviet bloc, and geopolitical concerns were relevant. They did not need to be predominant in the third world, however. When third-world peoples were insurgent, when they expressed anger toward the United States and its European allies, it was not fundamentally because they were allied with the Soviet Union. It was because they were crying out against the injustice of their poverty and exclusion. The rich countries could have joined with them in their struggles, but for the most part, they turned a blind eye. Now that the war on terrorism seems to have replaced the cold war as the dominant principle in international affairs, we are in danger of repeating the same tedious story. It is not necessary, however, to do this.

Sometimes the argument is made by well-meaning people in the rich countries that they cannot afford to help the disadvantaged abroad until they have met the needs of the poor at home. This sentiment is expressed especially frequently in the United States, which suffers from a much higher poverty rate than do most European countries. One can understand the argument, but the historical evidence does not support it. In the 1960s, the United States undertook major new initiatives to help the poor both at home and abroad. At the time, the two policies did not seem contradictory. The United States withdrew from its foreign commitments in later years, but not in order to redouble its efforts at home. At the same time, it was pulling back from its antipoverty initiatives at home as well. The two fronts—foreign and domestic—are best seen as closely related parts of the same withdrawal.

For the rich to stand against the advancement of the poor is dangerous for their own future health, wealth, and safety. They would be much more secure living in a world in which basic rights and a decent living were guaranteed to all people. Most of the rich take only a narrow view of their self-interest, however. To extend a helping hand to the poor would require a sacrifice, they believe, and they have made enough sacrifices.

Is there a way out? The best answer would be for the rich countries to awaken to their global responsibilities and redirect their foreign policies to bring them into alignment and partnership with the aspirations of the poor. It is not impossible that this could happen. In the recent past, some leaders in the rich countries have made attempts—people such as Willy Brandt, Jimmy Carter, Robert McNamara, Olof Palme, Lester Pearson, and Andrew Young. As the new millennium begins, this spirit could be rekindled. As the cold war fades in memory, the industrialized world could reduce its military budget and direct some of the savings toward aid. Freed of the need to see every struggle in the world in geopolitical terms, it could offer a hand of friendship to the poor. In the long run, such a policy is the best way, perhaps the only way, to eliminate the threat of terrorism.

Notes

1. The information in this paragraph comes from Stephen G. Brooks and William C. Wohlforth, "American Primacy in Perspective," *Foreign Affairs* 81 (July/August 2002), 20–33.

2. Brooks and Wohlforth.

3. For a remarkable survey of the worldwide threat of infectious diseases, see Laurie Garrett, *The Coming Plague: Newly Emerging Diseases in a World out of Balance* (New York: Farrar, Straus and Giroux, 1994).

4. Brooks and Wohlforth, 31.

5. Data in this paragraph from United States Department of State, Bureau of Verification and Compliance, *World Military Expenditures and Arms Transfers 1999–2000* (Washington, D.C.: GPO, 2002).

6. *World Military Expenditures and Arms Transfers.*

7. For a good historical background to the Persian Gulf War, see Joe Stork and Ann M. Lesch, "Why War? Background to the Crisis," *Middle East Report* (November–December 1990): 11–18.

8. For an account of the conflict, see Mark Bowden, *Black Hawk Down: A Story of Modern War* (New York: Atlantic Monthly Press, 1999).

9. The emergence of the United Nations as a force for peace is analyzed in Cameron R. Hume, *The United Nations, Iran and Iraq: How Peacemaking Changed* (Bloomington: Indiana University Press, 1994).

10. For a good introduction to U.S. human rights policy, see Robert F. Drinan, *Cry of the Oppressed: The History and Hope of the Human Rights Revolution* (San Francisco: Harper and Row, 1987).

11. Quoted in Drinan, *Cry of the Oppressed,* 86–87.

12. Jeane Kirkpatrick, "Dictatorships and Double Standards," *Commentary* 68 (November 1979): 34–35.

13. The figures in this paragraph are from United Nations Development Programme, *Human Development Report 2002* (New York: Oxford University Press, 2002), Table 15.

14. Quoted in ACTIONAID, *The Reality of Aid 95* (London: Earthscan Publications Limited, 1995), 97.

15. ACTIONAID, *The Reality of Aid 95,* 98.

16. For a balanced assessment of U.S. aid policy, see Robert F. Zimmerman and Steven W. Hook, "The Assault on U.S. Foreign Aid," in Steven W. Hook, ed., *Foreign Aid toward the Millennium* (Boulder, Colo.: Lynne Rienner, 1996), 57–73.

Suggestions for Further Reading

See Bibliography for full details.

Andrew J. Bacevich. *American Empire: The Realities and Consequences of U.S. Diplomacy.*

Stephen G. Brooks and William C. Wohlforth. "American Primacy in Perspective."

Catherine Caufield. *Masters of Illusion: The World Bank and the Poverty of Nations.*

Christopher Hitchens. *The Trial of Henry Kissinger.*

Steven W. Hook, ed. *Foreign Aid toward the Millennium.*

Samuel Huntington. *The Clash of Civilizations and the Remaking of World Order.*

Chalmers Johnson. *Blowback: The Costs and Consequences of American Empire.*

Stanley Karnow. *Vietnam: A History.*

Paul Kennedy. *The Rise and Fall of the Great Powers: Economic Change and Military Conflict from 1500 to 2000.*

Henry A. Kissinger. *Does America Need a Foreign Policy? Toward a Diplomacy for the 21st Century.*

Charles A. Kupchan. *The End of the American Era: U.S. Foreign Policy and the Geopolitics of the Twenty-first Century.*

Chapter Eight

The Future: Justice in an Age of Globalization

I believe the time has come for higher expectations, for common goals pursued together, for an increased political will to address our common future.

—Gro Harlem Brundtland,
Our Common Future

What we need is an enthusiastic but calm state of mind and intense but orderly work.

—Mao Tse-tung

The promise of the independence movements has largely been lost. The optimism the Indians felt as the British flag was lowered, the enthusiasm of the Ghanaians as theirs became the first of the newly autonomous African countries, the cheering of the Vietcong as they entered Saigon in triumph and renamed it Ho Chi Minh City, the earnest determination of Salvador Allende's followers as they took over the reins of government in Chile—these hopes and countless others throughout the third world have crumbled. No doubt it was inevitable that the euphoria of the moment would be short-lived; the expectations were infinite and could not possibly be fulfilled. Over the last several decades, though, so little has changed. Although there have been pockets of success, there have also been vast areas of deterioration. Populations have continued to grow, and today more people live in poverty in the third world than did so in the period just after the Second World War.

The hopes for alleviating poverty and for asserting human dignity have been largely unfulfilled. Both were battered in the age of imperialism. Third-world economies were exploited for the benefit of the colonialists. Third-world peoples were treated as inferiors. It was the task of the independent countries to reverse this, to bring material welfare as well as hope and pride to the majority who had been denied them. For the most part, however, the independent countries failed, and they were abetted in this failure by the rich countries.

In the twenty-first century, we face the challenge of creating a more just world, in an era of globalization.

Globalization

Globalization is a fundamental attribute of the modern world, and it is not going to disappear.[1] Nor is it a new phenomenon; global empires and global economic systems have roots tracing back centuries. Still, the decades after the Second World War witnessed major changes in international relationships.

The late 1940s and the 1950s saw the reconstruction of international economic institutions, following the severe disruptions of the depression and the war. The 1960s and 1970s were marked by an explosion of multinational corporations, gigantic institutions operating in many countries simultaneously and hence subject to the control of none. In the 1970s, the international trading and financial system was thrown into turmoil by the increase in oil prices, and this in turn led to the great debt crisis of the 1980s, when poor countries found they could not service their financial obligations. Trade and foreign investment in the 1990s led to the rapid growth and then, in some cases, collapse of formerly poor economies in East Asia and elsewhere. Investors sent enormous sums of money across national borders and subsequently, almost on a whim it seemed, pulled them back again, leaving not only financial panics but real economic depressions in their wake. Along with the increase in financial flows, and facilitating that flow, came sophisticated electronic technology, which brought efficiencies in production, but also instability, because it is used to switch funds halfway around the world in an instant.

The new globalization has brought with it a new ideological orthodoxy: uncontrolled markets, neoliberalism, and free trade. Governments have backed off from the controls they formerly imposed on private markets. Where once they saw these controls as necessary to direct capitalism in ways that served people, not just capital, now they regard them as fetters that reduce the efficiency of capitalism and

make people poorer. Governments cut budgets, reduce taxes, eliminate tariffs and currency controls, take away subsidies and licenses,
and generally make the free market freer. The changes occur internally, as many countries pare back social expenditures, and externally
as well, as they lift restrictions on trade and investment. The International Monetary Fund (IMF) has made these sorts of "reforms" the
conditions that countries in distress have to meet before they can
receive financial help from outside. The World Trade Organization
(WTO) has ruled many national subsidies and restrictions on trade to
be illegal in the new world of free, unconstrained trade. The world
seems to be withdrawing its faith in governments and replacing it with
a new faith in unregulated capitalist markets. This is the meaning of
globalization as we begin our journey through the twenty-first century: not just a dense network of international relationships, but the
primacy of the capitalist market.

The international market has brought dynamic growth to some
areas, for some periods, but the growth has been fraught with instability. Globalization has led to increasing gaps between the rich and
the poor, both within countries and between them. The discipline of
international markets has reduced the ability of sovereign states to
make policy decisions, on behalf of their citizens, that are at variance
with international norms.

If we are committed to justice, if we believe that we should adopt
at least some minimal moral standards internationally, if we want to
respond constructively to the crushing poverty that blights so much of
the world, what can we work for? Some of the protesters who have
taken to the streets since the late 1990s seem to have been attacking
capitalism and globalization themselves. Their intentions are, for the
most part, honorable, but I think that this sort of blanket opposition
to the most powerful trends in our modern world is fated to fail. We
live in a system dominated by international capitalism, and it is hard
to discern any competing system with the strength to displace it.
Nevertheless, we can develop a long agenda of constructive actions.

We can work to restrain and guide the global capitalist system in
much the way we have restrained and guided capitalism on a national
scale. At the national level in economically advanced countries, businesses are not free to operate in any way the capitalists see fit. During
a long period in the development of capitalism, they were much less
controlled than they are now. A hundred years ago, the indigent had
no social safety net, business practices faced no legal restrictions, and
national governments took almost no responsibility for unemployment, inflation, and the rate of economic growth. Labor unions were
outlawed as illegal constraints of trade. All that has changed now.

Governments take the responsibility for guiding and restricting capitalist enterprises inside their countries, and unions exert countervailing power against employers.

The locus of government control has evolved from the local or state level to the nation. The United States has long been an enormous free-trade zone, with virtually no restraints on commerce between its different areas. The European Community is now a similar free-trade zone. Free trade exists within the boundaries of both Europe and the United States, but this does not mean that business enterprises within those areas are free to do whatever they please. They are confronted by powerful labor unions, which have the legal right to bargain with them in good faith about wages, hours, and working conditions. They face government regulation with respect to a bewildering array of their operations, including accounting standards, disclosure of ingredients, safety standards, fair labor practices, environmental impacts, competitive practices, truth in advertising, and much more. Governments impose retirement, unemployment, and disability insurance schemes on firms, and they engage in countercyclical monetary and fiscal policy in order to smooth the business cycles that are inherent in free-market capitalism. All these government policies have a dual purpose: to protect individuals against the excesses of capitalism and to keep the system on a prosperous trajectory. At the time they were established, each of these policies was opposed by the captains of industry, who claimed that they were too restrictive and that they would kill the goose that laid the golden egg. As it turned out, the national regulatory policies did nothing of the sort. The long-run profitability of capitalist enterprises is much greater now than it was before these measures were instituted. In the capitalist system at the national level, private enterprises compete against each other for profits, but are regulated by national governments and constrained in their labor relations by unions of workers.

To recount this familiar history is to make clear that nothing like it exists on the international level. Capitalism is global in scope, but the controls it faces at the global level are laughably weak. This is what we have:

We have the United Nations, an organization that does good works but is starved for funds. As an international peacekeeper, it depends upon consensus of the great powers that are the permanent members of the Security Council. Its economic policy is controlled by the General Assembly, in which each country has a vote; consequently, the poor countries dominate. For that reason, the rich countries have been unwilling to allow it to claim much power. The UN lacks the authority to regulate the global economic system.

We have human rights resolutions and several regional and international courts to adjudicate them. The problem with the system of international courts is that the verdicts cannot be enforced without the agreement of the countries concerned.

We have the World Bank, the IMF, and the WTO. These institutions are controlled by the rich countries, not the poor, so they are given more authority than the United Nations. The World Bank is, on the whole, a positive influence on global justice, helping to direct international investment funds to the needs of the poor. Its allocations are often controversial, however, especially from an environmental perspective, and in any case, the funds it controls are relatively small. The IMF is charged with helping countries deal with temporary financial crises, and it often does this while imposing free-market ideology; it requires countries to reduce their controls over international economic activities. The purpose of the WTO is to reduce the tariffs and other restrictions that governments impose on trade. The WTO has the authority to rule that certain policies of national governments are inconsistent with international rules and must be rescinded. In other words, the IMF and the WTO have authority at the international level, but the authority is used to constrain national governments, not international corporations.

We have free-trade areas in many parts of the world: in Europe, in Latin America, in Asia, and in North America. The agreements setting up these areas typically have strong enforcement powers. The North American Free Trade Agreement (NAFTA), for example, sets up administrative bodies that can ban policies adopted by any of its national governments in such areas as the cultural content of media, environmental and health protections, and subsidies for distressed areas. Like the WTO, NAFTA restrains the authority of countries, not companies.

In sum, the international institutions that might possibly control the excesses of international capitalism are relatively weak. The international institutions that are larger and more powerful are directed for the most part to freeing international markets of restrictions imposed by governments. When people concerned with justice on an international scale protest this unevenness, they are frequently given lectures about the virtues of free trade. They are told that they should study a little economics and learn what every freshman learns in the introductory principles course: that restrictions on trade hurt all countries, whereas open, unconstrained trade enriches all countries. These lectures are beside the point. Free trade may well be a good policy, but all it means is the absence of tariffs restricting the passage of goods across national boundaries; it does not mean the absence of all regulations. Why could we not work for a set of regulations governing the international operations of businesses, parallel to the extensive regulations that exist within the economically developed countries?

Something like this was proposed in the 1970s under the name of the New International Economic Order (NIEO), described in Chapter 6. Along with the stabilization of commodity prices, the NIEO called for an international money supply and a common monetary policy, and also for a code of conduct to be adhered to by multinational corporations operating in poor countries. The code would have established common standards with respect to working conditions, tax holidays, environmental pollution, bribery, and other corporate issues. With the collapse of world oil prices, however, the NIEO proposals disappeared. The NIEO was controversial, and quite likely some of its proposals would have been difficult to implement or would have led to unintended harmful consequences. In spite of its imperfections, though, it could have provided a base for the construction of a system of international regulations that would have protected the global capitalist system from its own instabilities and advanced the cause of justice. That opportunity was lost. The twenty-first century could see a revival of the idea that the international operations of large corporations can be regulated at the global level, in the interest of the world's people. The following is a nonexhaustive list of topics that cry out for regulation:

Wages. Wage rates cannot be equalized around the world. The attempt to do so would eliminate economic activity in many low-income areas. Still, minimum-wage regulations that are appropriate to different societies and different levels of economic development should be applied to corporations operating in more than one country.

Hours. Maximum hours should be set, beyond which overtime rates of pay would be mandatory.

Working conditions. Simple minimum standards should be developed, having to do with cleanliness, toxic chemicals, safety, first aid, and related topics.

Child labor. Enforceable standards should be agreed to.

Labor unions. Uniform rights should be established for workers to organize and bargain collectively in good faith about wages, hours, and working conditions.

Nondiscrimination. Companies operating internationally should be held to standards of nondiscrimination with respect to race, gender, sexual orientation, social class, nationality, faith, and political opinion.

Taxation. Minimum tax levels should be established for corporations operating in foreign countries in order to end the practice of companies bargaining with countries for "tax holidays."

Disclosure. Companies operating in foreign countries should be required to disclose the sort of information that is now required by securities' regulators in the rich countries. This would ensure that people buying the securities and financial obligations of the companies would have a fair chance of understanding what they were buying. Consumers should know the ingredients of the products they buy.

Banking practices. Because banks hold the people's money, and because people's deposits in banks are typically insured by a government agency, the business practices of international banks should be closely regulated, with an eye to seeing that prudent decisions are made.

Crime and corruption. International standards should be established—enforceable in international courts—forbidding corruption, bribery, and other crimes.

Human rights. Corporations operating in foreign countries should be held to all the injunctions contained in the human rights treaties.

Environmental protection. International standards of environmental protection should be developed.

Capital flows. Now that capital moves in such huge amounts and so instantaneously, countries have reason to slow it down and make it less volatile. One good idea, proposed by economist James Tobin, is a small tax, say half a percent, on new capital flows into a country.[2] The purpose of the tax would be to curtail the fast movement of billions of dollars into and out of countries in search of tiny advantages in interest rates. If there were a cost of moving capital from one country to another, it would move only when the advantages were substantial.

International taxation for foreign aid. Rather than leave foreign aid up to whatever charitable inclinations the rich countries have, amounts could be assessed by an international tax agency, imposing predetermined tax rates upon changing levels of national income in the rich countries. This would be analogous to the shift in the responsibility for the welfare of poor people in the rich countries, from private charities to the government and its taxpayers.

Culture. One of the victims of free trade has been the integrity of national cultures. The power of Western movies, pop stars, music, and images of all sorts to submerge local and national cultures around the globe can hardly be exaggerated. Under the rules of free trade, countries often find that they lack the tools to combat the globalization of popular culture. To the extent that local and national cultures disappear, the world will be terribly impoverished, so exceptions to the rules of free trade should be made in culturally sensitive areas.

Enforcement. Infractions of regulations in all these areas should be prosecuted in international courts.

To people familiar with the economies of the economically advanced countries, none of these proposals should appear in any way radical.

Regulations like these are the meat and potatoes of capitalism at the national level in these countries.

One might reasonably ask why national regulations should not suffice, even in an age of globalization. The answer is that countries, particularly but not exclusively poor countries, are under pressure to weaken their regulations in order to attract the business of international corporations. A low-income country that was serious about enforcing its child labor laws might lose business to a neighboring country that was not so careful. Many of these standards will not be enforced at all unless they are enforced collectively by many if not all of the world's countries.

The main obstacle to moving toward a regime of uniform controls over international corporations is that we have no international government. At the level of the nation-state, regulations are imposed by passing laws in the legislature. This mechanism is not available internationally, because the United Nations is not a world government. Its officials are not elected by the world's people, and it has no authority independent of the nations that constitute its membership. This is not an oversight; its charter requires it to respect the sovereignty of the member states.

There is no possibility of world government in the future that any of us can foresee. The people in the rich countries are greatly outnumbered by those in the poor countries, and they would never agree to subject themselves to a democratic process in which their interests could be overridden. Even people living in the poor countries are unlikely to think that a global government would serve their long-run interests or would advance the cause of justice. A global government, even if fully democratic, would have to operate at such a distance from people that they would feel virtually no connection to it. We are not going to achieve uniform regulation of global capitalism through the laws of a global government. The only answer, therefore, is the slow and painstaking creation of international treaties, documents to which sovereign nations accede voluntarily and to which they agree to bind themselves.

We already have many international treaties, covering relationships between countries on a wide array of issues. We have treaties on human rights, on the use of the oceans, on standards for the treatment of refugees, on the coordination of national tax systems, on tariffs and trade, on rivers that flow between different countries, on the extradition of criminals, on the nonproliferation of nuclear arms, and much more. Countries sign treaties of their own volition. Once they sign, however, the treaties have the force of law and can be enforced by courts within the different countries. One way to view a treaty, therefore, is that by signing one, a country gives away some of its sovereign authority. It is sometimes willing to do so in order to secure the promise of other countries to cede a certain degree of their sovereign authority in a parallel way.

Sovereign nations could accede to treaties establishing a more robust set of international regulations than currently exist. Canadian scholar Sylvia Ostry has suggested, for example, the creation of a new World Environmental Organization to parallel the WTO and to have the responsibility for creating global standards relating to emissions and environmental preservation.[3] She has also suggested that the International Labor Organization be strengthened by having the responsibility for the regulation of global labor standards. Such treaties and institutions will be difficult to create because of the conflicting interests that exist in the world. At the present time, for example, representatives of poor countries tend to be skeptical of environmental and labor standards that are proposed by groups in the rich countries. Corporate interests can be counted upon to resist any new regulations on their activities. In the absence of a world government, however, no alternative exists to the slow, negotiated development of international standards and the mechanisms for enforcing those standards if globalization is not to be a synonym for injustice.

A Hope for Partnership

I take it as a matter of faith that the rich could join in a partnership with the poor, that they could adopt the struggle against world poverty as a common endeavor. The betrayal documented in these chapters is a tragedy precisely because it is not inevitable. This is a controversial view, one on which the schools outlined in Chapter 3 take different positions.

Most dependency theorists have no hope that the rich countries will do anything to help the poor in their development. They have created a long literature criticizing foreign aid, the World Bank, foreign investment, technology transfer, trade patterns, military actions, and the many other ways in which the rich countries interact with the third world. Through the prism of dependency theory, all these connections between the North and the South are seen as ways of exploiting the world's poor and crippling them, not as ways of helping them. People in the dependency school often argue that the third world has been most successful when and where it has been left on its own, having little contact with the wider world system. The Marxists tend to agree with the dependency theorists that the rich countries are unlikely to be helpful to the poor. Their disagreement lies in the fact that the Marxists do not see the external connections of the third world as being so important; they focus instead on the internal class structure.

Only the modernizationists believe that policies undertaken by the rich countries can make a real contribution to the development of the third world. This is the heart of the modernization approach, and it is seen as naive by the other two schools. The dependency theorists and the Marxists generally believe that most government policy is illusory, that the forces of capitalism are too strong to permit mere policy to change outcomes. They criticize the modernizationists for not understanding the interests of the rich countries and the fact that these interests constrain their policies. It would be irrelevant and hopelessly sentimental, they believe, for people of goodwill and representatives of the poor to try to persuade the governments of the rich to behave differently.

They may be right, but I do not believe it. The people in the prosperous countries are not of a single mind; they engage in debate and political competition, and they argue over policy. It is possible for them to behave responsibly. The fact is that the rich countries engage in policies that affect the poor. They have enormously powerful tools: their military policy, their trade policy, their diplomatic policy, their financial policy, and more. There is no question that these tools will be used; the question is whether they will be used helpfully or harmfully. People in the rich countries who are concerned about world poverty have a responsibility to work to see that they are used as helpfully as possible. Whatever the barriers to creating a constructive relationship between the rich and the poor, one should work for it. This was the approach taken by the successive international commissions led by Canada's Lester Pearson and Germany's Willy Brandt. Although they recognized all the obstacles to partnership, they called for a long list of policy reforms in the rich countries to advance the cause of the poor.

Why should people in the rich countries take on the responsibility of being helpful to the world's poor? The answer is that the world is completely interdependent; the rich are fundamentally affected by the third world, just as third-world people are affected by the rich. In one of the great works of social science in the twentieth century, *The Great Transformation*, Karl Polanyi showed how in nineteenth-century Britain the classical economists' model of society—a model in which individuals are thought of as pleasure-seeking individuals with concern only for themselves and not for their neighbors—was put into practice and collapsed. The market society glorified by the economists brought riches to some but left millions destitute; after about a generation, the society discovered that it could not tolerate this. Polanyi proposed the idea of a society as a single organism in which the individual cells are connected to and dependent on one another. If one part of an organism is injured, the entire organism is threatened, and all the other parts rush to its defense. So in Britain, when millions were abandoned to poverty by the laissez-faire policies of the time, the society eventually crafted a safety net as a collective response to their plight.

Can one think of the entire world as an organism in this sense, an organism in which the rich cells will come to the defense of the poor cells for the purpose of saving the organism? It is a compelling image, because there are many ways in which we are dependent on one another.

In terms of economic prosperity, the developed countries require expanding markets for exports, and desperately poor people cannot provide those markets. The military security of the developed countries requires the alleviation of poverty in the third world. For now the threat is terrorism; in the future the threat may be more serious if nuclear, chemical, and biological technology spreads. If AIDS is not eliminated in Africa, it will continue to kill people in Europe and North America regardless of the public health measures they adopt. If the rain forests of South America and Africa are cut down, the increase in carbon dioxide in the atmosphere will lead to higher temperatures in all parts of the world with destructive impacts on ecosystems. If employment cannot be found in the third world, migration to the rich countries will increase regardless of police measures taken at the borders, and homelessness and poverty will spread everywhere. If wars persist between and within third-world countries, the armed forces of the North will be sucked into them.

So the people of the rich countries have strong self-interested reasons to remove their blinders and seriously address the problem of world poverty. The threats to their way of life are real. But threats are not sufficient. For the most part, threats provoke defensive, siegelike reactions, not generosity of spirit. Generosity of spirit can follow, perhaps, from a renewed understanding that we are, after all, of the same species; we share a common planet and a common future. To use Polanyi's image, we are a single organism. In the end, we should address the problem of world poverty because it is intolerable for us, as human beings, to turn our backs on our sisters and brothers.

The task is not easy. Most people care deeply about their immediate families, about their spouses, their parents, their children, and perhaps a few friends. Beyond that, the ties are weaker—not absent, but weaker. One has acquaintances one knows and cares about, somewhat. Perhaps some have school spirit or civic pride or even a connection to the local football team. Some have an ethnic identity that is important. Patriotism for their country may be meaningful for some. But identification with the poor people of the world? Far-fetched. Yet without some identification, some understanding that there is a common fate for humanity, there is not much hope.

In some respects, hope is fading. Third-world governments have far too often mismanaged their affairs and thrown away the chance to address the needs of their people. The rich countries have moved backward and closed their eyes. Narrow self-interest has been substituted for vision, partnership, and commitment.

From another perspective, though, hope is growing. More countries in the third world are turning toward democracy and toward a renewed respect for human rights. As the global security concerns of the cold war recede, Americans and Europeans may be able to see the needs of third-world people for what they really are. Most people in the third world are poor and need the help of those who are better off; they are not communist insurgents seeking confrontation.

It is not beyond hope that Mauwa Funidi's family will reclaim some economic security and dignity; that the villagers of Berat will amass enough savings to tide them comfortably through the drought years; that the Mossi will reverse the desertification of their land and make the fields green again; that the workers of Siglo XX will acquire title to their homes, safety in their mines, and freedom to bargain collectively; and that the Indian cultures of Guatemala will be treated with respect. It is not beyond hope, but the achievement of these goals will require dramatic changes in behavior by the world powers—and dramatic changes in understanding and commitment by the world's peoples.

Along with preventing a nuclear holocaust, the alleviation of world poverty is the most urgent task facing humankind. We have done badly. There is a chance that we could do well in the future. The people of the rich countries could take seriously the problems that beset third-world people—they could learn from their wisdom, take pleasure in their achievements, be enriched by their cultures, and join with them in their struggles.

Notes

1. Much of the material that follows on globalization is adapted from Chapter 8 of John Isbister, *Capitalism and Justice: Envisioning Social and Economic Fairness* (Bloomfield, Conn.: Kumarian Press, 2001).

2. James Tobin, *Full Employment and Growth: Further Keynesian Essays on Policy* (Cheltenham, England: Edward Elgar, 1996), 222.

3. Sylvia Ostry, "Foggy in Seattle," *National Post* (Toronto), November 26, 1999, A16.

Suggestions for Further Reading

See Bibliography for full details.
Robert L. Heilbroner. *An Inquiry into the Human Prospect.*
John Isbister. *Capitalism and Justice: Envisioning Social and Economic Fairness.*
Paul Kennedy. *Preparing for the Twenty-first Century.*
Richard Sandbrook, ed. *Civilizing Globalization: A Survival Guide.*
Harry Shutt. *A New Democracy: Alternatives to a Bankrupt World Order.*
Leslie Sklair. *Globalization: Capitalism and its Alternatives.*

Bibliography

Abernethy, David B. *The Dynamics of Global Dominance: European Overseas Empires, 1450–1980.* New Haven: Yale University Press, 2000.

Achebe, Chinua. *Arrow of God.* New York: Doubleday, 1969.

————. *A Man of the People.* New York: Doubleday, 1967.

ACTIONAID. *The Reality of Aid 95.* London: Earthscan Publications Limited, 1995.

Adamson, Peter. "The Rains." In James P. Grant, *The State of the World's Children, 1982–83.* New York: Oxford University Press, 1982.

Allen, Tim, and Alan Thomas, eds. *Poverty and Development into the 21st Century.* Oxford: Oxford University Press, 2000.

Amin, Samir. *Unequal Development: An Essay in the Social Formations of Peripheral Capitalism.* New York: Monthly Review Press, 1976.

Argueta, Manli. *One Day of Life.* New York: Vintage Books, 1983.

Arndt, H. W. *Economic Development: The History of an Idea.* Chicago: University of Chicago Press, 1987.

Avineri, Schlomo, ed. *Karl Marx on Colonialism and Modernization.* Garden City, NY: Doubleday, 1969.

Azuela, Mariano. *The Underdogs: A Novel of the Mexican Revolution.* Trans. E. Munguia Jr. New York: New American Library, 1962.

Bacevich, Andrew J. *American Empire: The Realities and Consequences of U.S. Diplomacy.* Cambridge: Harvard University Press, 2002.

Bairoch, Paul. "International Industrialization Levels from 1750 to 1980." *Journal of European Economic History* 11 (fall 1982): 269–333.

Baran, Paul. *The Political Economy of Growth.* New York: Monthly Review Press, 1957.

Barrios de Chungara, Domitila. *Let Me Speak: Testimony of Domitila, a Woman of the Bolivian Mines.* Ed. Moema Viezzer. New York: Monthly Review Press, 1978.

Beckford, George L. *Persistent Poverty: Underdevelopment in Plantation Economies of the Third World.* New York: Oxford University Press, 1972.

Bhalla, A. S., and Frederic Lapeyre. *Poverty and Exclusion in a Global World.* London: Macmillan Press Ltd., 1999.

Bisilliat, Jeanne, and Michele Fieloux. *Women of the Third World: Work and Daily Life.* Trans. Enne Amann and Peter Amann. Cranbury, N.J.: Associated University Presses, 1987.

Block, Robert. "The Tragedy of Rwanda." *New York Review of Books* 41 (October 20, 1994): 3–8.

Blomstrom, Magnus, and Björn Hettne. *Development Theory in Transition: The Dependency Debate and Beyond: Third World Responses.* London: Zed Books, 1984.

242

Bowden, Mark. *Black Hawk Down: A Story of Modern War.* New York: Atlantic Monthly Press, 1999.

Brandt, Willy. *Common Crisis: North-South: Cooperation for World Recovery.* Cambridge, Mass.: MIT Press, 1983.

Brooks, Stephen G., and William C. Wohlforth. "American Primacy in Perspective." *Foreign Affairs* 81 (July/August 2002): 20–33.

Caufield, Catherine. *Masters of Illusion: The World Bank and the Poverty of Nations.* London: Pan Books, 1998.

Chamberlain, M. E. *Decolonization: The Fall of the European Empires.* 2d ed. Oxford: Blackwell Publishers Ltd., 1999.

Chambers, Robert. *Whose Reality Counts? Putting the First Last.* London: Intermediate Technology Publications, 1997.

Coale, Ansley J., and Edgar M. Hoover. *Population Growth and Economic Development in Low-Income Countries: A Case Study of India's Prospects.* Princeton, N.J.: Princeton University Press, 1958.

Cohen, Joel E. *How Many People Can the Earth Support?* New York: Norton, 1995.

Conrad, Joseph. *Heart of Darkness.* New York: Penguin Books, 1973.

Critchfield, Richard. *Shahhat, an Egyptian.* Syracuse, N.Y.: Syracuse University Press, 1978.

Cueva, Agustin. "Problems and Perspectives of Dependency Theory." Trans. Jose Villamil and Carlos Fortin. *Latin American Perspectives* 3 (fall 1976): 12–17.

Curtin, Philip D. *Death by Migration: Europe's Encounter with the Tropical World in the Nineteenth Century.* Cambridge: Cambridge University Press, 1989.

De Jesus, Carolina Maria. *Child of the Dark.* New York: E. P. Dutton and Company, 1962.

Dos Santos, Theotonio. "The Structure of Dependency." *American Economic Review* 60 (May 1970): 231–36.

Drinan, Robert F. *Cry of the Oppressed: The History and Hope of the Human Rights Revolution.* San Francisco: Harper and Row, 1987.

Eldridge, C. C. *Victorian Imperialism.* London: Hodder and Stoughton, 1978.

Emecheta, Buchi. *The Joys of Motherhood.* New York: George Braziller, 1979.

Fanon, Frantz. *The Wretched of the Earth.* Trans. Constance Farrington. New York: Grove Press, 1968.

Feffer, John, ed. *Living in Hope: People Challenging Globalization.* London and New York: Zed Books, 2002.

Fieldhouse, D. K. *The Colonial Empires: A Comparative Study from the Eighteenth Century,* 2d ed. London: Macmillan, 1982.

Foster-Carter, Aidan. "From Rostow to Gunder Frank: Conflicting Paradigms in the Analysis of Underdevelopment." *World Development* 4 (March 1976): 167–80.

———. "Neo-Marxist Approaches to Development and Underdevelopment." *Journal of Contemporary Asia* 3 (1973): 7–33.

Frank, André Gunder. *Capitalism and Underdevelopment in Latin America.* Rev. ed. New York: Monthly Review Press, 1969.

Freire, Paulo. *Education for Critical Consciousness.* New York: Seabury Press, 1973.

———. *Pedagogy of the Oppressed.* Trans. Myra Bergman Ramos. New York: Herder and Herder, 1970.

Friedman, Thomas L. *The Lexus and the Olive Tree: Understanding Globalization*. Rev. ed. New York: Random House, 2000.

Fuentes, Carlos. *The Death of Artemio Cruz*. Trans. Sam Hileman. New York: Farrar, Straus and Giroux, 1964.

Galeano, Eduardo. *Open Veins of Latin America: Five Centuries of the Pillage of a Continent*. New York: Monthly Review Press, 1973.

Gallagher, J. A., and R. E. Robinson. "The Imperialism of Free Trade." *Economic History Review*, 2d ser., 6 (1953): 1–15.

Gandhi, Mohandas K. *An Autobiography: The Story of My Experiments with Truth*. Boston: Beacon Press, 1957.

Garnaut, Ross, and Guonan Ma. "How Rich Is China? Evidence from the Food Economy." *Australian Journal of Chinese Affairs* 30 (July 1993): 121–46.

Garrett, Laurie. *Betrayal of Trust: The Collapse of Global Public Health*. New York: Hyperion, 2000.

———. *The Coming Plague: Newly Emerging Diseases in a World out of Balance*. New York: Farrar, Straus and Giroux, 1994.

Gilpin, Robert. *The Challenge of Global Capitalism: The World Economy in the 21st Century*. Princeton, N.J.: Princeton University Press, 2000.

Glover, Jonathan. *Humanity: A Moral History of the Twentieth Century*. New Haven, Conn.: Yale University Press, 2000.

Goldman, Michael R. "'There's a Snake on Our Chests': State and Development Crisis in India's Desert." Ph.D. dissertation, Board of Studies in Sociology, University of California, Santa Cruz, 1994.

Greider, William. *One World, Ready or Not: The Manic Logic of Global Capitalism*. New York: Simon & Schuster, 1997.

Hadjor, Kofi Buenor, ed. *New Perspectives in North-South Dialogue: Essays in Honour of Olof Palme*. London: I. B. Tauris, 1988.

Hagen, Everett. *On the Theory of Social Change: How Economic Growth Begins*. Homewood, Ill.: Richard Dorsey, 1962.

Haq, Mahbub ul. *The Poverty Curtain: Choices for the Third World*. New York: Columbia University Press, 1976.

Heilbroner, Robert L. *An Inquiry into the Human Prospect*. 2d ed. New York: W. W. Norton, 1980.

Hiebert, Murray, and Susumu Awanohara. "The Next Great Leap." *Far Eastern Economic Review* (April 22, 1993): 68–71.

Hinton, William. *Fanshen: A Documentary of Revolution in a Chinese Village*. New York: Random House, 1966.

Hitchens, Christopher. *The Trial of Henry Kissinger*. London: Verso, 2001.

Hobsbawm, E. J. *The Age of Empire, 1875–1914*. London: Weidenfeld and Nicolson, 1987.

Hobson, J. A. *Imperialism: A Study*. Ann Arbor: University of Michigan Press, 1965.

Hook, Steven W., ed. *Foreign Aid Toward the Millennium*. Boulder, Colo.: Lynne Rienner, 1996.

Hulme, David, and Michael Edwards, eds. *NGOs, States and Donors: Too Close for Comfort?* New York: St. Martin's Press, 1997.

Hume, Cameron R. *The United Nations, Iran and Iraq: How Peacemaking Changed*. Bloomington: Indiana University Press, 1994.

Huntington, Samuel. *The Clash of Civilizations and the Remaking of World Order*. New York: Simon & Schuster, 1996.

Hyden, Goran. *Beyond Ujamaa in Tanzania: Underdevelopment and Uncaptured Peasantry*. London: Heinemann, 1980.

Isbister, John. *Capitalism and Justice: Envisioning Social and Economic Fairness*. Bloomfield, Conn.: Kumarian Press, 2001.

James, Robert Rhodes. *Winston S. Churchill: His Complete Speeches 1897–1963*. Volume VI, 1935–1942. New York: Chelsea House Publishers, 1974.

Johnson, Chalmers. *Blowback: The Costs and Consequences of American Empire*. New York: Henry Holt, 2000.

Kamarck, Andrew M. *The Tropics and Economic Development: A Provocative Inquiry into the Poverty of Nations*. Baltimore: Johns Hopkins University Press, 1973.

Karnow, Stanley. *Vietnam: A History*. New York: Viking Press, 1983.

Kennedy, Paul. *Preparing for the Twenty-first Century*. New York: Random House, 1993.

———. *The Rise and Fall of the Great Powers: Economic Change and Military Conflict from 1500 to 2000*. New York: Random House, 1987.

Khusro, A. M. *The Poverty of Nations*. London: Macmillan Press Ltd., 1999.

Kirkpatrick, Jeane. "Dictatorships and Double Standards." *Commentary* 68 (November 1979): 34–35.

Kissinger, Henry A. *Does America Need a Foreign Policy? Toward a Diplomacy for the 21st Century*. New York: Simon & Schuster, 2001.

Korten, David C. *Getting to the 21st Century: Voluntary Action and the Global Agenda*. West Hartford, Conn.: Kumarian Press, 1990.

Kristof, Nicholas D. "In Congo, a New Era with Old Burdens." *New York Times*, May 20, 1997, A1.

Krueger, Anne O. "The Political Economy of the Rent-Seeking Society." *American Economic Review* 64 (June 1974): 291–303.

———. "Trade Policy and Economic Development: How We Learn." *American Economic Review* 87 (March 1997): 1–22.

Kumar, Sehdev. "Third World Toils to Feed the West." *Globe and Mail* (Toronto), April 15, 1988, A7.

Kupchan, Charles A. *The End of the American Era: U.S. Foreign Policy and the Geopolitics of the Twenty-first Century*. New York: Alfred A. Knopf, 2002.

Lacouture, Jean. *Ho Chi Minh: A Political Biography*. New York: Random House, 1968.

Landes, David. *The Wealth and Poverty of Nations: Why Some Are So Rich and Some So Poor*. New York: W. W. Norton, 1998.

Lappé, Frances Moore, Joseph Collins, and Peter Rosset, with Luis Esparza. *World Hunger: Twelve Myths*. 2d ed. New York: Grove Press, 1998.

Lappé, Frances Moore, Rachel Schurman, and Kevin Danaher. *Betraying the National Interest*. New York: Grove Press, 1987.

Lenin, V. I. *Imperialism, The Highest Stage of Capitalism*. Moscow: Progress Publishers, 1975.

Lewis, Bernard. *What Went Wrong? Western Impact and Middle Eastern Response*. New York: Oxford University Press, 2002.

Lewis, Oscar. *The Children of Sanchez: Autobiography of a Mexican Family*. New York: Random House, 1961.

Lewis, W. Arthur. "Economic Development with Unlimited Supplies of Labor." *Manchester School of Economic and Social Studies* 22 (1954): 139–91.

———. *The Theory of Economic Growth*. London: Allen and Unwin, 1955.

Lower, A. R. M. "Two Ways of Life: The Primary Antithesis of Canadian History." *Canadian Historical Association Report* (1943): 5–18.

Lubeck, Paul M., ed. *The African Bourgeoisie: Capitalist Development in Nigeria, Kenya and the Ivory Coast.* Boulder, Colo.: Lynne Rienner, 1987.

Maddison, Angus. "A Comparison of Levels of GDP per Capita in Developed and Developing Countries, 1700–1980." *Journal of Economic History* 43 (March 1983): 27–41.

Mao Tse-tung. *Quotations from Chairman Mao.* Ed. Stuart R. Schram. New York: Frederick A. Praeger, 1967.

Marx, Karl. *Capital: A Critique of Political Economy.* Vol. 1. New York: International Publishers, 1967.

Marx, Karl, and Friedrich Engels. *The Communist Manifesto.* Trans. Paul Sweezy. New York: Monthly Review Press, 1964.

McClelland, David C. *The Achieving Society.* Princeton, N.J.: Van Nostrand, 1961.

McClelland, David C., and David G. Winter. *Motivating Economic Achievement.* New York: Free Press, 1969.

McKellin, William. "Putting Down Roots: Information in the Language of Managalase Exchange." In *Dangerous Words: Language and Politics in the Pacific,* ed. Donald Lawrence Brenneis and Fred R. Myers. New York: New York University Press, 1984.

Memmi, Albert. *The Colonizer and the Colonized.* Boston: Beacon Press, 1965.

Menchú, Rigoberta. *I, Rigoberta Menchú.* Ed. Elisabeth Burgos-Debray. London: Verso Books, 1984.

Merriam, Alan P. *Congo: Background of Conflict.* Chicago: University of Chicago Press, 1961.

Mortimer, Robert A. "Algeria: The Clash between Islam, Democracy, and the Military." *Current History* (January 1993): 37–41.

Nair, Kusum. *Blossoms in the Dust: The Human Factor in Indian Development.* New York: Frederick A. Praeger, 1961.

Narayan, Deepa, and Patti Petesh, eds. *Voices of the Poor, From Many Lands.* New York: Oxford University Press and the World Bank, 2002.

National Research Council. *Population Growth and Economic Development: Policy Questions.* Washington, D.C.: National Academy Press, 1986.

Nehru, Jawaharlal. *Independence and After.* New York: John Day, 1950.

Nkrumah, Kwame. *The Autobiography of Kwame Nkrumah.* London: Thomas Nelson and Sons, 1957.

Orwell, George. *Burmese Days.* London: V. Gollancz, 1935.

Ostry, Sylvia. "Foggy in Seattle." *National Post* (Toronto), November 26, 1999, A16.

Pearson, Lester B. *Partners in Development: Report of the Commission on International Development.* New York: Praeger, 1969.

Polanyi, Karl. *The Great Transformation.* Boston: Beacon Press, 1944.

Prebisch, Raúl. *Change and Development—Latin America's Great Task.* New York: Praeger, 1971.

Rao, Raja. *Kanthapura.* London: George Allen and Unwin, 1938.

Rheingold, Howard. *They Have a Word for It.* Los Angeles: Jeremy P. Tarcher, 1988.

Rosset, Peter, and John Vandermeer. *Nicaragua: Unfinished Revolution. The New Nicaraguan Reader.* New York: Grove Press, 1986.

Rostow, Walt W. *The Stages of Economic Growth: A Non-Communist Manifesto.* 2d ed. Cambridge: Cambridge University Press, 1971.

Said, Edward. *Orientalism.* New York: Random House, 1978.

Sandbrook, Richard, ed. *Civilizing Globalization: A Survival Guide.* Albany: State University of New York Press, 2003.

Schlegel, Stuart A. *Wisdom from a Rainforest: The Spiritual Journey of an Anthropologist.* Athens: University of Georgia Press, 1998.

Schultz, Theodore W. *Transforming Traditional Agriculture.* New Haven, Conn.: Yale University Press, 1964.

Sen, Amartya. *Development as Freedom.* New York: Random House, 1999.

Senghor, Léopold Sédar. *Chants d'ombre.* Paris: Edition du Seuil, 1956.

———. *The Collected Poetry of Léopold Sédar Senghor.* Trans. Melvin Dixon. Charlottesville: University Press of Virginia, 1991.

Shutt, Harry. *A New Democracy: Alternatives to a Bankrupt World Order.* London and New York: Zed Books, 2001.

Sklair, Leslie. *Globalization: Capitalism and its Alternatives.* Oxford: Oxford University Press, 2002.

Springhall, John. *Decolonization Since 1945: The Collapse of European Overseas Empires.* Houndsmills, Basingstoke, Hampshire: Palgrave, 2001.

Stannard, David E. *American Holocaust: The Conquest of the New World.* New York: Oxford University Press, 1992.

Staudt, Kathleen. *Policy, Politics and Gender: Women Gaining Ground.* West Hartford, Conn.: Kumarian Press, 1998.

Stiglitz, Joseph. *Globalization and Its Discontents.* New York: W. W. Norton, 2002.

Stoll, David. *Rigoberta Menchú and the Story of All Poor Guatemalans.* Boulder, Colo.: Westview Press, 1999.

Stork, Joe, and Ann M. Lesch. "Why War? Background to the Crisis." *Middle East Report* (November–December 1990): 11–18.

Streeten, Paul. *First Things First: Meeting Basic Human Needs in Developing Countries.* New York: Oxford University Press, 1981.

Tobin, James. *Full Employment and Growth: Further Keynesian Essays on Policy.* Cheltenham, England: Edward Elgar, 1996.

Todaro, Michael. *Economic Development.* 7th ed. Reading, Mass.: Addison Wesley, 2000.

Turnbull, Colin M. *The Forest People: A Study of the Pygmies of the Congo.* New York: Simon and Schuster, 1962.

United Nations, *Department of Economic and Social Affairs. Demographic Yearbook.* United Nations, New York: annual.

United Nations Development Programme. *Human Development Report.* New York: Oxford University Press, annual.

United States Department of State, Bureau of Verification and Compliance. *World Military Expenditures and Arms Transfers 1999–2000.* Washington, D.C.: GPO, 2002.

Walker, Thomas W., ed. *Nicaragua: The First Five Years.* New York: Praeger, 1985.

Wallerstein, Immanuel. *The Capitalist World-Economy.* Cambridge: Cambridge University Press, 1979.

———. *The Modern World-System: Capitalist Agriculture and the Origins of the European World-Economy in the Sixteenth Century.* New York: Academic Press, 1974.

Weaver, F. Stirton. "Positive Economics, Comparative Advantage, and Underdevelopment." *Science and Society* 35 (summer 1971): 169–76.

Williams, Eric. *Capitalism and Slavery.* New York: Russell and Russell, 1961.

Woods, Donald. *Biko.* 2d ed. New York: Henry Holt, 1987.

World Bank. *World Development Report.* New York: Oxford University Press, annual.

World Commission on Environment and Development. *Our Common Future* (the Brundtland report). New York: Oxford University Press, 1987.

Yergin, Daniel. *The Prize: The Epic Quest for Oil, Money and Power.* New York: Simon & Schuster, 1991.

Yergin, Daniel, and Joseph Stanislaw. *The Commanding Heights: The Battle for the World Economy.* New York: Simon & Schuster, 2002.

Zimmerman, Robert F., and Steven W. Hook. "The Assault on U.S. Foreign Aid." In *Foreign Aid toward the Millennium,* ed. Steven W. Hook. Boulder, Colo.: Lynne Rienner, 1996.

Acknowledgments

Grateful acknowledgment is made for permission to reprint previously published and copyrighted material from the following sources:

From *The Autobiography of Kwame Nkrumah* by Kwame Nkrumah (London: Thomas Nelson and Sons, 1957). Used with permission of the publisher.

From *The Poverty Curtain: Choices for the Third World* by Mahbub ul Haq (New York: Columbia University Press, 1976). Used with permission of the publisher.

From *Arrow of God* by Chinua Achebe (New York: Doubleday, 1969), and from *A Man of the People* by Chinua Achebe (New York: Doubleday, 1967). Used with permission of HarperCollins Publishers and Octopus Publishing Group Library.

From *The State of the World's Children, 1982–83* edited by James P. Grant (New York: Oxford University Press, 1982). Used with permission of Oxford University Press.

From *Let Me Speak: Testimony of Domitila, A Woman of the Bolivian Mines* by Domitila Barrios de Chungara, edited by Moema Viezzer (New York: Monthly Review Press, 1978). Copyright 1978 by Monthly Review Press. Used with permission of Monthly Review Foundation.

From "The Structure of Dependency" by Theotonio Dos Santos, *American Economic Review* 60 (May 1970): 231–36. Used with permission of the American Economic Association.

From *The African Bourgeoisie: Capitalist Development in Nigeria, Kenya and the Ivory Coast* edited by Paul M. Lubeck (Boulder, Colo.: Lynne Rienner Publishers, 1987). Used with permission of the Social Science Research Council.

From *Development Theory in Transition: The Dependency Debate and Beyond: Third World Responses* by Magnus Blomstrom and Björn Hettne (London: Zed Books, 1984). Used with permission of the publisher.

From *Congo: Background of Conflict* by Alan P. Merriam (Evanston, Ill.: Northwestern University Press, 1961). Used with permission of the publisher.

From *Biko,* revised and updated by Donald Woods (New York: Henry Holt, 1987). Used with permission of the publisher.

From *The Colonizer and the Colonized* by Albert Memmi (Boston: Beacon Press, 1965). Used with permission of Penguin USA.

From *Quotations from Chairman Mao* by Mao Tse-tung, edited by Stuart R. Schram (New York: Frederick A. Praeger, 1967).

From *Kanthapura* by Raja Rao (London: George Allen and Unwin, 1938). Copyright 1963 by New Directions Publishing Corporation. Used with permission of New Directions Publishing Corporation.

From *Nicaragua: Unfinished Revolution. The New Nicaraguan Reader* by Peter Rossett and John Vandermeer (New York: Grove Press, 1986). Used with permission of the publisher.

From "Interview with Daniel Ortega" by Jerry Brown, *New Perspectives Quarterly* (fall–winter 1984–85). Used with permission of the publisher.

From *Chants d'ombre* by Léopold Sédar Senghor (Paris: Edition du Seuil, 1956). Used with permission of the publisher.

From *The Wretched of the Earth* by Frantz Fanon, translated by Constance Farrington (New York: Grove Press, 1968). Used with permission of the publisher.

From *Open Veins of Latin America: Five Centuries of the Pillage of a Continent* by Eduardo Galeano (New York: Monthly Review Press, 1973). Copyright 1973 by Eduardo Galeano. Used with permission of Monthly Review Foundation.

From "Economic Development with Unlimited Supplies of Labor" by W. Arthur Lewis, *Manchester School of Economic and Social Studies* 22 (1954): 139–91. Used with permission of Basil Blackwell, Ltd.

From *Preparing for the Twenty-First Century* by Paul Kennedy (New York: Random House, 1993). Used with permission of the publisher.

From *New Perspectives in North-South Dialogue: Essays in Honor of Olof Palme* edited by Kofi Buenor Hadjor (London: I. B. Tauris, 1988). Used with permission of the publisher.

From *Cry of the Oppressed: The History and Hope of the Human Rights Revolution* by Robert F. Drinan (San Francisco: Harper and Row, 1987). Copyright 1988 by the Society of Jesus of New England. Used with permission of HarperCollins Publishers.

Index

abortion, 158, 190*n*15
Achebe, Chinua, 7, 84–85, 144–145
Afarat, Yasir, 126
Afghanistan, 110, 127–128, 193, 195, 199–200, 205
Africa, 54, 78, 91–92, 94, 103, 129, 174
  authoritarianism in, 128, 132
  democracy in, 130, 132, 216
  European imperialistic carving up of, 73–74, 77
  health issues for, 129, 174, 205
  human rights issues of, 216–217
  income in, 17*t*, 152
  land expropriated from, 91
  languages of, 81
  nationalism of, 104, 106–107, 139–142
  nationalism/independence of sub-Saharan, 104, 128–132
  negritude, black consciousness and, 139–140, 141–142
  non-development, except Boers, of, 70
  population growth, economic growth and, 24*t*, 25, 157
  religion and, 84–85
Africa, French West, 139–140, 223
Africa, South
  African National Congress, democracy winning in, 130, 145
  Afrikaners in, 129
  apartheid in, 129–130, 141, 195
  Boers in, 70, 91, 129
  British in, 73–74, 129

  constructive engagement by U.S. in, 195
  international pressures against, 130, 218
  nationalist movement of, 104, 130, 141–142
  religion, culture and, 83–84, 85, 141–142
African National Congress (ANC), 104
Afro-Asian Solidarity, First Conference of, 201
agriculture
  colonial export, 68, 70, 77, 88, 89–93, 94, 96
  dependency theory and, 44
  developed nations migration from, 166
  fertilizers needed for, 9
  food aid, U.S. farm support and, 222
  government regulation/support, prices and, 167, 222, 225
  green revolution of, 168
  Guatemalan migrant, 13–14
  individual plots returned for, 164
  (imperialist's) land expropriation for, 91, 96, 129, 140
  land ownership instituted for, 119
  land reclaiming, irrigation and, 150–152
  land reform for, 134, 139, 187
  large landowners of, 150–151, 168
  manufacturing needs improvement in, 162, 166, 168, 187

251

destructive values of, 55
development of, 33
of East Asian NICs, 23, 184–187
globalized, 230–232, 236
government as partner with, 34,
  48, 162
growth of, 23, 24t, 25, 34–35,
  55
mode of production, Marxism
  and, 50–51
modernization and, 33–35, 47
nationalism, Marxism and, 105
political freedom for, 35
poverty and, 31, 35, 42, 60
product markets needed,
  imperialism and, 76–77
raw materials/foods needed,
  imperialism and, 76–77
science, technology and, 34–35,
  79–80, 87
slave trade, Britain and, 43–44
social change and, 62–63
social structure of third world
  changed by, 43, 47
system of, 34, 53
from third estate/bourgeoisie, 16
third world capitalism v., 48
third world's growth of, 40, 50,
  55
without controlling governmental
  plan, 162, 185
workers in, 35
Cardoso, F.H., 42
Caribbean, 24t, 43–44, 70, 76, 81
Carter, Jimmy, 202, 212
  human rights' advocacy by, 137,
    195, 215, 217–218, 227
Castro, Fidel, 105
Catholic Church, 211
  abortion opposed by, 158
  Indian conversions by, 168
  Indian teachings and, 14
  liberation theology of, 85
Chamorro, Pedro Joaquín, 137
Chamorro, Violeta, 138–139
Chiang Kai-shek, 111–112
children, 98, 181, 234

Chile, 24, 216, 229
China, 17t, 22, 62, 78, 97, 198
  British new imperialism of, 75
  central economic planning retreat
    by, 164–165, 184
  Chinese language used in, 81
  communism of, 111–112, 115,
    118, 163–164
  economic growth of, 23–24, 113,
    149, 153, 164–165, 219
  Gang of Four of, 113
  Great Leap Forward of, 112–113
  health care for, 23, 174
  industrial output of, 95t
  Japan and, 75, 111
  nationalism of, 110–111
  population growth/control of, 23,
    157, 158, 190n15
  Proletarian Cultural Revolution
    of, 113, 163, 164
  revolution of, 86, 105, 106,
    110–112, 113–114
  student demonstrations in, 113,
    218
  Vietnam and, 114, 115
Christianity, 57–58. *See also*
  Catholic Church
  benefits of, 85
  indigenous culture's disruption by,
    83–85
  intolerance of, 68, 70, 83
Churchill, Winston, 106
city(ies)
  migration to, 45, 67, 88, 91, 92,
    166, 168
  poverty, 3, 8, 45, 161, 168
class
  capitalist, 45–46, 52, 53, 55, 60,
    93–94, 237–238
  imperialism shattering, 67, 92–93,
    103
  middle, 93–94, 143–144
  non-change in, 89–90, 92–94
  peasant, 112
  ruling, 54, 60, 92–93
  structure, 31, 49–51, 67, 92–93
  workers, 112

Clinton, Bill, 125, 212, 215,
218–219
Cold War
arms spending and, 193, 194,
197, 206–207
end of, 193–194
foreign aid as "weapon" of,
221–222
globalism and, 194–196, 207
colonialism, 39
nationalism, exploitation and, 3,
15
neo, 160
varying kinds, same results of, 44
Columbus, Christopher, 67, 68
communism
anti, 133, 136, 138, 194–195,
215, 218
blacks and, 196
central economic planning retreat
by, 164–165, 184
Chinese, 111–112, 115, 118, 163
Marxist, 55, 60
Russian, 112, 115
Vietnamese, 118, 196
Congo, 7–9, 18, 27, 74, 90, 91, 96,
99, 131–132
Conrad, Joseph, 99
corporations
disclosure, 234–235
multi-national, 45, 46, 170
regulations of, 234–236, 237
crime, 234
Critchfield, Richard, 9–10
Cuba, 60, 61, 76, 91, 105, 133,
138, 163, 193, 216, 218
benefits of, 153, 175
Cueva, Agustin, 52
culture. See also traditional society
Christianity's disruption influence
on, 83–85
conqueror's cultural influence on
indigenous, 82–83, 103
free trade and, 235
of imperialism, 81–87, 103
indigenous language's loss
influence on, 81–82

(European) secular ideologies
influence on, 85–87
currency, 182, 197

da Gama, Vasco, 68, 70
Dayton Accords, 211
de Gaulle, Charles, 121
Death of Artemio Cruz, The1
(Fuentes), 135
debt crisis, 176, 180. See also loans
imported goods payment spurred,
181
oil and, 180, 181
restructured economies for relief
from, 182–183, 185
standard of living reduced from,
182
world bank system threatened
with, 181
democracy
abandoning of, 3–4, 145
foreign policy of (rich), 204–207,
213–214
industrial revolution and forming
of, 35–36
pluralism with, 138
in third world nations, 121–122,
130, 132, 136, 138, 145, 216,
218, 240
wealth with, 16
Democrats, 215, 219
Deng Xiaoping, 164
dependency, 30
capitalism and, 31, 42–43, 45–47,
53–54, 55, 62, 237–238
capitalist class, 45–46, 52
current perspective of, 45, 47
definition of, 31, 41–42
East Asia, semiperiphery and,
55
economic subservice for
political subservice and, 47
for government planning, 161
historical perspective of, 42–44
imperialism and, 66–67
interconnectedness of world and,
47, 61–63

Marshall Plan, 169, 170
Marx, Karl, 49, 51, 56, 77, 86, 99, 105
Marxism, 30. *See also* socialism
  capitalism as precursor for, 55
  capitalism's mode of production and, 50–51, 55
  capitalist class and, 52, 53, 55, 60, 237–238
  class structure and, 31, 49–51, 56, 60, 238
  classical, 112
  communism v., 55
  dependency and, 31, 49
  dependency theory different from, 50
  government's role in, 53–54
  imperialism and, 66–67, 86
  modernization's similarity to, 50, 55
  nationalism, capitalism and, 105
  neo-, 31
  poverty, class structure and, 31, 59, 60, 237–238
  production defined for, 50–51, 64n7
  social change dynamics of, 49–50
  workers, wage labor and, 51–52, 53
  as worldview, 62–63
mass consumption, 38
McClelland, David, 38
McNamara, Robert S., 153, 220
media, 210
Memmi, Albert, 102
Menchú, Rigobèrta, 13–15, 58, 69, 81
Menchú, Vincente, 14
Merrill College, ix–xi
mestizo, 69
Mexican War of 1846, 75, 133
Mexico, 55, 68, 96, 149, 168
  debt crisis of, 180, 181, 182
  NAFTA and, 186–187
  nationalism of, 135–136
  one party system of, 135

Party of Revolutionary Institutions (PRI) of, 135
  peasants, land reform and, 134
  revolution of, 134, 135–136
  U.S. immigration and, 200–201
  Zapatista revolt in, 134–135, 187
microcredit, 188
Middle East. *See also* Arab nations; Islam
  Arabic language used in, 81
  human right issues in, 216, 218
  population growth, economic growth and, 24t, 25
military, 77, 205
  bombing use in, 212
  for human rights, 209–210, 212–213
  interventions and consequences, 208
  isolationism and, 210–211
  for oil, 208–209
military spending
  Cold War, arms race and, 193, 194, 197, 206–207
  no peace dividend for, 207
  third world, 207
  United States, post Cold War and continued, 207
Milosevic, Slobodan, 212
mining, 44, 134, 162
  black slaves and, 70
  in Jamaica, 170
  in South Africa, 130
  Spanish, Americas and, 68, 69, 90, 92
  strikes, torture and, 12–13
Mobuto, Sese Seko, 8
modernization
  capitalism system and, 33–35, 47, 238
  continued growth essential for, 40
  definition of, 31
  government's role and, 34–36, 41, 53–54, 59–60, 162
  imperialism and, 66
  liberal, 41, 48
  Marxism's similarity to, 50

About the Author

John Isbister is a professor of economics at the University of California, Santa Cruz. He was raised in Ottawa, Canada, and studied history as an undergraduate at Queen's University in Kingston, Ontario. After working with Operation Crossroads Africa in Senegal in 1962, he decided to pursue the study of economic development in low-income countries. He received his doctorate in economics from Princeton University in 1969, then joined the faculty of the University of California, Santa Cruz, as a founding fellow of Merrill College, which concentrates on the study of the third world. From 1984 to 1999 he was the provost of Merrill College. He is the author of three other books, *The Immigration Debate: Remaking America* and *Capitalism and Justice: Envisioning Social and Economic Fairness,* both published by Kumarian Press, and *Thin Cats: The Community Development Credit Union Movement in the United States.* He teaches courses on economic development, economic theory, and ethics. He is married to the writer Roz Spafford and has four children and one grandson.